# Where the Muses Still Haunt

**Other Books of Interest from St. Augustine's Press**

Joseph Bottum, *The Decline of the Novel*

David Ramsay Steele, *The Mystery of Fascism*

James V. Schall, *On the Principles of Taxing Beer: And Other Brief Philosophical Essays*

James V. Schall, *The Praise of 'Sons of Bitches': On the Worship of God by Fallen Men*

Rémi Brague, *The Anchors in the Heavens*

Roger Kimball, *The Fortunes of Permanence: Culture and Anarchy in an Age of Amnesia*

Marvin R. O'Connell, *Telling Stories that Matter: Memoirs and Essays*

Josef Pieper, *Traditional Truth, Poetry, Sacrament: For My Mother, on her 70th Birthday*

Peter Kreeft, *Summa Philosophica*

John von Heyking, *Comprehensive Judgment and Absolute Selflessness: Winston Churchill on Politics as Friendship*

Gerard V. Bradley, *Unquiet Americans: U. S. Catholics and America's Common Good*

David Lowenthal, *Slave State: Rereading Orwell's 1984*

Gene Fendt, *Camus' Plague: Myth for Our World*

Nathan Lefler, *Tale of a Criminal Mind Gone Good*

Nalin Ranasinghe, *The Confessions of Odysseus*

Will Morrisey, *Herman Melville's Ship of State*

Roger Scruton, *The Politics of Culture and Other Essays*

Roger Scruton, *The Meaning of Conservatism: Revised 3rd Edition*

Roger Scruton, *An Intelligent Person's Guide to Modern Culture*

Stanley Rosen, *The Language of Love: An Interpretation of Plato's Phaedrus*

Winston Churchill, *The River War*

# Where the Muses Still Haunt

## The Second Reading
### ANNE DRURY HALL

ST. AUGUSTINE'S PRESS
South Bend, Indiana

Manufactured in the United States of America.

1 2 3 4 5 6  28 27 26 25 24 23

**Library of Congress Control Number: 2022933796**

Paperback ISBN: 978-1-58731-539-8
Ebook ISBN: 978-1-58731-540-4

∞ The paper used in this publication meets the minimum
requirements of the American National Standard for Information Sciences –
Permanence of Paper for Printed Materials, ANSI Z39.48-1984.

St. Augustine's Press
www.staugustine.net

# TABLE OF CONTENTS

# ACKNOWLEDGMENTS

Many people deserve my thanks for teaching me important things. Some were my teachers at Wellesley college: Robert Garis, who stressed the importance of literary judgment, Beverley Layman, who showed the riches of Shakespeare, and David Ferry, who attended carefully to the music of poetry. Others were my teachers at Stanford University, Fred Robinson, who delighted in etymologies, and Wesley Trimpi, who loved the classics. One more was the composer, Harold Boatrite, who taught me much about music and shared with me wise observations about contemporary life. I feel special gratitude to Prof. Larry Goldberg of the University of North Carolina at Chapel Hill, who, from 1991–1998, shared his wisdom with me in a course in the great books; officially, we taught this course together, but the truth is that I was as much a student as the undergraduates; many things that I learned in those classes appear in this book. I also thank those many students, at the University of North Carolina, at the University of Pennsylvania, and at the Rosenbach Library in Philadelphia for their willingness to read difficult books carefully and for their insights into what they read. Then thanks are due to friends with whom I have discussed books over many decades and who now live in the far-flung places where graduate students tend to end up. Finally, I would like to thank St. Augustine's Press for publishing this endeavor and especially the editor Katie Godfrey.

When I think about my friends, Isabel's reflections on Ralph Touchett in Henry James's *Portrait of a Lady* come to mind. Isabel "had been constantly wondering what fine principle was keeping him alive; she had decided that it was his love of conversation." I am very grateful to my friends—in person and by email—for their learned, thoughtful, and often droll conversations.

Finally, I thank members of my family and in particular my husband, Philip Cohen, for their good spirits and encouragement.

This book is intended for the general reader. It is based on my reflections from 50 years of teaching. If I have failed to acknowledge some scholarly insight, I offer my apologies here.

---

If you canoe the ocean to my igloo,
bring lampoil, please, and word of my old logoi.

Julia Stockton,
Bynum, North Carolina, 1994

# INTRODUCTION

The title of this book comes from the invocation to Book 3 of Milton's *Paradise Lost*. In the beginning of the invocation, Milton reverently addresses the Holy Light, "offspring of Heaven firstborn; / Or of the eternal coeternal beam / May I express thee unblamed?" He praises the light as the first act of God's creation. Soon after these opening words, however, the poet falls to lamenting his own darkness, that is, his blindness.

> but thou
> Revisit'st not these eyes, that roll in vain
> To find thy piercing ray, and find no dawn.

Then he struggles to find resolve:

> Yet not the more,
> Cease I to wander where the Muses haunt,
> Clear spring, or shady grove, or sunny hill,
> Smit with the love of sacred song, but chief
> Thee, Sion, and the flowery brooks beneath
> That wash thy hallowed feet, and warbling flow,
> Nightly I visit....[1]

The passage starts with a declaration that he will not succumb to bitterness: —"Yet not the more"— but the path he takes seems aimless, as he "wanders" among "[c]lear spring, *or* shady grove, *or* sunny hill." "Wander" is as crucial a word as "fall" becomes later in the poem, for wandering is what

---

1    John Milton, *Paradise Lost*, ed. with intro. by David Scott Kastan, based on the edition of Merritt Hughes (Indianapolis/ Cambridge: Hackett Publishing Company, Inc., 2005). All references to *Paradise Lost* are to this edition.

fallen human beings do. At the end of the poem, Adam and Eve leave Paradise "with wandering steps and slow." In his wandering, the poet hears the familiar songs of the Bible, but rather than giving him resolve, the songs offer only a vague sense of being in the outer realms of truth. This invocation parallels the plot of the whole poem: the joy of admiration, fall, despair, and finally the realignment of the soul Still, the sense of being only in the realms of truth offers some comfort.

And so it is with re-reading great books. Re-reading is one of life's joys. One goes back to great books to listen, slowly and meditatively, and then, suddenly, to hear something one had not heard before. It is like listening again to a favorite piece of music or looking again at a favorite painting. Hearing again a piece of music not listened to for a while or opening a book read long ago or seeing again a much-loved painting is like visiting an old friend, who is still there, with her intelligent dismissal of things not worth bothering about and her enthusiasm for an artist who asked a lot of himself. The experience brushes away the trivia of daily life. One feels the pull of something steady and reliable.

When, long ago, Plato talked about the importance of the arts in education, he emphasized music. In the category "music" he included poetry. For him music-poetry is good for human beings because it brings harmony to the soul's war between the reason and the senses. The achievement of harmony in the soul sets free the reason, which works at its best when it is not distracted by its duty to control the emotions. The calm that harmony brings gives reason flexibility and acuity. The soul can then notice, sift, survey, compare, connect, appreciate, and admire with all the connotations of the Latin *admirare*, "to wonder at." This latter activity is, for Plato, the highest human pleasure.

Although Platonism is often summed up as otherworldly Forms and careful logic, Plato presented his philosophy by way of poetry. He did not write treatises; he wrote dramatic presentations in dialogues. He wanted his dialogues to be psychagogic, to lead the soul. He wanted, first, to lead the soul of the reader either to clarity or to a more serious understanding of why something was a problem and, second, to represent the movements of the soul as it comes to clarity. He used characters; he gave those characters a disposition; he put them in a setting; he had the characters interact with each other, sometimes with tension, sometimes with ease. Through all these means, which we are accustomed to calling "literary," Plato could lead his reader by way of the senses to careful thought and, through thought, to a world of abstraction. At that point, the soul would understand the fundamental order of things which, in the end, it could not articulate but could only "see" (the Greek word for what the soul sees—a Platonic Form—is *eidos*, which is related to the Greek verb "see," *oida*). What the souls sees is, ultimately, the harmonious order of the truth. Perhaps the harmonious order of truth is never fully seen and understood; but one can get closer to it.

Some of the interlocutors whom Plato put before his readers are adults; some of them are youths. The point of getting youths to converse with Socrates is to direct them toward the importance of continuing their poetic-musical education into adulthood. In the *Laws*, the Athenian stranger remarks:

> Now this education which consists in correctly trained pleasures
> and pains tends to slacken in human beings, and in the course
> of a lifetime becomes corrupted to a great extent as one becomes
> older.[2]

Surely Plato was right. In college, we could concentrate. As adults, we dimly remember those times when fierce concentration created a wall of silence between us and the various shuffling and thumping noises of a college library, or when we were at one with the silence of post-midnight hours in a dorm room. It took work to get to that almost otherworldly silence, but following a writer through a complicated argument to its end offered the satisfaction of having understood why something was a problem. For many reasons, it is hard, in adulthood, to revive that power of concentration. Picking up Chaucer or Milton after these books have stood unopened on

---

2    Plato, *The Laws*, 653c, translated with notes and an interpretive essay by Thomas L. Pangle (Chicago: University of Chicago Press, 1980). All quotations from *The Laws* are from this translation.

the shelf for a decade or more seems a daunting task; and besides, there are so many easier books to read. Here, I am counting on my reader's memory of that moment, when one began to feel the urgency of a writer who had something important to say, to recognize that hers was a mind seasoned by much experience and much thought, and to become aware that concentration had changed from self-discipline to appreciation.

The books I talk about here used to belong to the category of the so-called, or erstwhile-called, "Great Books"—erstwhile because few people use the phrase "great books" any more except ironically because there is an odd view that there is no such thing as "greatness." But the fact is, some books really are better than others and deserve being called great. Perhaps the very category of "great books" is displeasing because the books are old and because old, foreign, and because foreign, difficult, or they are old, and because old, not relevant anymore, and because not relevant anymore, a waste of time.

It is not age alone that made—or makes—the great books great. They are great because their authors are hard on themselves. They strive to address fundamental problems common to all readers insofar as they are in the general category "human," not because they are doctors, lawyers, or interpreters of literary texts—that is, they are addressed to a general reader, not a specialist. Although their authors believe that reason can discover remedies for the ills of life, they also see that finding those remedies is difficult—for those remedies do not always work. They also see that reason can be dangerous because it may swerve off the path into cunning. Then, too, the search for remedy can turn a thinker into an addict, someone who isolates himself from the common difficulties of life in order to have the freedom to ponder absorbing puzzles. Most important, the activity of remedy-finding can obscure the truth that life will never live up to our imagination of what it might be. Finally, great authors ponder how fundamental human problems should be talked about, for surely if the problems are fundamental, they are also complex, and there is something repugnant about confronting life's difficulties with stock formulas of hope or perseverance.

Wise teachers want to persuade their students to appreciate complex thought. These teachers think less about the requirements needed for a students to graduate and more about but what is going to be good for the student after she has graduated. I had such a teacher in college, although I did not recognize his wisdom at the time. At the end of my first semester in college, in a course called "The Critical Essay," the professor, Robert Garis, had his students write an essay on a recently published book of poems or a novel; and he meant by that a true "critical essay," an essay that showed understanding of a collection of poems or of a novel and then went on to evaluate it—in short, to write a piece of criticism along the lines of a review that might appear in a newspaper or literary magazine. This effort was way over our heads because, not having read enough to make appropriate comparisons, our judgments were not seasoned.

But Garis was teaching us for the sake of the long view. He set a goal for reading throughout our lives. This is why one reads, to ask the question, "In the great scheme of literature, is this a good book?" To answer that question fully, one has to sink into the book and, for the sake of fruitful comparison, have sunk into a lot of other books and especially into books that have been greatly admired, or "have stood the test of time." One has had to learn to recognize slack thinking. One has had to learn not to be dazzled by novelty. One has had to learn not to be seduced by sentimentality. Indeed, one could say that the success of a college education should be measured by what students choose to read *after* college, for that choice will show if the graduate wants to live a serious life.

The education that introduces students to wise judgment is what is called a "liberal arts education." The "liberal" in "liberal education" comes from Latin *liber,* meaning "free," free, that is, from having to work for a living, in a trade or a craft, and thus having leisure to read and think. Here lies a difficulty, of course. Many of us—most of us—do not have the time to read and consider because we have to make a living. While students are in college, however, they are, insofar as they have the freedom to let their minds range over many questions, living the lives of aristocrats; they have the time to ruminate. After college, when they settle down to making a living, their lives as aristocrats are curtailed; they must concentrate on the narrow fields of their jobs. Then the problem is to find time to let the mind range freely over many questions, even the question of how one should face difficulties, but also what one, as a human being, should be striving for, because that question gnaws even after college. What does Tocqueville say? When Americans are young, they have no time to let the mind muse on life-questions because they are making money; and when they have made their money, they no longer have the inclination. One remedy might be to re-read some of those books that one *had* to read in college. With such re-reading comes an important reward, for it often happens that age brings fuller understanding of what earlier the reader was too callow to understand.

The works I have chosen to discuss here—works by Plato, Homer, Chaucer, Shakespeare, Milton, and Melville—are about finding a deeper understanding of life. Reading them, one feels as if one were following thinkers who, to alter King Lear's line, took upon them the mystery of things as if they were God's spies. At first, the experience is difficult, as many students complain. Certainly, the first time through *Paradise Lost* is like climbing over large, sharp boulders and, the other side of the boulders being out of view, we can only groan when what looked like the summit shows still more rocks to climb. But the second time, the ascent is not so hard; in fact, there are sections along the way that feel like lying down on a lawn and gazing at the clouds in a clear sky. My goal is to help the reader get over the boulders and lie down on the soft grass. Few people have, after college, read the books I talk about here; the exception is perhaps Shakespeare. My hope is to persuade people to read them again, if only to measure contemporary books against them. I am fairly sure that what these old books have to say will offer a view of life that is more thoughtful than much contemporary literature.

The heart of these books is the drama of choice. Because choice is both liberating and terrifying, it makes for good tales. One of the greatest dramatizations of choice occurs in the third chapter of Genesis, when Eve admits her actions: "The serpent beguiled me, and I did eat." Whoever put together the story in Genesis was just stating the facts; this is what Eve said. But it is hard not to weigh Eve's admission against the previous grandeur of the creation story, and hear, in the stark simplicity of her words, the contrast between her blindness to what has been lost and our all-too-full awareness of it. Kant remarked on this profound moment in the Bible; he said that when man was given choice, he "stood on the brink of an abyss."

Plato and Aristotle too are concerned with choice, not as a decision made once but for a whole life. They present the problem of choice with philosophical clarity. For Aristotle, what kind of life a human being chooses to live falls into three categories—the life of pleasure, the life of honor, or the life of thinking. We should reject the life of pleasure because it is not a life that is chosen at all; one just slides along, satisfying the senses. Not putting too fine a point upon it, Aristotle called it the life of a beast. The next choice is the life of honor. Here one really must choose because the life of honor requires moral discipline, and for this life a person must think as well as act. The man of honor finds nobility in statesmanship because it builds cities where people are able not just to live but to live well. Aristotle spends a great part of the *Nicomachean Ethics* outlining the balanced and serious soul of the man who leads a city. His word to describe the tragic hero—*spoudaios*, or "serious, weighty"—might apply also to his view of the life of honor. When great books put before the reader the view from a higher plane, what really happens is the choice to lead a serious life. The specialists help certain people in certain areas, but the choice to lead a serious life helps the city, in the Aristotelian sense, that one lives in.

Shakespeare understood the importance of the "deliberate" part of deliberate choice. In a passage from Act 2 of *The Tempest,* a pair of aristocrats are making sarcastic jokes about their shipwrecked situation. On the stage with them is Gonzalo, the counselor loyal to the deposed duke Prospero. While the sour-tempered aristocrats are snapping out complaints, Gonzalo patiently tries to cheer his comrades up by imagining an ideal state:

> All things in common nature should produce
> Without sweat or endeavor. Treason, felony,
> Sword, pike, knife, gun, or need of any engine
> Would I not have; but nature should bring forth,
> Out of it[s] own kind, all foison, all abundance,
> To feed my innocent people.[3]

This passage comes almost word for word from Montaigne's essay "On Cannibals":

> These nations then seem to me to be so far barbarous, as having
> received but very little form and fashion from art and human

---

3   *The Tempest*, 2.1.164–69, ed. Robert Langbaum (New York: Signet Classics, 1998). All references to *The Tempest* are to this edition.

invention, and consequently to be not much remote from their original simplicity. The laws of nature, however, govern them still. It is a nation wherein there is no manner of traffic, no knowledge of letters, no science of numbers, no name of magistrate or political superiority; no use of service, riches or poverty, no contracts, no successions, no dividends, no properties, no employments, but those of leisure, no respect of kindred, but common, no clothing, no agriculture, no metal, no use of corn or wine; the very words that signify lying, treachery, dissimulation, avarice, envy, detraction, pardon, never heard of.[4]

Shakespeare thought Montaigne had not gotten to the heart of the matter because after Gonzalo utters his last line—"[t]o feed my innocent people"—Shakespeare has the old courtier add a phrase not in Montaigne: "no sovereignty."

Shakespeare adds this phrase because, in this play, the heart of the matter is just this—sovereignty, that is, authority and the necessity for authority. He has Sebastian, one of the aristocratic plotters, sneer at Gonzalo's utopian fantasy: "Yet he would be king on't." Needless to say, this ridicule of Gonzalo's utopia backfires on Sebastian, for Gonzalo is merely exhibiting what Shakespeare would call "courtesy," generously trying to keep up his companions' spirits with a fantasy. Sebastian does not understand the courtesy behind Gonzalo's little dream.

As the play goes on to argue, human communities need kings—Gonzalo's "sovereignty"—because human nature will never achieve such wisdom or such love of neighbor as to make an arbitrator unnecessary. As all readers of Shakespeare say, the verse in his plays is magnificent, and it is especially so in *The Tempest*; but also magnificent is the play's rumination on the connections among human nature and political leadership and courtesy. For the wise leader, these connections are complex. There are things in human nature he must encourage, things he must correct, things he must honor, things he must condemn. To think out those responsibilities requires more than dreamy musing. Surely Shakespeare was right. All societies have some kind of authority, and what legitimizes that authority may be power; but what most people want in authority is wisdom.

4    Montaigne, *Essays,* quoted in Langbaum, *The Tempest,* p. 103.

The brink of the abyss inherent in choice is powerfully represented in Homer's *Iliad*. Achilles must choose between a long life with friends and family and a short life with honor and fame. That choice is mentioned in Book 1 and again in Book 9, but Achilles does not actually make the choice until Book 18, and there it is Homer, much more than Achilles, who makes us realize its gravity. Honor requires deliberate choice, but it also requires courage, and the test of courage is how much one is willing to sacrifice to defend what one loves. Homer uses the musical similarities and contrasts of song, the second word in the poem. The poem turns out to be a song of praise for courage and a song of mourning, and not just for Achilles or for Hektor or for Priam, but for all human beings.

While Aristotle describes the man of honor and Homer sings of the life of honor, Shakespeare *examines* the man of honor. In *1 Henry IV*, Shakespeare gives Prince Hal an early soliloquy where he considers his situation: the prince knows his current companions are wastrels; he knows that people are whispering about his feckless life; he knows he is disappointing his father; but he is not yet ready to be what his father and the kingdom expect; he will become, when he is ready, the man he knows he wants to be. Shakespeare also gives the prince a scene where he considers the simple soul of an indentured servant who would run from his service in a second if he could, while Prince Hal knows he cannot, but also knows part of him does not want to. Then, too, Shakespeare brings into sharp focus Hal's deliberations when he has his audience measure him against the hotheaded Hotspur and the man of sensual pleasure, Falstaff.

In *Measure for Measure*, Shakespeare shows the man of honor as a statesman who must direct the souls of his subjects, some of whom have erred and know it, some of whom are inclined to err and do not know it, some of whom do not know how to forgive the faults of those they love, and finally, some of whom are sophisticates who do not take misdeeds seriously. Prospero in *The Tempest* is also a man of honor but a more complex one even than the Duke in *Measure for Measure*. Like the Duke in that play, Prospero arranges the union of souls he is fond of, and he also brings a group of wayward souls to their better selves, to the extent that he is able. What he really wants to do, however, is to lead into Aristotle's third choice—the life of thinking and contemplation of a transcendent world. In *The Tempest*, the transcendent world belongs to goddesses, and Prospero watches rapt as classical goddesses descend to his island to celebrate the marriage of his daughter and her devoted log-man Ferdinand. Then, suddenly, his political responsibilities intrude. He has to control the sensualist whom he has tried to raise from a bestial state (Caliban), and also the dolts whom he himself has ship-wrecked and against whom he must protect the people he is fond of. Shakespeare is showing how a man of true wisdom longs for the life of contemplation but nevertheless does his political duty as a man of honor, until old age sets him truly free.

In *Paradise Lost*, Milton takes a more critical view of the life of honor. It is, he argues, more a temptation than a goal, for the happiest life is unquestionably the life of thinking and contemplation. For people who are intelligent and who wish to change the political situation in which they find themselves, it is a great temptation to pursue a life in politics, for in politics one can pursue a cause and bring a better life to people, but one can also fall to the temptations of fame.

No one understood better than Milton the temptations of honor and fame, and no one understood better than Milton that those temptations frustrate deliberate choice. The dwellers in the hell of *Paradise Lost* deliberate in council, for they must decide what path to take now that they have been defeated. They can storm heaven; but God is almighty, as all the devils concede because they refer to him as "the Almighty," and, because he is the Almighty, he will defeat the rebels; thus, that alternative is eliminated because even devils want *some* kind of life, even if one devilish rhetorician, Moloch, shrugs off life as not worth the regret. As a second choice, they might try to win back the Almighty's favor by not annoying him with obvious disobedience. This possibility is eliminated because the devils have souls in conflict. On the one hand, they rather like feeling they have been badly treated because they can then claim to be fighting the good fight for justice. On the other hand, somewhere deep in their souls, they want to participate in the Almighty's fullness of being; otherwise they would not continue to call him "the Almighty." The third choice would be to get accustomed to being in hell and, like the honorable man, build a city and find happiness on their own terms; but Milton shows that city-living in hell would be a cramped existence down in the darkness, fire, soot, and smoke. Milton counts on his audience's intuitive rejection of this life as miserable. If devils had deliberated successfully, they might see that in fact they have a way out—through repentance and reconciliation—but in the universe of *Paradise Lost*, a good life must be grounded in awe of God, a stipulation that is, for the devils, unacceptable right from the start. Awe of God assumes devotion to Him, and through that devotion comes service to human beings. It is a hard life. It demands much self-denial and steady courage, but it is quietly assured.

For Chaucer, the highest life is thinking about the human soul and pondering the attitude that the good Christian should take toward other souls. Chaucer considers human souls by way of the tales they choose to tell, their self-justifications, and their attitude toward their audience. He also considers the part of Christian love in assessing these souls. Milton's poem struggles to find a ground that mixes humility and hope, and he offers the possibility to his reader. Chaucer, by comparison, is more detached, more irenic, less hopeful. In *The Canterbury Tales*, the pilgrims' yarns suggest that human beings will always wrap themselves in self-justifying stories, and there is little a wise leader can do in the way of a remedy except keep the peace. The resulting detachment is a cheerful, almost serene, acceptance of the various human types that life presents and of God's wisdom in sorting them out.

Melville, too, dramatizes a choice about a remedy. The remedy is the rule of law as opposed to the rule of men. As a remedy to the capricious rule of kings, the rule of law will give to all men and women equal standing before authority. But in its search for equality before the law, the rule of law cannot take into account differences in the depth of soul among those ruled. *Billy Budd* follows the deliberate choice of Captain Vere, as he strides back and forth in the cabin of the ship, trying to explain to his officers why they must follow the letter of the law. The officers see in Billy Budd only a fundamentally innocent man, despite his having killed an officer. They abide by the old law, which holds that the merciful rules of a transcendent world should override the strict dictates of earthly law. Vere is sympathetic with this argument; Billy Budd does indeed seem to come from a place of unearthly innocence. But Vere sees that he should obey the letter of the earthly law because in the modern world, in which men have decided that earthly order is more important than a vaguely-defined transcendent order, judgments should be made strictly from an earthly point of view.

Painfully, Vere sees the difficulty of any remedy he chooses. Melville's goal is to make the reader see the nub of the choice that Vere faces: the innocence of the man who stands before him as opposed to the preservation of what "the times" have agreed is a better political system. Melville also wants his reader to see that many men in positions of authority—clergymen, military officers, doctors—educated though they may be, often have a limited understanding of the complexity of political decisions. Although they may feel compassion for a man who acted out of honor and who is, in the great scheme of things, innocent, the person with authority must choose between, first, allegiance to a good higher than human law but which history has shoved aside as no longer relevant; and, second, allegiance to a new law that has limitations but will at least form a wall against mob rule. Or perhaps it should be phrased another way: a man who understands the complexities of justice must choose between the eternal word of God, which few people—educated or uneducated—pay attention to anymore, and a human law that is authoritative until it is changed by "the times" but which is regarded by most people—the readers of newspapers—as the deterrent to be counted on. God may or may not punish the law-breaker, but the earthly law will indeed.

In discussing these books, I will assume that the writers followed Plato's advice that good arguments should be presented with good music. As has been discussed, that music was, for Plato, the dialogue and all the various kinds of verbal music that accompanies it. Education in the music of poems and prose is a problem I have ruminated on for many years. It is a problem because it is difficult to explain how the music affects meaning. Readers who can hear musical effects have something like "a good ear" and can give reasons why some literary works are better than others because those works are more attentive and more subtle, avoiding sentimentality on the one hand and flat-footedness on the other. Avoiding sentimentality and flat-footedness are the result not only of craft in the arrangement of narrative matter but, crucially, the craft of the music of the prose or the poetry.

There is a difficulty, of course. Inevitably, the judgments about what work is better than others lead to questions of taste, especially when one is talking about literary works, not philosophy; and the reader will have noted that all the "great books" I have chosen here are literary works. For me, the problem of taste arose in a standard English Department survey of "English Literature: Romantics to the Moderns." The professor, a young Ph.D. from a nearby university, still unsure of himself in the classroom, was asked by a very self-confident student why we had to read "all this old stuff." Considering the question, the professor thought for a long moment. Then he said, "To extend your range of taste." At the time, I found this answer feeble. It had the ring of "the right set," those who buy their clothes at certain expensive emporia. Perhaps, however, by the phrase "good taste" he meant, "loving things that suggest beauty and truth." If so, he meant a connection between good taste and wisdom. Some may balk at the phrase "good taste," but I doubt anyone would argue that a 40-year-old woman who still liked to play with Barbie dolls had good taste. I have come to realize that it would take a lot of explanation to get at what that professor meant by "taste" and the thinking behind it. But he probably sensed that his student questioner would have neither the patience nor the range of experience, in life or in reading, to understand his explanation.

When colleges say that their goal is to teach "critical thinking," they do not mean "critical thinking about taste." Some people dismiss the very idea of arguing about taste because, they say, there is no disputing it—*de gustibus* and all that. Still, it depends on what taste you are talking about. It is hard to convince one to like spinach; no amount of reasoning will work. But it is possible to give the reasons why a certain composer is one's favorite, and those reasons may be persuasive. Moreover, we can and should grow out of the preferences we had when we were young. Youth tends to like books and poems that pulse with great drama of life. But taste requires something beyond luxuriating in feeling or luxuriating in violence or, for that matter, luxuriating in cynicism. It requires restraint, the restraint that comes with sufficiently steadying one's emotional involvement in a story or argument to evaluate the appeal to the part of one's soul that tends, all too much, to like tension, pathos, bitterness. Taste about music leads to differences of opinion. There are people who much prefer Baroque music to nineteenth-century romantic music, and they can tell you why. If one's musical experience has started with Beethoven, Mendelssohn, and Brahms, it is interesting to hear why someone else prefers Vivaldi or Bach.

While the "music" that Plato recommends to young children is not difficult, the "music" of the poetry—in the widest sense—that students meet in college is often difficult. But the language in which these books are sometimes talked about is strange. Cicero warned that, in speeches, technical terms were to be avoided because good rhetoric, like good literature, should speak to the community, not to specialists. Much modern teaching of literature might benefit from Cicero's warning. Nowadays, English departments generally agree that literature should be read through complex literary theories, with technical terms that require much practice in the handling. Thus, what used to be aimed at the generally educated public is presented by way of a language with many gears, screws, and sharp edges clanking around in a toolbox. Poetry begins in the "foul rag and bone shop of the heart"—Yeats's line. Talking about the rags and bones of poetry's source by way of an opaque professional argot turns the work to dust.

Then, too, in today's university, students have been seduced by not only critical high tech but by the notion that nothing legitimizes authority, a claim that is implicitly at work in the various theories that students read or have heard about and which, oddly, they regard as "authorities," oddly because most of these books argue that there is no such thing as authority. They have learned mockery, not unlike Sebastian's in *The Tempest*. It provides great satisfaction to ask of someone, in the accents of shocked disbelief, if she is so naïve as *still* to believe in "the truth" or in "universals" (at her age!). Montaigne was trying to open the world's eyes to differences in custom, and as different customs have become known, we have learned not to be rattled by cultural differences; Montaigne was not appalled by cannibalism. Anthropology has backed him up in his acceptance of differences; different peoples have different customs—many ways of eating, many ways of marrying, many ways of solving quarrels. Awareness of these differences is crucial to the modern virtue of tolerance and to the belief in cultural relativism.

But there are troubles with this comfortable acceptance of different ways of doing things. At the same time that tolerance is much lauded, the traditional respect for human rights is also much lauded because there is something in human nature—without quotation marks around that phrase—that should not be violated. As I said above, the human creature has the power to think about what a good human life might be; that creature deserves to have rights. There is a problem, however, in holding to cultural relativism on the one hand and on the other to a notion of "rights," because if there is no such thing as something inviolable in every human being, then there cannot be such a thing as human rights; there would, after all, be nothing in the individual human being to be violated. Even the cultural relativists are sure that there are certain things that should not be done to human beings. If there are certain things that cannot be done to human beings (they should not be tortured, the practice of clitorectomy is barbaric, slavery is de-humanizing, throwing babies down wells is inhuman), then one is assuming, or at least appealing to, a standard that is higher than an array of cultures, all practicing tolerance toward each other.

The concentration in the library that lifts minds to a higher plane cannot withstand the onslaught of there-is-no-such-thing-as-truth. When we argue, we believe that some views are closer to the truth and some farther away; but we could not hold that one position is closer if there is no standard. Mathematicians may say that there are problems that have no solution, but mathematicians agree on the difficulties that make a solution impossible.

Without some notion of what is at least in the arena of agreed-upon arguments, we would never be able to decide what arguments make more sense than others. Without these agreements, discussion devolves into wily maneuvers. As the wise man Sun Tzu said about warfare, the best way to deal with an opponent is to attack, attack, attack. Reading and discussing becomes combat. For many of the young, the thrill of clever icon-smashing has taken the place of illumination. Patiently allowing an author to make his case through argument or, in a work of fiction, through the slow unfolding of incident, is regarded as pitiable naiveté. Hence, the student with an up-to-date education is on the alert. She has been taught that every author is hiding something, and her task is to discover it. The psychology of "coming to understand" has been changed to the distrustful interrogation of a perpetrator of non-truths. But if there is no standard for weighing claims to truth, then no claim is true or false; there can be no such thing as a non-truth.

Another attack is by way of politics. A student has heard a professor say that literature is a semiotics of power, and if a reader reads carefully, he can detect the author's subtle attack on the political injustices of his day or his subtle reinforcement of the power of a dominant class. The question about any one of Shakespeare's plays, is—what was going on in England at the end of the sixteenth and beginning of the seventeenth centuries? A weak student finds the argument nifty and feels he is in the know when he asks of *Midsummer Night's Dream*, "What was going on in Athens at this time?" as if the play had anything to do with the political situation of Athens in the late sixteenth century or at any other time. He has heard the argument, but he does not understand it, and if he did perhaps understand it, his teacher did not ask him to consider its limitations.

When an author is not attacking the injustices of the society in which he wrote, he is often hiding something, and then his method is dubbed "mystification." Authors who talk about honor and decency and justice are indulging in mystification of the truth that all societies are built on oppression. Any lines spoken by a once-denominated tragic figure—a Hamlet or a Cordelia or a Lear—are, it is argued, so many tangled threads obscuring the hard fact of power subduing the powerless. A fancier version of this argument attacks education itself. One way to reinforce the power of one group of people over another—or at least to intimidate them—is to amass the "cultural capital" of learning. The very people who relish the phrase "cultural capitalism" are the ones who have accepted the argument that all higher-planed education is an enforcement of class distinctions. But what is the phrase "cultural capitalism," used with an air of wise sophistication, except itself an advertisement of cultural capital?

Yes, education can be used for self-promotion; we all know the type who wraps herself in quotations from Shakespeare, and we have come to know the teacher who can wield nimbly some strange, complex words. It is true that philosophy sometimes needs new and strange terms. But, except for *Finnegan's Wake*, writers did not write for Ph.D's in literature or literary theory. Moreover, if the modern de-mystifyers of power are sure that cultural capital is a way of maintaining power, why did they go into teaching?—for, at the very least, to teach undergraduates that anything difficult to read is a power grab risks having the tables turned on the teacher herself.

Of course, "thoughtfulness" leads to the subject of wisdom, and I am back at the oft-heard rejoinder, "whose wisdom?"—uttered as the irrefutable dismissal of wisdom itself. But wisdom is worth discussing because, as Aristotle's argument goes, all human beings seek happiness, and for this goal, it might help to ponder what happiness is. The pondering will probably require very long discussion. The thinkers presented here all agreed that a connection with a transcendent world is necessary to wisdom. If the gods do not exist, then neither does there exist the mysterious source of human reason, which impels the human creature to seek for something higher. Perhaps a human connection with a transcendent world is a subject that cannot be argued. In the tenth book of Plato's *Laws*, one of the three old men discussing how to construct the best possible human city holds that belief in the gods is necessary for the investigation at hand and that therefore a proper prelude for their conversation would be a prayer (*Laws*, 887c–88d). The prayer sets the tone for a respectful view of the gods. Another figure, however, the Athenian stranger, the wise man of the three interlocutors, muses to his two fellow inquirers that they ought to consider the arguments of the atheists. He warns that the discussion will take a long time; his dispassionate and thorough presentation does indeed take a long time. His is an important point. Most of the questions that come up about any truly serious question require consideration of the other side; measuring the two sides may take a long time—months, years, a lifetime.

In college, I knew of a professor who wrote on a student's paper that he had to give it an A because the paper analyzed the play so well; but he could tell that this student had regarded her task as performing an exercise and that she had no love for the play. As a professional, he did his job and credited her with having performed the exercise well. Perhaps he thought to himself, it is not the student's job to love the books she is assigned; her job is simply to show that she has learned the skills the course claimed to teach. But an argument can be made on the other side. The professor was reaching for considerations that were outside the realm of "skills," for facility with mere skills is not a difficult accomplishment. True education is something else. It is learning to appreciate a well-considered exploration of a problem. Some kinds of appreciation are restricted to specialized disciplines; scientists learn to appreciate descriptions of nature's complex operations; philosophers learn to appreciate a well-constructed argument. But the most important appreciations are not confined to a specific "field" or a "discipline." It is appreciation of the works of human beings who have struggled to see into the heart of things. When the professor did not dock the student's grade, he was rightly acting according to an unstated law between academic evaluators and student learners; but in his comment on the paper, he put into the student's mind something to think about.

# PLATO'S MUSIC

## 1. Persuasion of the Ordinary Citizen

Explaining why some books are great may be a fruitless effort because, as Socrates would say, if a soul is not ready to admire them, no amount of explaining will help. In his view, to understand greatness, one has to be prepared to see it, and that preparation requires an early start in childhood and some refresher exercises thereafter.

I start with one of Plato's shorter dialogues, the *Crito*, because its ending has raised controversy and because the terms of that controversy involve Plato's views about the importance of childhood education, about educability in general, and also about the place of music in persuasion. For Plato, there are some people who cannot hear the music of poetry and cannot therefore hear the complexities of an argument. For Plato, this was a central educational problem, and also a central political problem.

Plato structures the *Crito* by beginning with an educational problem and finishing with a political problem. He obscures the educational problem by focusing on a character who is not a student. Early in the morning, Crito, a friend of Socrates, visits him in prison. Having been condemned by the Athenian jury, Socrates awaits the arrival of the ship from Delos that will allow Athens to carry out the verdict of execution. After its arrival, the hemlock will fulfill the sentence of the Athenian jury. When Crito arrives, he remains silent until Socrates awakes before proposing a means to facilitate Socrates' escape—a bribe for the jailer. When Socrates refuses Crito's proposal, Crito becomes distressed and wants to know why Socrates is not also distressed. He fires off a series of arguments about why Socrates should accept his help in escaping from prison. First, Socrates should not worry about his children if he has to flee to another city; Socrates' admirers will care for them. Second, if Socrates does not allow Crito to help him escape, other people will question Crito's devotion to his philosopher friend; surely

18

Socrates realizes that people will say Crito should have used his great wealth to engineer Socrates' escape. Third, it is unmanly of Socrates not to try to escape; Socrates may say he is not interested in the opinions of others, but it is a fact of life that the opinions of others can drive a mob to come after you at any moment.

> *Crito*: But, Socrates, tell me this. Surely you aren't worrying, are you, on behalf of me and the rest of your companions, over the prospect that if you leave here, the informers will make trouble for us on the ground that we stole you away from here, and we will be compelled to lose either our whole substance or a lot of money, or even to suffer something else besides this? If you fear some such thing, leave it aside. For surely it is just for us to save you and run this risk, and one still greater than this, if need be. But obey me, and do not do otherwise.

> *Socrates*: I am worrying over the prospect of these things, Crito, and of many others.[5]

In other translations, the line is: "I am considering this, Crito, and many other things," and elsewhere, "I do have these things in mind, Crito, and many others." It is the phrase "and many others" that counts. The line sounds weary and distracted. It is remarkable for its restraint; one wonders why Socrates does not specify at least some of the "many other" things he has on his mind. One has to have read other works of Plato to surmise what the "many others" might be. I will return to this passage in the *Crito* at the end of the chapter.

Socrates' response may have a slight undertone of exasperation because he has reason to doubt that Crito understands his philosophy. That doubt goes to the heart of Plato's wider doubt, not just doubt about Crito but about human nature. For Plato, the highest happiness lies in the longing for and love of an idea connected to a transcendent world. The Greek word

---

5    *Four Texts on Socrates*, trans. Thomas G. West and Grace Starry West (Ithaca and London: Cornell University Press, 1984). All quotations from the *Crito* are from this translation.

for this love is *eros*. The transcendent world in which reside Beauty and the Good is the anchor human beings can count on. To create in the soul love for this world is the ultimate goal of Plato's educational program. Plato is, however, quite aware of the distractions that lure human nature away from this goal—ambition, impatience, fascination with precision in small fields of inquiry, laziness, sentimentality, and cowardice. Crito is a rich symbol of the last three—laziness in thinking, sentimentality, and cowardice. In the course of teaching over four decades, I sympathize with Socrates' sense of futility. As the years passed, I began to see many of my students as the prisoners that Plato imagines in his cave, prisoners of an education that has taught them glibness instead of thoughtfulness. Instead of cowardice, other figures with whom Socrates converses show another kind of fault—energy wrongly directed. I have seen that, too.

Student resistance to the Platonic goal derives from mistaking clever debunking for reflection. For Plato, thoughtfulness is crucial to erotic love of Beauty and Good. Distinguishing between the false and the true shines a light on sophistry. In my teaching days, I knew of a professor, a person with a good deal of charm, who told his students that it is small wonder Socrates was put to death, that he was an irritating old busybody whose incessant talk about virtue and the examined life missed the obvious truth that having a family or having a successful career are greater satisfactions than being a philosopher. But this characterization of Socrates' position is not true. Socrates does not say the philosophical life is for everybody (and what Socrates means by "philosopher" is not an "intellectual"), but he does say that inquiry into the questions of virtue and truth must undergird any happiness a person can achieve.

Inquiry must undergird any life for two reasons, the first having to do with politics and the second having to do with happiness. As an endeavor related to politics, the inquiry into virtue and truth will govern the individual's speech and actions, and those speeches and actions will in turn influence those around him. This is the argument by aggregate; people tend to follow those whose company they keep. Moreover, as an endeavor related to personal happiness, inquiry into virtue and truth tunes the soul to the highest in human beings. That "highest" is the greatest happiness. If most of us non-philosophers cannot get to the state of the true philosopher, then the closer we get, the better for us.

The argument by aggregate is the force behind Socrates' question to Meletus in the *Apology*. "Does anyone want to live in a polity with bad citizens? No? Then why are you accusing me of corrupting the young? Why would I want to live in a polity with corrupt citizens?" (26c–d, paraphrase). Much hangs on what kind of people the city wants the next generation to be. Socrates-the-fussbudget is an easy jibe and a sure way to persuade all too receptive students that dwelling with Plato is not a good use of their time. The point is not that one should consider oneself uneducated if one has not read Plato; it is that Plato thought out crucial problems in morality and politics with a complexity appropriate to the difficulty of those problems. If those questions have been thought out with the same profundity by another author, that author should by all means be read.

The professor's quip that the Athenians were well rid of Socrates was made for laughs, and to that end, successful; the students regarded Socrates as a joke. It is a great temptation for a teacher to persuade students that he shares their skeptical view of "greatness," for the professor gets the reputation of being cool. But a laughing dismissiveness toward a philosopher who taught the importance of reason in guiding human lives is a worse corruption of the young than asking them, as Socrates did, to examine their lives, precisely because of the affect in which the corruption is couched. The advertised goal of a secondary education is for students to be challenged, but for an adult to talk in the breezy, shrugging argot of the young is not to challenge but to flatter. For Plato, a citizen cannot become good in a city in which citizens are not encouraging each other to become better people.

To persuade the young to the pursuit of a philosophical life, Plato strives for ordinary language used precisely. For his unphilosophical hearers, on the other hand, Plato admits a language that does not rely on precise abstractions. He calls this less-than-the-most-precise-language *mousike,* or music. When in Book 3 of the *Republic*, Plato discusses the necessary regulation of art in the beautiful city, he includes under *mousike* both the sounds played on a musical instrument and, significantly, poetry.[6] Music and poetry shape the souls of children; in the *Republic*, Plato refers to "the muse of philosophy" (499c).

---

6   Plato, *Republic*, 376e, translated G. M. A. Grube with revisions by C. D. C. Reeve (Indianapolis and Cambridge: Hackett Publishing Company, 1995). All references to the *Republic* are from this translation.

But *mousike* can also shape the soul to ill by arousing the passions and thereby creating confusion. Therefore, music and poetry must be regulated. Regulated *mousike* prepares the soul for understanding true harmony:

> Education, I say, is the virtue that first comes into being in children. Pleasure and liking, pain and hatred, become correctly arranged in the souls of those who are not yet able to reason, and then, when the souls do become capable of reasoning, these passions can in consonance with reason affirm that they have been correctly habituated in the appropriate habits. (*Laws*, 653b)

Later in the child's education, musical harmony may be superseded by more precise languages—mathematics and finally dialectic—both of which enable the soul to "give an account," in one of Plato's favorite phrases, of what harmony is and why it should be sought. But the nonverbal arguments of music must be kept alive even in adulthood because they reinforce the harmony of the soul gained through reason. Although Plato has a reputation for being opposed to art, we have only to read the dialogues to realize that he is keenly aware of the power of poetry's music to move the soul. As Socrates's line to Crito suggests, even the philosopher needs music to harmonize his soul, for he must constantly negotiate between people as they are and people as they might be, the world as it is and the world as it might be. This essay, then, might be called "Platonic *Mousike* for an Imperfect World."

## 2. Music and the Soul's Harmony

In the world of a college education, there are many shortcuts. When students say they have read Plato ("Oh, I've *done* Plato"), they mean that they know—or they have heard about—the Forms, the divided line, the allegory of the cave. They know that the *Phaedrus* is about love, that the *Symposium* means "drinking together," and that in that dialogue there is indeed a lot of drinking, and that Aristophanes has a funny story about egg-like ovoids cut in half. But above all, they know that Plato recommended political lies, approved the censorship of art, and insisted on careful logic. The first two charges are the ones that are most frequently leveled because they offer an easy way to argue that Plato is not as great as some have thought and that therefore he does not have to be read with serious attention. Plato's endorsement of censorship flies in the face of modernity's confidence that art is the arena in which can be questioned all that the great powers assume. If art is seductive, as Plato thought, it is, for the modern student, seductive for the good. Since art has taken over the place of religion (in *Doktor Faustus*, Thomas Mann calls it "culture without the cult"), students think it boorish to suggest that perhaps art sometimes stimulates in ways that are pernicious. Plato's arguments about art are, however, more complicated than most students are willing to see.

In teaching Plato, however, the teacher's greatest difficulty is with the intelligent student who insists, with some justification, that Plato opposed art not only because it taught unwise things about the gods or aroused the emotions but, more fundamentally, because it had no true cognitive power. This reader points to Plato's emphasis on careful logical thinking and his favorite distinction between experts and laymen. True, Plato concedes that non-philosophers can also use precise knowledge. He draws on common human experience to make his case. When a person is ill, he wants to be treated by someone who knows about diseases—a doctor; when passengers on a ship find themselves in the midst of a storm, they want someone experienced in sailing ships—a pilot. The advantage of philosophic precision as opposed to the precision of specialized skills, however, is its universality. In the *Meno*, the phrase for the knowledge derived from logic is "the tie of the cause" (*aitias logismos*).[7] In that dialogue, Socrates makes the analogy between inquiry into the logical steps of an argument and discovering the invariable relationship expressed in the Pythagorean theorem. That invariable relationship is the *aitias logismos*. The logic of geometry guarantees stability; the theorem will always be true. As Socrates says in the *Crito*:

> Dear Crito, your eagerness is worth much if some correctness
> be with it. If not, the greater it is, the harder it is to deal with.
> So we should consider whether these things are to be done or

---

7   *Meno*, 98a, in *Plato: Five Dialogues,* 2nd ed., translated G. M. A. Grube, revised John M. Cooper (Indianapolis, Cambridge: Hackett Publishing Company, 2002).

not, since I not only now but always, am such as to obey nothing else of what is mine but that argument which appears best
to me upon reasoning. (46b)

Once the argument—the *logismos*—is understood, one must submit to
its logic until a better argument presents itself. In Plato's view, the risk of
art is its lack of strict logic. Its appeal to the senses dulls the power of reason and undermines it. Perhaps the best word for summing up Plato's attitude to art is to say he thought it was "charming," with all the
ambiguities of that word. Despite Plato's emphasis on logical precision
and expertise, he is willing, nevertheless, to grant some cognitive power
to the intuitions of *mousike*.

Indeed, the cognitive power of intuition is the foundation of childhood education. In childhood, the soul is still fluid and uncomposed.
But if the child is raised in an orderly, stable, and beautiful environment,
he learns through the senses to recognize symmetry, proportion, and balance: " ... when children play the right games and absorb lawfulness from
music and poetry, it follows them in everything and fosters their growth"
(*Rep.*, 425a). When the soul matures, it will know by intuition when
something is unbalanced or disordered. The right kind of music cannot
define the soul's true home, but training in music will help to steer the
soul in the right general direction. If a child is taught order and proportion by the harmony of his surroundings, he will have:

> the right distastes ... praise fine things, be pleased by them, re-
> ceive them into his soul. He'll rightly object to what is shameful,
> hating it while he's still young and *unable to grasp the reason*,
> but, having been educated in this way, he will welcome the rea-
> son when it comes and recognize it easily because of its kinship
> with himself. (*Rep.*, 402a; italics added)

As poets and novelists have known for a long time, the way people speak
and the tone of their voices signal the difference between those who have
made progress on the path to a thoughtful life and those who have fallen
by the way. In the *Republic*, Plato calls his balancing kind of music "the
song of dialectic," the Greek for which is, interestingly enough, the same

word for "law," or *nomos* (*Rep.*, 532a). The song of dialectic articulates the harmony suggested only in outline by music. Dialectic teaches the hearer to enjoy defining, distinguishing, ordering. The music of dialectic is simple but precise. Its timbres—patient, careful—teach the right attitudes toward the philosophical quest.

Most important, souls on the way to Beauty and Goodness can, more surely than others, see in the philosopher the representative of a happy life (*Rep.*, 433b–d). Intuiting the harmony in the philosopher's soul prompts the auditor to inquire into its foundation. The auditor will know, by the calm and harmony of the philosopher's speech, that he is accustomed to reasoning soundly. In this way, a teacher's *mousike* is crucial to education because it can gently discipline the soul and thereby teach it composure, which reinforces justice, the soul's overarching principle:

> However, [justice] isn't concerned with someone's doing his own externally, but with what is inside him and *what is truly himself and his own.* And when he does anything, whether acquiring wealth, taking care of his body, engaging in politics, or in private contracts—in all of these, he believes that the action is just and fine that *preserves the inner harmony* and helps achieve it, and calls it so, and *regards as wisdom the knowledge that oversees such actions.* (*Rep.*, 443c–e; italics added)

Justice is the articulated principle that harmonizes the parts of the soul. This principle steadies "that which is truly himself." A soul ruled by justice is not easily swayed by turmoil around it.

In showing how Socrates' harmony of soul attracts the distracted young, Plato is arguing that the soul's internalization of justice can itself be a political act. Indeed, Socrates' skill in dialectic combines forcefulness without anger in facing down arrogance, irony in depreciating folly, hesitation in stating conclusions, courtesy in reminding interlocutors that discussion should be carried on slowly, thoroughly, and graciously. By contrast, when disorder, or lack of moderation, is allowed into the musical part of education, that lawlessness "flows over little by little into characters and ways of life" (*Rep.*, 424d). The moderation essential to the citizenry of a well-ordered polity starts with a musical education.

### 3. Souls in Progress

The most obvious way Plato puts his literary or musical gifts to work is in characterizing souls who have gone in the wrong direction. He would agree with Ben Jonson's line, "Speech most shows a man; speak that I may see thee." He portrays various pseudo-philosophers who present themselves as teachers hoping to acquire a reputation for such wisdom. In the *Meno*, it is hard to know which Meno Plato wishes us to envision, a man who is very young and impatient with serious thinking or a man who, though young, is nevertheless imperious. The opening of the dialogue can be read as the breathless question of a young man or a challenge from someone who is accustomed to giving orders:

> Can you tell me, Socrates, can virtue be taught? Or is it not teachable but the result of practice, or is it neither of these, but men possess it by nature, or in some other way?

Meno assumes the teachability of virtue can be explained in readily available nuggets. In the *Symposium*, the drunken Alcibiades announces his love for Socrates, but his incoherent ramblings show he does not fully understand him. In the *Phaedrus*, because a young man's enthusiasm for speeches bubbles up out of him like the water of a spring, Socrates must, before he can teach him anything, dampen that enthusiasm. In the *Euthyphro*, a professional priest's paralyzed habits of thinking will not suffer any rearrangement. In the *Protagoras*, a famous man has learned that elegant volubility can capture the admiration of a large audience seeking confirmation of its prejudices. In the *Gorgias*, a young-man-on-the-move angrily dismisses anything that smacks of traditional piety. As has long been pointed out, Plato can make the dialogue a true drama, where characters are doing something ("doing" in Greek is related to the Greek word for "drama"). Their "doing" is taking action, sometimes with stolid determination, sometimes with aggression.

One of the most pointed of these actions is the confrontation between Callicles and Socrates in the *Gorgias*. The two are battling over the question of whether or not a man of virtue should aim for power or wisdom. Callicles heatedly argues that a man who does not know how to pretend to be wise will always be at the mercy of ignorant people, and for Callicles, such a position is a humiliation. Does Socrates not recognize this obvious fact? Socrates replies with weary dispassion:

> *Socrates*: Of course I do, Callicles. It isn't only you who've been telling me: I hear it time and again from almost everyone in Athens. But I've got something to tell you too. [The man who can fake wisdom] may well kill him [the man who cannot, that is, the philosopher], if he wants, but it'll be a bad man killing a paragon of virtue.

Callicles then bursts out with:

> *Callicles*: Yes, and isn't that exactly what makes it infuriating, on top of everything else?[8]

Somewhere in Callicles' turbulent thinking, there is, after all, a fundamental agreement with Socrates; a man with superior knowledge should not be vulnerable to the whims of the ignorant.

Callicles' exasperation resonates with anyone who has read the *Apology*; it is not *right* for a more thoughtful person to be at the mercy of the less thoughtful; it is infuriating that a great philosopher should be put to death by people who think in the clichés of the day. For Callicles-the-operator, however, one does not have to submit to such a vulnerable position; one can *do* something about it; one can scramble for power. The confidence of these "doers" is easy to portray because their speeches are so noisy. Plato has Socrates meet Callicles' attack not by a louder shouting but by calm. In short, Socrates' harmony of soul emphasizes by contrast how much his interlocutors, no matter how confident their aggression, have souls in conflict; they are full of bravado, but they are also fearful.

Nowhere is the conflict in the soul more obvious than in tragedy. It is small wonder that Plato objects to tragedy because, by giving the tragic hero a passionate *mousike*, the playwright glorifies the fighting within the

---

8    *Plato: Gorgias*, 511b, translated Robin Waterfield (Oxford and New York: Oxford University Press, 1994). All quotations from the *Gorgias* are from this edition.

soul of the hero and thus invites the audience to sympathize with him. The turmoil in the tragic hero, however, is at its heart a fight against the limits of human life, limits established by the gods. Moreover, the gods see the future, but human beings cannot. As a result, human beings move around in their environment like blind animals (see the semi-articulate exclamations and murmurings of Io in *Prometheus Bound*). Human beings know they will die but do not know when or how. As Homer emphasizes over and over, human life is measured against the gods-who-live-at-ease.

But of all the beings the gods created, human beings have one advantage. They do not have to regard suffering as irremediable. Unlike animals, they can use their cleverness to ameliorate the harshness of their lives. In *Prometheus Bound*, the chorus describes how human beings discovered shelter, medicine, and prophecy. In *Oedipus Rex*, Oedipus solves the riddle of the sphinx and frees Thebes from the plague. In *Antigone,* Creon points out that human politics and law have made the city, and in the city, human beings can enjoy friendship. Although human reason can improve human life, however, those improvements risk being a challenge to the fundamental distinction between gods and human beings. For that challenge, the human being must be punished. The tragic hero—warrior or philosopher—sets out to make life better for himself or for his people, but then encounters unforeseen consequences for himself or for those around him.

The distinguishing characteristic of being human—what makes it possible not be constrained to live the life of a beast—is, then, a painful mystery. Nowhere is the mystery more painful that in *Oedipus Rex*. Oedipus uses his intelligence to solve the riddle of the sphinx and save his city. When another plague attacks the city, he thinks, justifiably, that he can do so again. In order to do so, he must find out the source of the curse on the city. Sophocles emphasizes Oedipus' nobility in the pursuit of the truth by putting next to him the self-protective Jocasta, who wishes to evade it. When Oedipus cries out, "What have you designed, O Zeus, to do with me?"[9] Sophocles is dramatizing the paradox in life introduced by human intelligence. Human beings, unlike animals, have a power by which they can rise

9    *Oedipus the King*, line 738, in *Sophocles 1,* David Grene and Richmond Lattimore, 3rd ed., edited by Mark Griffith and Glenn Most (Chicago: University of Chicago Press, 2013).

above the life of beasts; at the same time, that power can lead human beings to imagine they can overcome human nature and the human condition. It was foretold that Oedipus would kill his father and marry his mother, and although Oedipus, wishing not to offend the gods, did everything in his power to avoid such a fate, he did in fact kill his father and marry his mother. Human beings are free and yet they are not. Tragedy both allows and encourages the audience to protest against that mystery. Such a protest is, for Plato, fruitless. A tragedy is not helping human beings when it encourages an audience to suffer with the tragic hero (*Rep.*, 605c). The *mousike* that better accompanies the effort to improve human life will encourage composure in the soul, clarity of thought, and acceptance of some of life's difficulties.

## 4. *The Composed Soul and the Composed Work of Art*

A tragedy moves toward a stunned silence that both elicits and expresses catharsis. There is nothing more to say, as Albany remarks at the end of *King Lear*. For Plato, however, the artistic work should concentrate less on the heroic soul than on the composed one, or as he would say, the just one. As Plato recognizes, however, a play about a good man will not appeal to a popular audience because the good man is not *doing* anything, at least not doing anything that is satisfyingly dramatic. To draw admiration for Socrates, Plato surrounds him with obviously uncomposed souls.

In some dialogues, however, Plato has a different solution—to compose the whole dialogue as a work of art. In this way, "the beauty of the good," as Plato calls it in Book 6 of the *Republic*, lies not only in the good man but in the beauty of the dialogue as a musical whole. It is musical insofar as it has one tone, and then another, and then another, and then a conclusion, something that *closes them* all up together, i.e., *concludes* them.

In the *Phaedrus*, Plato gives some sign that he has thought about philosophical conclusions. While discussing rhetoric with Phaedrus, Socrates asks his eager pupil a question:

> And suppose someone approached Sophocles and Euripides and
> claimed to know how to compose the longest passages on trivial
> topics and the briefest ones on topics of great importance, that

he could make them pitiful if he wanted, or again, by contrast, terrifying and menacing, and so on. Suppose further that he believed that by teaching this he was imparting the knowledge of composing tragedies—

*Phaedrus:* Oh, I am sure they too would laugh at anyone who thought a tragedy was anything other than the proper arrangement of these things: *They have to fit with one another and the whole work.*[10]

In a well-constructed piece of art, the parts will "fit with one another and the whole work." The harmony among those parts expresses the harmony of a philosophical soul (*Rep.*, 433c–e). It teaches that everything is connected to everything else (*Rep.* 537c). In Plato's beautiful city, students should see, by the age of twenty, that "the subjects learned in no particular order [when they were children] ... must now bring together to form a unified vision of their kinship both with one another and with the nature of *that which is*" (*Rep.*, 537b–c; italics added).

## 5. The Music of the Educator

Strangely enough, after a first reading of the *Phaedrus*, the dialogue does not seem to be well orchestrated at all. Instead, it seems to fall into two distinct parts—the first part ending in the so-called Great Speech, in which Plato pulls out all the stops in describing what love truly is, and the second part arguing about what rhetoric teaches. The first part has long sections where Plato allows Socrates, or perhaps Plato himself, to indulge in an extended satire followed by an ecstatic depiction of love of Beauty, Truth, and the Good. Then, in the second part, by contrast, the dialogue is broken up in short snippets, as Plato allows Socrates to do his usual question-and-answer. The dialogue concludes with the Myth of Theuth and an apparent renunci-

---

10 *Plato: Phaedrus*, 268 (see also 263e), translated with introduction and notes, by Alexander Nehemas and Paul Woodruff (Indianapolis and Cambridge: Hackett Publishing Company, 1995), italics added. All quotations from the *Phaedrus* are from this translation.

ation of the dialogue itself, for Socrates argues that the best discourse is never written down, when obviously Plato wrote it down and so thought there must be some point in writing. What holds all these disparate parts together?

One harmonizing part of the *Phaedrus* is the changes in the titular character. Phaedrus is, at the beginning, a charming young man, enthusiastic about altogether too many things. Both the *Phaedrus* and the *Lysis* have at their beginning the question, *poi de kai pothen?*—"where and whence?" or "where have you come from and where are you going?" A properly educated soul should be reaching out for "everything human and divine as a whole" (*Rep.*, 486a). A good depiction of this eagerness to reach out will show both its potential and its danger. Phaedrus starts as a young man who is easily impressed. He has found a copy of a speech of Lysias, and, because it has a novel argument, he thinks the speech is marvelous. It takes little effort on Socrates' part to induce Phaedrus to take from his cloak the scroll on which Lysias' speech is written and to recite it. In a desultory fashion, Lysias' speech argues that it is better for a youth to be pursued by a non-lover than a lover, because the non-lover is calculating and therefore level-headed, and if level-headed, then reasonable. It is better to be loved by a reasonable man—reasonable, of course, in a certain definition of that word. Phaedrus is amazed by this cleverness.

Socrates counters with his own version of Lysias' speech. He does not, however, renounce the argument that a non-lover is better for the beloved than the lover. Socrates' improvements are instead logical clarity. He starts with a definition of love and then becomes, as he himself confesses, positively dithyrambic with the elaboration of his examples (238d). When this speech finishes, however, Socrates disavows its import, recanting the argument that a non-lover is better for a young boy than a lover. In a third speech written by one Stesichorus, which Socrates recites, the argument swings around in favor of *eros*. A man who is in love is in fact the best of all gifts for a youth, but only with a certain understanding of "love." A true lover of youth will desire not the youth's body but the readiness of the youth's soul to pursue a vision of the Good. In this account, Socrates starts with a definition, then presents the stages of love—falling in love with the beauty of a body, then the beauty of a soul, and finally the beauty of a vision of the whole. At that point, the lover travels with the gods and looks down on the whole world:

31

> But when the souls we call immortals reach the top [of the rim of heaven], they move outward and take their stand on the high ridge of heaven where its circular motion carries them around as they stand while they gaze on what is outside heaven. (246b–c)

There follows the allegory of the charioteer and his two horses, which culminates in an image of the lover's sight of the truth. This vision persuades the lover to follow his favorite boy "with reverence and awe" (254e). When the boy matures, he comes to understand that "all that friendship he has from his other friends and relatives put together is nothing as compared with this friend who is inspired by a god" (255b).

In Phaedrus' view, Socrates now surpasses the celebrity speech-maker so admired at the beginning of the dialogue. For the reader, however, Socrates' speech teaches a new understanding of *eros,* and its *mousike* teaches the *feeling* of that new understanding of *eros.* When Phaedrus admits to admiring the speech for the feeling it has inspired in his soul, he has moved beyond the admiration for mere cleverness to the deeper pleasure of ecstatic absorption into something higher—ecstatic in the root meaning of the word, "standing outside oneself."

His education is not, however, complete. Phaedrus is right to be enthusiastic about speeches; and he is right to be enthusiastic about the connection between an erotic friendship and an education in philosophy; and he is certainly right to be enthusiastic about Socrates. But enthusiasm risks being an untempered joy merely in being enthusiastic—that is, *in being young.* In this dialogue, Plato gives a free rein to youth in the character of Phaedrus himself, in allowing Phaedrus to recite the speech of Lysias, and then entering himself into a speech competition, and finally, permitting himself unrestrained exuberance in the rhetorical extravagance of the so-called "Great Speech."

> *Socrates*: Now this takes me to the whole point of my discussion ... that which someone shows when he sees the beauty we have down here and is reminded of true beauty; then he takes wing and flutters in his eagerness to rise up, but is unable to do so; and he gazes aloft, like a bird paying no attention to what is down below—and that is what

brings on him the charge that he has gone mad. This is the best and noblest of all the forms that possession by a god can take for anyone who has it or is connected to it. (*Phaedrus*, 249d–e)

The speech soars into the realm of the gods, floating above the world and viewing with mild disinterestedness everything outside of the center of order, balance, and steadiness. Socrates knows that this sort of expansive optimism is what Phaedrus really wants to hear, not the cramped, sophisticated cynicism of Lysias—he wants to hear it and needs to hear it. The recitation is the philosopher's concession to the eagerness of youth, for Plato says in the *Republic* that "great and numerous labors belong to the young" (*Rep.*, 536d). Or perhaps "measurement" is a better word than concession; Plato is *measuring* youth. The speech is at once Plato's admission that youth is charming in its eagerness to embrace new ideas, but it is also an assessment of the liabilities of that eagerness.

In allowing youth its hour in the sun, Plato provides the dialogue with comedy's reassurances. First, as in Shakespeare, there is beneficent nature. Socrates and Phaedrus are outside the city in the fresh air where all of summer seems to combine to promise eternal life—warm sun, cool stream, a plane tree, grass to lie down on, cicadas singing. Then too, like many comedies, this one has the piquancy of sex. The whole encounter provokes the question—who is seducing whom? Phaedrus thinks he is seducing Socrates:

*Socrates*: Lead the way then, and find us a place to sit.
*Phaedrus*: Do you see that very tall plane tree?
*Socrates*: Of course.
*Phaedrus*: It's shady, with a light breeze; we can sit, or, if we prefer, lie down on the grass there. (229a–b)

And:

*Socrates*: I'll cover my head while I am speaking. In that way, as I am going through the speech as fast as I can, I would get embarrassed by having to look at you and lose the thread of my argument.

*Phaedrus*: Just give your speech! You can do anything else you like. (237a)

And:

*Socrates*: Where then is the boy to whom I was speaking? Let him hear this speech, too. Otherwise, he may be too quick to give his favors to a non-lover.
*Phaedrus*: He is here, always right by your side, whenever you want him. (243e)

Part of the comic shield over the whole is the naiveté of Phaedrus, who thinks he is the one doing the seducing when it is actually Socrates leading Phaedrus onward to something he knows only "musically" that he wanted. Comedy is both charmed by youth and also condescending to it, for its sages, like Feste in *Twelfth Night*, measure its enthusiasms against a more sober view of life.

Comedy facilitates the transition from Socrates' exaggerated self-mockery to a more serious probing of love. First, Socrates mocks himself by covering his head as he recites the revised version of Lysias' speech. Then he mocks himself by exclaiming over his slide into dithyrambs and his slide from lyric to epic. Although Socrates switches to question and answer, his questioning is in the manner of the *Republic,* that is, "in play" (*Rep.,* 536c). In the second part of the dialogue, with its more serious probing, the goal is to temper Phaedrus' enthusiasm.

Socrates now abandons encomiastic speeches about love altogether and instead addresses art, or artifice. Phaedrus thought the best part of Lysias' art was his diction. Using once again his favorite analogy between education and the medical art, Socrates argues that the best part of any speech is not so incidental a thing as diction but rather knowledge. Just as a doctor needs to know the facts of medicine, the good rhetorician must know the nature of the soul and the "world as a whole" (270c). Socrates then denigrates the rhetorician's resort to "the likely" when he ought to be concerned with the truth. The argument is carried on with many references to the contemporary rhetoricians, thereby introducing the exciting combats of who's in and who's out on the Athenian rhetorical scene.

Plato now brings the dialogue to an appropriate ending by showing not only that Phaedrus' attitude has changed but also that Socrates' tone has changed. He gives the dialogue a new scope and depth by introducing the myth of Theuth and the entire question of speech-making and speech-writing. What are they good for? This is a question that Plato had suggested and then elided at the beginning when he said, somewhat wryly, that any speech that did something for the polis was certainly a good idea ("contribute to the public good" [227d]). In introducing this criterion for a good speech, he raises doubt about Lysias' intention to do more than make a name for himself as a clever speaker. Now Plato returns to the question of the public good, not in the context of the latest star rhetoricians in contemporary Athens, however, but in the dark past of myth. The ancient Egyptian myth told of one Theuth, a clever man who discovered the technical advance of writing. Theuth presented his discovery to King Thamus with enthusiasm. Wise Thamus was dubious about the advantages of writing, for, he argued, it will teach subjects forgetfulness by having a device for retrieving information, and it will thereby persuade citizens that they know something when they do not. In this mysterious world of Egypt of long ago, with an ambitious clever man and a sage ruler who listens silently to the proposal for improving human life, Plato addresses the tendency of all artists—both artists who create beautiful things, but also artists in the Platonic sense of craftsmen or inventors—to seek admiration for themselves without thinking about the long-term effects on citizens. Plato too is an artist, and his having written down his dialogues makes him liable to the very charge he implicitly levels against Lysias. Therefore, he must exhibit the humility proper to any philosopher worthy of the name. He does so by measuring himself.

The next couple of lines, then, juxtapose youth's confidence against the calm and slightly sorrowful wisdom of the old. Phaedrus exclaims breezily that Socrates is very good at "making up stories." Socrates' reply, invoking the old prophecies that came from the oak of Dodona, captures the oracular wisdom of Thamus. Old stories have something true in them, and that is why they last; stories that depend on novelty, like those of Lysias, are produced for acclaim and therefore they do not. Far more important in the realm of "doing something good" is conversation between philosophical seekers. Plato the artist is casting his eye not only over the head of youthful enthusiasm but also over his own activity in an arena that may be suspect.

Silently, the myth of Theuth is an admission of his own complicity in something tainted. It is the music of this doubt that is the last note of the dialogue. In leaving behind contemporary references to Athenians and instead using an ancient Egyptian myth, dialectic gives way to the *mousike* of oracular wisdom. This more sober knowledge now reverberates with the earlier allusions to the gods—in the story of the nymph ravished by Boreas (229b), and on the human beings who, having stopped eating upon hearing the Muses sing, were turned into cicadas (259 b–d), and in the conclusion of Stesichorus' speech, where the lover follows his boy "with reverence and awe" (254e). While those stories were treated with a facetiousness, the myth of Theuth rumbles with solemnity.

Finally, surprisingly, the rhetorician Isocrates receives praise, for, says Socrates, he has "a divine impulse for more important things" than making elegant speeches. Gone is the condescending geniality with which Socrates had treated the enthusiasm of youth. Now the note is a generous praise for a rhetorician. Quietly, the dialogue ends on the philosopher's wise humility of knowing that one's own writings will always be secondary to the love of a philosopher who wants to educate and the love of a student who wants to be educated. That is the oldest story, older, certainly, than the latest rhetorical novelties, and even older than putting words on paper. Restraint in calling attention to one's own excellence is also a matter of "doing something good" for the polity.

The dialogue ends with a brief prayer. Plato has retuned the raptures of love and concluded with the music of a poised, harmonious, and grateful soul, alert to messages from the gods. Plato is his own literary critic. He sums up the decorum of the dialogue:

> We used a certain sort of image to describe love's passion; perhaps it had a measure of truth in it, though it may have also led us astray. And having whipped up a not altogether implausible speech, *we sang playfully but also appropriately and respectfully, a story-like hymn to my master and yours, Phaedrus—to Love, who watches over beautiful boys.* (265b–c; italics added)

It is an artistic whole difficult to resolve—to mix the ecstasies of love, and even the philosopher's version of love, with the philosopher's precision.

### 6. *The Music of Courage*

The *mousike* of the ending of the *Apology* is also finely calibrated. Its final note is appropriate for the underlying premise on which the speech rests—that courage is, as Socrates says in the *Republic*, knowing what is to be feared and what is not to be feared (*Rep.*, 429–30). Socrates accepts the vote of the jury. He urges his friends to stay with him so that they can tell stories "as long as it is possible."[11] With characteristic tentativeness, he tells them he is not sure how to regard the vote of the jury: "Probably what has occurred to me has turned out to be good" (40b). His consolation also is tentative: "Let us also think in the following way how great a hope there is that it is good" (40c), for, he says, perhaps death will be peaceful. He follows with a string of conditional clauses: for "if in fact there is not perception [after death] ... if death is like a journey ... if one who arrives in Hades ..."; then he imagines meeting Orpheus, Musaeus, Hesiod, Homer, and the Greek generals at Troy, and then, moving to a climax, as in the Great Speech of the *Phaedrus,* he imagines that the dead enjoy immortality "for the rest of time." After a string of hypotheses of the happiness in the next life, he concludes with a deflationary condition: "at least if the things that are said are in fact true" (41c). Socrates cheers up his friends with the old stories, but then reminds them, with a wry aside, that they are merely old stories. The promise of association with wise men in the next life rises and swells with hope of rich conversation—and then hesitates. The old myths provide great consolation, but the philosopher concedes that those myths may be only fictions.

And anyway, perhaps death should be regarded as release from "troubles." (The Greek is wonderful here. In two sentences, Plato twice uses the Greek word *pragmata,* which can be translated neutrally as "matters, affairs" or more dismissively as "troubles" [*Apology*, 41d].) The whole dialogue then ends: "But now it is time to go away, I to die and you to live. Which of us

11  *Apology,* in *Four Texts on Socrates,* trans. by Thomas G. West and Grace Starry West (Ithaca and London: Cornell University Press, 1984), p. 94.

goes to a better thing is unclear to everyone except the god." The indict-ments against the poets, politicians, and artisans were carried on as narration of facts. The dialogue then became heated with the contentious back-and-forth with Meletus. It gathered intensity in the Socrates' claim to have been called by the god to a mission, one that he has never abandoned, even in the short time he has been in public service, and even further intensity when he ar-gued that villainy is worse than death. While the ending might have reverted to a declaration, it ends instead with almost a shrug: only the god knows whether life or death is better. In the middle part of the speech, Socrates paints himself as a heroic soldier, placed at his post by the god. At the end he puts that heroism aside, for implicit in the customary notion of heroism is the common human fear that death is terrible and the hero faced that terror bravely. Socrates makes no such claim for himself; for him, bravery in dying is simply not an issue.

It is, as Socrates says in the *Republic*, knowing what is to be feared and what is not to be feared (*Rep.*, 429–30). Socrates accepts the vote of the jury. He urges his friends to stay with him so that they can tell stories "as long as it is possible."[12] With characteristic tentativeness, he tells them he is not sure how to regard the vote of the jury: "Probably what has occurred to me has turned out to be good" (40b). His consolation also is tentative: "Let us also think in the following way how great a hope there is that it is good" (40c), for, he says, perhaps death will be peaceful. He follows with a string of conditional clauses: for "if in fact there is not perception [after death] … if death is like a journey … if one who arrives in Hades …"; then he imagines meeting Orpheus, Musaeus, Hesiod, Homer, and the Greek generals at Troy, and then, moving to a climax, as in the Great Speech of the *Phaedrus,* he imagines that the dead enjoy immortality "for the rest of time."

In the dialogue Plato has beautifully balanced *eros*, irony, and solemnity. The *mousike* of the ending of the *Apology* is also finely calibrated. Its final note is appropriate for the underlying premise on which the speech rests—that courage is knowing what is to be feared and what is not.

---

12 *Apology,* in *Four Texts on Socrates,* trans. by Thomas G. West and Grace Starry West (Ithaca and London: Cornell University Press, 1984), p. 94.

## 7. The Music of Gratitude

Earlier, I discussed Plato's opposition to tragedy, and now I return to that question, for it bears on Socrates's line in the *Crito* with which I began this essay. As argued above, at the heart of tragedy is a paradox. The human creature deserves dignity, and to that end human beings strive to improve their world; but there are things in the world that cannot be changed. In the *Republic*, Plato embarks on perhaps the most ambitious of those im-prove-ments: to design a superior political order by re-educating the citizens.

Whether the *Republic* treats this goal as achievable is debated. For those who argue that Plato thinks his new political order is possible, a passage in Book 6 is the touchstone. Up to this point, Socrates has hesitated about suggesting that his city is possible, frequently reminding the young men listening to him that they are describing merely a city in theory, for in cities as they exist the philosopher's life is threatened:

> Then there is … only a very small group who consort with philosophy in a way that's worthy of her. Now the members of this small group have tasted how sweet and blessed a possession philosophy is, and at the same time they've also seen enough of the madness of the majority [and realized also that] hardly anyone acts sanely in public affairs. Taking all this into account, they lead a quiet life and do their own work.

> Thus like someone who takes refuge under a little wall from a storm of dust or hail driven by the wind, the philosopher— seeing others filled with lawlessness—is satisfied if he can somehow lead his present life free from injustice and impious acts and depart from it with good hope, blameless and content (*Rep.*, 496 a–e).

But by the end of Book 6, Socrates has edged toward a more positive statement:

> Then, if in the limitless past, those who were foremost in philosophy were forced to take charge of a city or if this is happening

now in some foreign place far beyond our ken or if it will happen in the future [the string of conditional clauses is to be noted], we are prepared to maintain our argument that, at whatever time the muse of philosophy controls a city, the constitution we've described will also exist at that time, whether it is past, present or future. *Since it is not impossible for this to happen, we are not speaking of impossibilities.* That it is *difficult* for it to happen, however, we agree ourselves. (*Rep.*, 499c–d, italics added)

The city is not impossible it seems, despite all the previous hesitations. At the end of Book 7, Socrates says, "Then do you agree that the things we've said about the city and its constitution aren't altogether wishful thinking, that it's hard for them to come about but not impossible?" (540d). Ever so tentatively, Plato now suggests that his beautiful city might be founded after all.

After this statement, however, Socrates wavers. Early in Book 7, he asks the students listening to him to decide which group they are talking to, a group that believes there is in every soul an instrument that can be purified or a group that thinks such an idea is nonsense (527d–e). He ends with a question to Glaucon:

Or are your arguments for neither of them [these two groups] but mostly for your own sake—though you won't begrudge anyone else whatever benefit he's able to get from them? *Glaucon*: I want to speak, question, and answer mostly for my own sake.

In the end, the argument is not for the noble city that might be; it is for the individual soul, just as the analogy between the soul and the city at the beginning of the dialogue implies. By the end of Book 9, Socrates reiterates the point that his noble city is only a model for the private man:

*Glaucon*: I understand. You mean that he'll [the philosopher] be willing to take part in the politics of the city we were founding and describing, the one that exists in theory, for I don't think it exists anywhere on earth.

*Socrates*: But *perhaps*, I said, *there is a model of it in heaven*, for anyone who wants to look at it and *to make himself its citizen* on the strength of what he sees. It makes no difference whether it is or ever will be somewhere, for he would take part in the practical affairs of that city and no other. (*Rep.*, 592; italics added)

Thus, in Books 6 and 7, the *Republic* rises to a peak of hesitant optimism, and then it falls off. A philosophical city in the real world is impossible. Mixed in with the various kinds of music in Plato, all of them pointing to the way human beings can achieve happiness through their reason, is an elegy for both the complexities of the human condition. In this way, Plato's music is hesitant and ironic.

There might, however, be one more note in this complex music, the simple chanting of adoration. In the account of the divided line in Book 6 of the *Republic,* human inquiry leads to the higher music of the inarticulable vision of the Good. The mind has passed beyond images, beyond tangible things, beyond dialectic, to:

… that which reason itself grasps by the power of dialectic. It does not consider these hypotheses as first principles but truly as hypotheses [things "standing under"], stepping stones to take off from, enabling it to reach the unhypothetical *first principle of everything*. Having grasped this principle, it reverses itself, and, keeping hold of what follows from it, comes down to a conclusion without making use of anything visible at all, *but only of forms themselves, moving on from forms to forms, and ending in forms.* (*Rep.*, 511b; italics added)

"[M]oving on from forms to forms, and ending in forms"—the Greek chants as well: *eidesin autois, di' auton eis auta, kai teleuta eis eide.* This is the goal of philosophical quest, to go beyond searching to coasting from one beautiful and stable truth to another.

With this view, the human creature who has achieved philosophical wisdom will, unlike the tragic hero, not get caught. He will enjoy a perfect freedom:

One should achieve one of these things: learn the truth about these things or find it for oneself, or, if that is impossible, *adopt the best and most irrefutable of men's theories, and, borne upon this, sail through the dangers of life as upon a raft.*[13]

If you interpret the upward journey and the study of things above as the upward journey of the soul to the intelligible realm, you'll grasp what I hope to convey.... [T]his is how I see it: in the knowable realm, the form of the good is the last thing to be seen, and it is reached only with difficulty. Once one has seen it, however, one must conclude that it is the cause [*aitia*] of all that is correct and beautiful in anything, that it produces both light and its source in the visible realm, and that in the intelligible realm it controls and produces truth and understanding.... (*Rep.*, 517b–c)

The intelligible realm is the philosopher's dwelling place. Indeed, death for the philosopher is "a fitting destiny in that other place to the life [he has] lived" (*Rep.*, 498b). Perhaps the impossibility of a philosophical city does not matter because "true philosophic nature," says Socrates, "will not regard human life as anything great" (*Rep.*, 496b). Human life measured against the logic and beauty of the universe is a small thing. "[L]ove of the fine and the beautiful" (*Rep.*, 403c) is the philosopher's perfect freedom. This "first principle of everything" is utterly reliable because it exists in the universe, whether or not it is perceived by any human being or even by any god:

*Socrates:* And shall I add to the announcement that it holds, whether these things remain hidden from every god or human being or not?
*Glaucon:* Add it. (*Rep.*, 580c)

Human beings may pass away, the world may pass away, but the *logismos* that ties the universe together will not. The tragic hero submits to the gods' justice; the philosopher is one with it and with the beautiful order of the universe.

13  Plato, *Phaedo,* 123d, in *Plato, Five Dialogues: Euthyphro, Apology, Crito, Meno, Phaedo,*trans. by G. M. A. Grube, revised by John M. Cooper, 2nd ed. (Indianapolis and Cambridge: Hackett Publishing Company, ,2002). Italics added.

## 8. *The Danger of Music in Persuasion*

Let me now return to the line in the *Crito* with which I began this essay: "I am worrying over the prospect of these things, Crito, and many others." As I argued earlier, there is an undertone of futility in this line.

The central problem in the *Crito* is how to interpret the speech of the Laws at the end of the dialogue. These august figures present an argument that Crito needs to hear, the argument that Socrates owes Athens too much not to abide by to the court's punishment. This is meant to be the final argument against Crito's belief that since the court has handed down an unjust decision, Socrates has no duty to abide by that decision. The Laws point out that Socrates has lived all his life in Athens, that he never tried to leave it, that Athens has been like a father to him. When Socrates concludes this argument, he says that the Laws' speech is "booming" in his ears. If the parts of the dialogue must fit with the whole work, as Plato has Socrates maintain in the *Phaedrus*, then this line and the speech of the Laws at the end of the *Crito* fit together.

Plato emphasizes the connection between agitation and fear for oneself. At the beginning of the dialogue, he has Socrates ask Crito why he has come to the prison. Crito answers:

> To bear a message, Socrates, that is hard—not hard for you, as it appears to me, but for me and for all your companions it is a hard and grave one. And I, as it seems, would bear it the most gravely of all.

Socrates' silence at this point is itself a comment on Crito's self-absorption.

Crito's arguments in favor of Socrates' escape appear at the beginning of this chapter. Socrates should flee; Socrates should care more about the reputation of his friend; Socrates should be afraid of the mob. Crito then takes up an argument about character: it is not manly to accept death so passively. Socrates silently demurs; he knows that for the ordinary man, death is an event to be feared. For Socrates, however, manliness is not dominating people with one's forcefulness (compare Thrasymachus in the *Republic,* and Callicles in the *Gorgias*). The question is not, "what is it to be manly in the eyes of others?" but rather "what is it to be just in one's own eyes?" (*Rep.*, 522e), or perhaps "what is it to be a just member of a beautiful universe?" For Socrates, those with political power are not truly powerful because they are slaves to the mob; only those who are wise have power, and their power is not over the mob, but over themselves. The foundation of wisdom is not being terrified by death, neither one's own nor of a friend. What a philosopher worries about more than death is the possible corruption of his soul.

The irony in the *mousike* of this dialogue extends farther than Crito's initial self-absorption, for as it turns out Crito is immune to logic. His excitability, his anxiety, his sentimentality prevent him from understanding Plato's argument. With excruciating patience, then, Socrates endeavors to teach Crito what is important. He firmly states the principle that justifies more discussion:

> So we should consider whether these things should be done or not, since I, not only now but always, am such as to obey nothing else of what is mine than that argument which appears best to me upon reasoning?

Crito's frantic state, however, short-circuits his reason, and Socrates is forced to press:

> Was it said nobly ... or not, that one should pay mind to some opinions, but not others? Or was it said nobly before I had to die, while now it has become very clear that it was said pointlessly just for the sake of argument, and that in truth it was child's play and drivel? (*Crito*, 46b–d)

Socrates goes through the arguments once again, and a new note, besides weariness, sets in. When Socrates suggests to Crito that his thinking is that of the mob, his voice is stern:

> As for the considerations that you speak of concerning spending of money and reputation and nurture of children, I suspect that in truth, Crito, these are considerations of those who easily kill, and if they could, would bring back to life again, acting mindlessly: namely, the many. (48c)

Here the Mitylenian Debate in Thucydides' *History of the Peloponnesian War* is relevant. At the end of that debate, the Athenians vote to put to death the entire population of a city and the next day change their minds (*Peloponnesian War*, Bk.3. Par. 49). In the *Crito,* what is indicted is not vindictiveness, as it is in Thucydides, but sentimentality. Sentimental people are passionate; because of their passion, they kill people and then regret the killing. The indictment of Crito is clear. Indeed, by this point in the dialogue, Socrates shows glimpses of impatience. He says that if Crito cannot contradict his arguments, he should "stop telling me [Socrates] the same argument again and again" (48d).

It is here, after this momentary vexation, that Socrates invites Crito to imagine the Laws lecturing Socrates himself. This speech has been interpreted in at least two different ways. By one interpretation, Socrates endorses the Laws' argument. In paraphrase, the argument is, first, that the laws are given by the gods; Socrates could have left Athens whenever he wished, yet he remained in the city and lived 70 long years there. Second, Socrates acknowledges that for philosophy to survive, the democratic city must survive; in a strictly ordered city like Sparta, philosophical inquiry would have been impossible. therefore, the judgment of the Athenian court cannot be undermined. In the Laws' speech, then, Plato is making the concessions made necessary by the weakness of human nature.

There are other concessions in Plato's work that are also necessitated by the weakness of human nature. Most people are distracted by ambition and entertainment; for them, the happy life is excitement and pleasure. To lead these people to something higher, the philosopher must speak in metaphors and myths that will inspire awe. The famous "noble lie" of the *Republic* by which the citizens of the philosophical city are persuaded that they were born underneath the earth with gold souls, silver souls, or bronze souls is meant to persuade them of this acceptance. The myth presents the unavoidable fact, resisted by many, that some people are more intelligent than others, and also more courageous. Only in a city in which all citizens are of equally high intelligence and have had the right musical education is a lawgiver unnecessary. By this interpretation, then, the grounds of Socrates's endorsement of the Laws' speech is an appreciation of reality.

According to a second interpretation, however, Socrates does not endorse the Laws' speech. After all, in the *Apology*, the philosopher is subject to a threat more serious than having to take refuge by a wall. He is *not* being allowed to leave this life "blameless and content." Moreover, in the *Apology,* Socrates' attitude does not sound like a wise man's acquiescence to the imperfections of the city-in-reality. Much of it sounds like a sardonic indictment of Athens' leaders and its citizens. In that dialogue, as I have argued, Socrates says, as if with a shrug, that the law requires the defendant to make a defense, and so if he must, he will; but he knows that he cannot defend himself against years of rumor in so short a time. Moreover, the representatives of the city are shown not to have given a minute's thought to the education of the young. They live the lives of a large, lazy horse that must be bitten if it is going to wake up at all. If Socrates has lived a rich life as a philosopher, it has been in spite of the city and not because democratic Athens left him alone. After all, when a crisis comes, the once lazy horse turns into a vicious warrior-beast.

By this second interpretation, Socrates does not believe the arguments he has the Laws utter in the *Crito,* not even as a concession to political necessity. If the Laws are "booming" (54d), Plato is bitterly mocking the oratorical displays of sophists in other dialogues. In the *Protagoras,* Socrates slyly remarks on the deep voice of Prodicus, "whose voice [was] so deep that it set up a reverberation in the room that blurred what was being said."[14] Thus, with Crito, Socrates must also resort to rhetorical booming, which is not intended to justify Athenian law but rather is to bring calm to Crito's soul by a reminder of his citizenly duties. By this argument, Socrates tailors his speech to the earnest but unintelligent Crito in an effort to pull him out of his cave.

But there is a third consideration to be examined in this puzzle. In Book 6 of the *Republic,* Socrates suggests another reason to use a grandiose speech; it is necessary for the philosopher who wants to continue philosophizing. In the *Republic,* the wise man who has emerged from the cave must go back down into it, not because he has a mission to save others but because "his own life will be fuller," or in some translations, his own life will be more "complete" (*Rep.,* 496a). This is a

---

14  *Plato: Protagoras,* 316a, trans. Stanley Lombardo and Karen Bell, intro. Michael Frede (Indianapolis and Cambridge: Hackett Publishing Company, 1992).

puzzling statement. It could mean that the city is not just a convenience that the philosopher must tolerate. In fact, it offers something the philosopher cannot get on his own. Later in the *Republic,* however, when Socrates is talking about the city as it might be, a city in speech, he does not say that his life would be more "complete" by participating in a city as it exists in reality; it is complete only if the city leaves him alone. If the philosopher's life is complete only in an imagined city—not in a city that exists in reality—then a longing for that imagined city hangs over all of the conversations about the philosopher's wisdom as it connects to politics. Socrates gives the Laws a booming speech because he knows that booming speech is effective in intimidating an audience, that is, in some sense he is committed to it.

It is here we get to the deepest music of the *Crito*, and it is somber. Perhaps the gentle persuasion Socrates recommends in the *Republic* (500a) is not possible; perhaps the philosopher's effort to enter the political arena can end only in failure. Thus, in the first interpretation of the Laws' speech, Socrates is endorsing traditional law, which is confused but might tame at least somewhat the savagery of human nature. By the second interpretation, Socrates is being ironic. In the third interpretation, in Socrates' Laws' booming, myth-laden argument, he understands that Crito will not be persuaded by logical argument, nor is he mocking bombastic speech. Here Plato expects his reader to hear that Socrates is consciously spending the powers of his soul on calming a man who is a grown-up child. The speech is intentionally "booming," and the reader is supposed to understand that the booming is mixed with an apology to the gods for using a kind of speech that he concedes is necessary, but which he holds in contempt. By this interpretation Socrates' attitude toward the speech of the Laws has an exasperated and even despairing undertone. By the first interpretation, Socrates is speaking with conviction and fervor. By the second, he is weary with Crito. By the third, he is weary with the human condition, for the Critos of the world are not few.

Plato has offered evidence that we should be tuning our ears to this weariness because exasperation has been emphasized earlier in this dialogue. After Socrates has gone through the arguments about not listening to the opinions of others and the necessity of following the *logismos,* he warns Crito that the orators would marshal a defense of the city's law:

> For someone, especially an orator, would have many things to say on behalf of this law if it were destroyed—the law that orders that the judgments reached in trials must be authoritative. Or shall we tell them "The city was doing us an injustice and did not pass judgment correctly?" Shall we say this or what? (50b)

Here Socrates is deriding Crito's charge against the city, a charge Socrates has just gone to great lengths to undermine. After hearing all the arguments in support of the city's authority, however, Crito responds to Socrates' last question with charming—and depressing—alacrity: "Yes, this, by Zeus, Socrates!"—that is, "Yes, we should say that they did not pass judgment correctly!"—as if he had not heard any of the arguments that Socrates had just put forward.

At a later point, Crito seems to accede to the argument that it is worse to do evil than to suffer it. (He admits, quietly, "What you say is true" [49c]). Socrates then goes on:

> And see to it, Crito, that by agreeing to this, you aren't agreeing contrary to your opinion. For I know that this seems and will seem so only to a certain few. *So there is no common counsel* for those who hold this opinion and those who do not: it is necessary that they will have *contempt* for each other when they see each others' counsels. (49d; italics added)

"Contempt" is strong word, as is the statement that there can be no common counsel between those who agree about Socrates' arguments and those who do not. The view that Socrates' motivation in the Laws' speech is a pragmatic descent to necessity construes the relationship between the few and the many as cordial and condescending, in the aristocratic mode. But the view of Socrates' motivation in introducing the Laws' speech as a momentary concession to expedience in the case of a well-meaning but limited friend puts an uncrossable barrier between himself and Crito. When Socrates says to Crito, "I have these things on my mind, Crito, and many others," then, Socrates is aware that people who do not understand philosophical arguments as firmly as one understands the permanent ratio between the sides of a right angle and its hypotenuse will make politics impossible because they cannot recognize when they are wrong, and, as a consequence, they cannot be instilled with a desire to change their thinking. If, in the end, there can ultimately be "no common counsel" between those who are awed by thrasonical bombast and those who disdain it, there can be no political community.

In the speech of the Laws, Socrates is thinking about something he can say only to the reader, not to Crito: that he does not wholly believe what the Laws' speech is implying, that finally, for the sake of the polity, a speech that persuades by fear, resounding with the deep-throated gravitas of the orators and pious references to the gods, is necessary because philosophical arguments are futile, even the arguments that would give some purchase to legal tradition. If philosophy wishes to enter politics, it will always have to bow to the less than best. In resorting to persuasion by awe, the philosopher knows he is reinforcing everyman's satisfaction with being a child. To soothe his friend, Plato must contribute to his corruption.

The deepest and most somber music of the Crito, then, is the suspicion that politics is impossible because the souls of the majority are incapable of the knowledge that undergirds harmony in the city. The souls of sentimentalists are limited by the insistent belief that life in the body is what really counts. For such souls, the conviction that one cannot live without a particular beloved blocks reason's connection to the world of the intellect. For Socrates, grief is an indulgence that human beings allow themselves because they think that their grief stems from some injustice in the universe (as in tragedy), and that that injustice gives them license to be self-absorbed, as Crito is.

The music at end of this dialogue does not resolve, as does the music of the *Apology* or of the *Phaedrus*. Plato has one participant in the *Laws* say, "truth is a noble and a lasting thing, stranger [the Athenian stranger], but it is likely that it's not easy to persuade people of it" (663e), and the Athenian stranger does not disagree. In the same dialogue, Plato has the Athenian stranger remark that a discussion of politics requires a long view of history, in order to be fully aware that cities have come and gone, and that any city not ruled by a god will be subject to unrest and troubles (*Laws*, 676a, 709a–b, 713e).

In my experience, persuading students to appreciate Plato is difficult. The richness of a particular passage is hard to explain—because of the reluctance of the young to listen and wait, because of the shortness of the semester, because of one's own doubt about the meaning—for, after all, in the course of a lifetime, it has not been unusual for me to change my mind.

Outside of the building where I used to teach, after having just left the room where a group met for an evening discussion of Plato I would find my mind floating to other things. Last night's Plato reading group went well. There was a lot of Platonic drive in it, young people who love to argue. Fortunately, they could laugh at themselves. Two of the group were women. One of these had 7 children; she and her husband were founding a new high school in the suburbs, one with a strong education in the ancients. The other woman was a financial adviser in a bank. An older man, an Iranian with a Ph.D. who wrote his thesis on "The Logos and the Polis" and who just two months ago had come to the United States on a year's visa, agreed with me that even in the short dialogues, Plato is profound. There was one young man who would "cavil on the ninth part of a hair," as Shakespeare's Hotspur says of himself. Still, that eager pursuer of the truth set an example to the others. Participation in the group was entirely optional. It was the best kind of conversation in the university. Along the bike path, the mowers had just mowed the grass along. It was mere early summer, but soon the cicadas would be singing.

# HOMER'S *ILIAD*: "A SUMMER DIRGE"

## *1. The Hero's Courage*

In *Leviathan*, Hobbes argues that the human response a legislator can most count on is the fear of a violent death. In so doing, Hobbes pushes the definition of "man" toward "beast," and the solution for a merely bestial life is a sovereign who will pronounce what the law is and enforce it. One could say that at the heart of Homer's *Iliad* is also the fear of violent death and that life in Homer's *Iliad* is also bestial, perhaps even more so than in Hobbes because Homer only glimpses at the possibility of law.

In Homer, the fear of death is balanced against love of a community, as it is not in Hobbes. In the Hobbesian state of nature, one never fully banishes fear; even in a lawful regime, violence might break out at any time. In Homer, there is the same fear, but it at least it has the reward of honor, the energy of which Hobbes saw in warlike activities and therefore banished dueling from his state. For Homer, courage allows the hero to enter a world guaranteed by a singing poet to last after his death. Moreover, Homer diminishes the fear of death by love of one's comrades, who can be counted on in a fight. Still, a hero may also lose a comrade at the hand of his enemy. Hence, the poem is also about the pain of loss. That pain is ultimately in the hands of the gods, to whose power human beings must submit. The second word of the poem is "sing." The poem's meaning lies in the tenor of Homer's song of submission. The poem is essentially an elegy.[15] Despite the

---

15  Here I use the translation by Robert Fitzgerald, *Homer: The Iliad*, intro. Andrew Ford (New York: Farrar, Straus and Giroux, 2004). For scholars, this translation is too free; but to my my ear, the more literal translations are metrically unpleasant. On the other hand, this translation is preferable to translations that try to match Homer's dactylic hexameter because Fitzgerald's iambic pentameter is more familiar to readers of English poetry. This fact becomes important in Book 24 when Hermês escorts the grieving Priam to the tent of

length of the poem, the plot of the *Iliad* is simple. It follows the strict cause-and-effect logic of a vengeance plot. Akhilleus is dishonored by Agamemnon and stays in his tent. Because Akhilleus is absent from the battlefield, the Greeks are driven back to their ships. Pitying his dying comrades, Patróklos, Akhilleus' comrade, puts on the great hero's armor and fights the Trojans; he is killed by Hektor. Seeking to avenge the death of Patróklos, Akhilleus returns to battle and kills Hector, the son of the Trojan King. This is the bare bones of the story. But the artistic structure of the *Iliad* is a musical series of moods. The *Iliad* ends with Akhilleus mourning his friend and at the same time offering consolation to the father of the man who killed his friend. It is the emotional timbre of that confrontation that the whole poem is working toward.

The poem, then, is not proposing a definition of a good person or of a mature view of life or of true human wisdom. It seems merely to approach those questions—and to approach them with great tentativeness—and then go on to something else. Then it just stops in exhaustion and dazed perplexity, surveying the human situation with both wonder and pity.

The famous lines at the beginning of the *Iliad*—"Wrath, sing, goddess"—are a guide to reading the poem's paradoxes: wrath is both noble and frightening; the goddess, like the gods generally, is reassuring but also dismaying, for she is unpredictable; human life is bleak, but it is also beautiful. It is the singer singing who holds the whole together and "sounds" an argument without actually articulating it. The hexameter line sets the rhythm and the pace, and the singer, moving with it, sings the human power simply to endure.

## 2. The Primitive Appeal to the Senses

Reading Homer prompts the reflection that perhaps the foundation of epic is bewilderment; life does not stand up to too much explaining. Plato argued that philosophy is superior to literature because it is more articulate. In fact, one could say that poetry differs from philosophy insofar as its message

his enemy; there Fitzgerald changes to *rhymed* iambic pentameter to express the solicitude of the god. Fitzgerald refers to his epic's hero as "Akhilleus," not the more familiar "Achilles." I will follow his example with other Greek names.

is, finally, mute. Poetry uses words, of course, and epic uses lots of words; but poetry's first job is not rational articulation of an idea. Instead, it shows us something to "see," the word Conrad uses in the preface to *The Nigger of the Narcissus* to describe the cognitive act of comprehension at the end of story. If art in general does not offer articulate meaning, even less so does Homer. In my experience, students are puzzled by the *Iliad's* not offering a conclusion about human life. They wish at the end that Homer were making a statement about the rule of law being preferable to violence because eventually human beings will see reason and lay down their arms. But Homer does not offer that argument.

Others have characterized Homer's concentration on the senses as a blind man's groping his way through the furniture in a room. In this metaphor, Homer moves through his poem as if he were registering one perception after another. With his hands, the blind man feels objects one at a time, almost as an animal registers the particulars of unfamiliar territory. At any one moment, the information is vivid, startling, fresh. For Homer, human perception is nearer to that of the animals. The poem moves from one laden sensation—frightening or soothing—to the next.

In Hobbes, the prose and the political order go together. The fear-ridden state of nature is controlled by a rational solutions, and that rationality is legitimized by the prose of the Enlightenment philosopher. In contrast, the figures in Homer's poem, moving from one event to another without a causal justification, feel that their world is controlled by an inexplicable higher power, which they call "the gods." When in Book 1, Akhilleus harnesses his anger against Agamemnon, Athêna descends and takes Akhilleus by the hair. Akhilleus, who just a moment before was about to draw his sword, responds with surprising docility. The epic similes of the poem operate the same way. One can be in the midst of blood and dust and guts, and suddenly the poet is singing about human heads that, in death, droop like the blossoms on poppies. These changes of mood are crucial to the way Homer takes in the world.

Characters in Homer are not sharply differentiated from the larger "moods" of the poem. When in Book 9, Ulysses and others plead with Akhilleus to return to battle, Akhilleus is proud and dismissive:

> Now I think
> no riches can compare with being alive. (9.489–490)

He seems to be saying that, at this moment in his life, he prefers a life of safety to a life of constant danger for the sake of booty, for which the reward is insults from his leader. But when the outraged Akhilleus withdraws from battle, he is still "longing for battle and the war cry" (11.15–16). On the basis of this latter statement, modern readers might say that his declaration in Book 9 that he is going to hoist sail and go home to Phthía is "rationalization"—that is, what he really wants is to stay and fight. It is more accurate to say that a general feeling in the poem, for a moment, finds its articulation in a character. Although many passages in the poem argue that the greatest human fulfillment is victory on the battlefield, many others argue just what Akhilleus says in Book 9. Homer defends that feeling in countless paces in the *Iliad* when he talks about the beauty of snow, the beauty of leaves falling from a tree, the beauty of flowers, the beauty of wild animals, the beauty of women, the delight of babies. When in the *Odyssey*, Odysseus meets Akhilleus among the spirits in the underworld, Homer confirms this paradox: a great warrior's facing death on the battlefield is the best life; no, staying alive, even as a farmhand, is the best life.

Homer is also frustratingly inconsistent about the power of the gods. On the one hand, the human beings in the poem freely acknowledge that they have to submit to fate: Hektor says to Andrómachê that he knows in his heart that Troy will one day fall (6.520–22), and Nestor tells Diomêdês that the bolt of lightning that lit up in front of Diomêdês' horses is Zeus's denial of victory on that day (8.157–61). The mystery of higher powers is deepened in Book 16, when Hêra reminds Zeus that a limit is set for individual human lives, a limit set by a power higher even than that of Zeus:

> O fearsome power,
>  my Lord Zeus, what a curious thing to say.
> A man who is born to die, long destined for it,
> Would you set him free from that unspeakable end?
>  (16.513–16)

The cosmos is so set up, she implies, that human beings' lives are controlled; freedom from that control is not allowed them, nor is it allowed to a particular god to exempt a favorite from the general rule. Still, the poem shows the greatness of human courage; if human life is controlled by the gods and human beings cannot, therefore, decide and act, there is no such thing as courage, and there is no point in praising courage as Homer does over and over again. There is, then, a pervasive tension between these two views of human action. Human beings accept the gods' direction of human action, and yet human beings also believe that they too can determine whether or not a man is to die today; otherwise, they would not fight with as much concentrated fury as they do.

These two planes of the poem—gods and men—are connected to the characteristic feature of the telling—its parataxis, "arranging alongside," chiefly by the use of the coordinate conjunctions *and, but,* and *or.* It is implicitly in contrast with *hypotaxis. Hypotaxis* is what students learn in writing classes, how to "place things under" by using subordinate clauses, participial phrases, and conjunctive adverbs. Hypotaxis is the signature of the Ciceronian style of political rhetoric. Parataxis, by contrast, just states things as they come; the most obvious example is the language of the Bible. Parataxis is fundamental to Homer insofar as he is paratactic not only in syntax but also in thought: men are towering, powerful warriors; no, men are small, weak creatures.

Sarpêdôn's firm statement that war gives honor is followed by his equally emphatic statement that it is not the love of honor that drives him into battle, but survival:

> Ah, cousin, could we but survive this war to
> live forever deathless, without age,
> I would not ever go into battle again,
> nor would I send you there for honor's sake!
> But now a thousand shapes of death surround us,
> and no man can escape them or be safe.

So, soldiers fight to survive. But in his next breath, Sarpêdôn reasserts that glory is the goal:

> Let us attack—whether to give some fellow
> glory or to win it from him. (12.368–69)

Perhaps these contradictions are the result of stringing passages together from an oral tradition. But Homer saw that the parataxis and hence the disjointedness the oral tradition, if arranged in a certain way, could be used to make the point that, to the small creatures called human beings who cannot help striving to control what happens to them, life seems unintelligible. There should be justice, and yet there is none.

### 3. *The Three Songs of the* Iliad

#### First song: Fury

The parataxis of the poem arranges two basic musical moods, one that is tense and one that is at ease. The most prevalent music——the major key—is anger, just as the first word of the poem says. On the battlefield, life is about a soldier's courage, which is white hot with fury; the next second will determine whether he will kill his opponent or his opponent will kill him. His whole concentration is on winning this contest. To destroy a threat on the battlefield is full vitality. In the twentieth century, Yeats agreed:

> You that Mitchell's prayer have heard
> "Send war in our time, O Lord,"
> Know that when all words are said
> And a man is fighting mad,
> Something drops from eyes long blind
> He completes his partial mind
> And for an instant stands at ease.
> (*Under Ben Bulben*)

For Homer, "completing the partial mind" can be the summation of a man's life. The warrior's determination to kill his adversary concentrates the attention. On the battlefield in Book 5, Diomêdês is burning with wrath:

> If he had burned before
> To fight with Trojans, now indeed blood-lust
> Three times as furious took hold of him....
> So lion-like
> Diomêdês plunged on Trojans.
> First he killed

Astynoös, and a captain, Hypeirôn,
one with a spear thrust in the upper chest,
the other by a stroke of his great sword
chopping his collar bone at the round joint
to sever his whole body from his shoulder. (5.155–72)

Homer's concentration on the sensuous particular—the sweat and blood of killing or being killed—is one of his glories as a poet. He does not soften the terrors and satisfactions of the battlefield. Warriors eat fat lambs at feast:

and drink rare vintages, but the main thing is
their fighting power, when they lead in combat! (12.359–60)

Nor does Homer shy away from the horrors of war:

Our lot from youth to age
was given us by Zeus: danger and war
to wind upon the spindle of our years
until we die to the last man. (14.97–100)

Life has moments of relief, but battle is the main event.

In the later books, the "ardor for battle" becomes a tornado. Poseidon, having seen Zeus turn away from the battle, retires his horses to his underground cave but then joins the Greek army in the person of Khalkas. Ajax son of Oïleus tells Telmônian Ajax that it is not Khalkas but a god, and Telemônian Ajax then feels a new fervor in his body: "Power is rising in me I can feel / a springing freshness in my legs. I long / to meet this implacable Hektor face to face" (13.90–92). When Akhilleus returns to battle, he has no time for sacrifices: "Slaughter and blood are what I crave, and groans / of anguished men" (13.235–36). The ardor for battle culminates in Akhilleus' appearance in the armor that Hêphaistos has made for him. When he stands before the Greek army, he looks like "the Lord of Noon" (19.439). Finally, Akhilleus is fire itself:

A forest fire will rage
through deep glens of a mountain, crackling dry
from summer heat, and coppices blaze up

in every quarter as wind whips the flame:
so Akhilleus' flashed to right and left
*like a wild god*, trampling the men he killed.
(20.567–72; italics added)

Warriors fight as if a natural force were coursing through them. That force is fully unleashed when Akhillleus kills Hektor and drags his body around the walls of Troy.

The fury, however, is directed not only against the enemy. Deep in the poem lies the half-formed conviction that human fury might challenge the will of the gods. In Book 24, Akhilleus thinks that if he lacerates the body of Hektor with sufficient wrath, he might make it true that Patróklos has not been killed. Homer knows how powerful is the human desire to overcome the limits of the human condition simply by fierce denial of them. His artistic achievement might be, then, making use of the episodic and paratactic qualities of that tradition not to make a profound statement, but to offer a view into the human reaction to the irrevocability of death.

## Second Song: Release from Tension in "Turning Aside"

The second musical mode in the *Iliad* is the release from fury. It comes in three general categories: the ease of the body, the soul's submission to higher powers, and the ease of the singing imagination. Several episodes end with a detailed description of roasting meat on a spit and then going to sleep. This release from fury is the human version of divine ease, for although human beings cannot see the future as the gods can, they are allowed some respite from war. The gods too, after quarrels, escape to their banquet in the clouds of Olympus, drink nectar and ambrosia, and then go to sleep, sometimes with their consorts beside them.

The second kind of ease is acquiescence to the power of the gods:

… the flashing reins ran out of Nestor's hands. His heart
failed him, and he said to Diomêdês,
"Give way now; get the team to pull us out!
Do you not realize that power from Zeus
is being denied you?…
　　　　　　No man defends himself

against the mind of Zeus—even the ruggedest
of champions. His power is beyond us." (8.155–64)

Whatever has happened had to happen because it has happened.

The third kind of ease is the most important to the poem. It has two parts—refocusing of attention (what I will call a "turning aside") and mourning. In the "turning aside," the analogy between the movement of the *Iliad* and a blind man feeling his way through a room, is particularly apt. The blind man feels in an object something frightening; but the move to another object blots from his attention the previous object. The human creature can make reality go away simply by not looking at it. This same power belongs to the poet, especially in his epic similes. It is he who can turn aside from a thrust that kills or the death of a loved one and fix his attention on something else, as, for instance, in the famous metaphors of a poppy, the bees, the comber on the sea, the flies around a milk pan.

The freedom of the imagination feels especially powerful in Homer because of its sharp contrast with the constrained world of the warrior. This or that band of warriors may be defeated; an entire group may be defeated or a city destroyed; but through the singer's song, the image of those warriors or that band of people or that city will last. In those moments, when everything seems to stand still, the human imagination can, for an instant, dwell with the gods, without any threat of change or death.

The "turning aside" is closely connected to elegy. The poem admits that the permanence of beauty might be rooted in wish fulfillment. The beauty of song, which spreads its veil over the brutalities of life, is, like human beings, mortal or evanescent. Elegy mournfully begs for a reprieve from having to face bravely life's limitations, strewing flowers "with false surmise," as Milton has it in *Lycidas*. Sometimes the elegy in Homer is gentle.

> In the lead as he came on,
> he took the spear thrust squarely in the chest
> beside the nipple on the right side; piercing him,
> the bronze point issues by the shoulder blade,
> and in the dust he reeled and fell. (4.579–83)

Then the singer turns aside:

> A poplar
> growing in bottom lands, in a great meadow;
> smooth-trunked, high up to its sheath of boughs,
> will fall before the chariot-builder's ax
> of shining iron—timber that he marked
> for warping into chariot tire rims—
>  and, seasoning, it lies beside the river.
> So vanquished by the god-reared Aías lay
> Simoeísios Anthémidês. (4.583–91)

(Fitzgerald, the translator, must have felt a rush when he realized that that name all by itself was an iambic pentameter line.) Sometimes the "turning aside" seems to promise that peace will come again, as in the midst of Akhilleus' pursuit of Hektor around the walls of Troy:

> Just so, Akhilleus
> murderously cleft the air, as Hektor
> ran with flashing knees along the wall.
> They passed the lookout point, the wild fig tree
> with wind in all its leaves, then veered away
> along the curving wagon road, and came
> to where the double fountains well, the source
> of eddying Skamánder. One hot spring
> flows out, and from the water fumes arise
> as though from fire burning; but the other
> even in summer gushes chill as hail
> or snow or crystal ice frozen on water.
> *Near these fountains are wide washing pools*
> *of smooth-laid stone, where Trojan wives and daughters*
> *laundered their smooth linen in the days*
> *of peace before the Akhaians came.*
> (22.171–86; italics added)

Women doing the laundry is as dependable a sight as the sun coming up in the morning; and perhaps Trojan women will one day again wash clothes on the banks of the Skamánder. In the poem the common things of life—poppies, waterfalls, lions—gain their beauty and their comfort because they are made to seem as stable as "home," where death is not threatening. When in Book 9, Akhilleus announces his intention to "make it home to Phthía," the line gathers together the longing for home that is spread out in the many similes. These epic similes throw over even so frightening a thing as death a veil of comfort. There is nothing so terrible that a song cannot be made out of it.

## Fury and Ease in Alternation

Homer presents the alternations between tension and release from tension in the very beginning of the poem. Agamémnon and Akhilleus are at each other's throats; Athêna disciplines Akhilleus by catching him by the hair. With all the airy lightness of an immortal, his mother Thetis descends to comfort him; then she turns aside in elegy:

> Alas, my child, why did I rear you, doomed
> the day I bore you? Ah, could you only be
> serene upon a beachhead through the siege,
> your life runs out so soon.
> Oh early death! Oh broken heart! No destiny
> so cruel! And I bore you to this evil! (1.477–82)

This is the first elegy of a parent mourning the death of a son.

At the end of Book 1, there is another musical lull. With an easy turn, the fury and lament turn to comedy as Hêphaistos recalls the time when Zeus took him by the heel and hurled him out of Olympos. A whole day, he says, he was carried through the air, and when he landed on earth, a kindly people took care of "the fallen one" (Fitzgerald translates the Greek as "nursed a fallen god"), but part of the comedy is Hêphaistos' suggestion that he was just a bit of roadkill, at which the rest of the gods laugh. We the human listeners-to-the-song, however, hear the laughter of the gods with wistfulness; *their* quarrels can end in laughter because they are the gods-who-live-at-ease.

The pattern of fury-to-ease repeats. Book 2 recounts the peoples who followed Agamémnon's army. Then in Book 3, the poem addresses the motivation of the vengeance plot: what prompted the Greeks' assault on Troy? The answer is the abduction of Helen. But in the pattern of fury-to-ease, Helen herself functions as beauty's escape from the consequential logic of the plot. The voices of the Trojan elders on the upper floor of the gates of the city "sound[ed] like cicadas in dry summer / that cling on leafy trees and send out voices / rhythmic and long" (3.180–82). As Helen climbs to that upper floor, Priam and his elders turn and see her. Priam speaks:

> "We cannot rage at her, it is no wonder
> that Trojans and Akhaians under arms
> should for so long have borne the pains of war
> for one like this."
>                           "Unearthliness. A goddess
> the woman is to look at." (3.186–191)

Beauty's transcendence nullifies the chain of action-and-reaction in vengeance. Instead of inciting fury, beauty tunes the soul to detachment from daily events; it is part of human nature to stand rapt before it. In that detachment is the possibility of a seeing into the world of the gods. Another Trojan elder, however, presents the other side of the question:

> Ah, but still,
> still, even so, being all that she is, let her go in the ships
> and take her scourge from us and from our children. (3.191–193)

Priam ignores that objection:

> Come here dear child, sit here,
> beside me; you shall see your onetime lord,
> and your dear kinsmen.
> *You are not to blame.*
> I hold the gods to blame for bringing on

this war against the Akhaians, to our sorrow. (3.193–98; italics added)

Homer uses Priam to consider the disinterested view—that the enemy is no different from friends.

> O fortunate son of Atreus! Child of destiny,
> O happy soul! How many sons of Akhaia
> serve under you! (3.216–18)

Then Helen drifts into the poem's longing for home (and how powerfully Milton made use of this epic commonplace!). First, she identifies in Priam the various Greek heroes; then she looks for her brothers:

> I see
> all the Akhaians now
> whom I might recognize and name for you,
> except for two I cannot see, the captains
> Kastor, breaker of horses
>                        and the boxer Polydeukês,
> both my brothers; mother bore them both
> Were these not in the fleet from Lakedaimôn?
> Or did they cross in the long ships, but refrain
> from entering combat here because they dread
> vile talk of me and curses on my head? (3.278–88)

Helen searches for her brothers, who are part of home. Then the singer, the one who can see farther than Helen and Priam, breaks in:

> So Helen wondered. But her brothers lay
> motionless in the arms of life-bestowing earth,
> long dead in Lakedaimôn of their fathers. (3.289–90)

Helen is, briefly, a magic force even among the Trojans; then, with impassivity, the singer both embraces her and makes her small again.

## A Crescendo of Fury

When episodes not strictly related to the Akhilleus plot are introduced, Homer uses these digressions to tune ours ears to the alternation between intense fury and ease. In Book 5, Diomêdês rails at Aphrodítê for rescuing her son Aineías from battle:

> Oh give up war, give up
> war and killing, goddess! Is it not enough
> to break soft women down with coaxing lust?
> Go haunting battle, will you? I can see you
> Shudder after this at the name of war. (5.402–406)

The passage is not a prayer or a request; it is a demand. To Diomêdês, it seems only fair that Aphrodítê should "shudder" for crossing a line.

In the night raid of Book 10, when Diomêdês rouses the Greek captains to make a scouting expedition to the Trojan camp, Homer puts stillness into the already tense blackness of night. The Trojan captains are like "shepherd dogs" keeping "bristling watch," "their ears / pricked up at the approach of a wild beast." The Greeks creep into the camp and come across Dolôn, who gives them information that he thinks will spare him death; but Odysseus is unmoved. Dolôn

> leaned forward, reaching
> to touch his chin, beseeching; but he [Odysseus] brought
> his sword-blade in a flash down on the nape
> and severed the two tendons. (10.500–503)

Still in a fury, Diomêdês comes upon the charioteer who guards the horses of Rhêsos. Diomêdês, "whirling left and right … struck, / and pitiable sounds came from the bodies / cleft by the sword's edge. Earth ran red with blood" (10. 535–37).

When Patróklos enters the battle, the deaths become more savage:

> Pêneléos
> thrust at his neck below the ear and drove

the blade clear in and through; his head toppled
held only by skin (16.396–99)
—and the Akhaian [Patróklos]
got home his thrust on the right jawbone, driving
through his teeth ....
so from his chariot on the shining spear
he hooked him and face downward threw him. (16.469–77)

Patróklos attacks Hektor's charioteer, Kebríonês,

smashing his forehead with a jagged stone.
Both brows were hit at once, the frontal bone
gave way, and both his eyes burst from their sockets. (16.847–49)

Patróklos is killed; Zeus's son Sarpêdon is killed; Akhilleus resolves to return
to battle; Hêphaistos makes him a shield. When in Book 19, Akhilleus appears on the battlefield, he is the human version of the roar of Arês heard
in Book 5. "One heard his [Akhilleus'] teeth / grind hard together, and his
eyes blazed out / like licking fire" (19.400–402). He is the sign in the heavens that the Greeks have a demi-god on their side:

As when at sea to men on shipboard comes
the shining of a campfire on a mountain
in a lone sheepfold, while the gusts of night wind
take them, loath to go, far from friends
over the teeming sea: just so
Akhilleus' finely modeled shield sent light
into the heavens. (19.411–17)

Akhilleus now seems to embody the conviction that human fury can challenge the gods if it is sufficiently focused. Note the verbs placed at the beginning and end of lines:

Automédôn
and Alkimos with swift hands yoked his team,
making firm the collars on the horses,

placing the bits between their teeth, and pulling
reins to the war-car. Automédôn then
took in hand the shining whip and mounted
the chariot and at his back, Akhilleus
mounted in full armor, shining bright
as the blinding Lord of Noon. (19.431–39)

Akhilleus claims the center of the battle as his rightful place.

The fury increases. While Zeus remains at "ease upon a ridge," he sends his sibling-children gods back into battle. Poseidon makes the mountains shake; Apollo and Diana shoot arrows; the God of Fire Hêphaistos fights with the God of the Sea Poseidon; Hektor himself is longing to "glut the war god" with enemy bodies (20.91). Akhilleus is like a wildfire:

A forest fire will rage
through deep glens of a mountain, crackling dry
from summer heat and coppices blaze up
in every quarter as wind whips the flame.
So Akhilleus flashed to right and left
*like a wild god*, trampling the men he killed
and black earth ran with blood. (20.567–73; italics added)

The passage hurtles forward. The turning-asides of the epic similes hardly stop the demi-god warrior.

As when a countryman
yokes oxen with broad brows to tread out barley
on a well-bedded threshing floor, and quickly
the grain is husked under the bellowing beasts:
the sharp-hooved horses of Akhilleus just so
crushed dead men and shields. His axle tree
was splashed with blood, so was his chariot rail,
with drops thrown up by wheels and horses' hooves.
And Pêleus' son kept riding for his glory,
straining his powerful arms with mire and blood. (20.573–82)

Then, riding the forward pulse of the dactylic rhythm, Homer pushes the narrative beyond dirt and blood to a level beyond the fury of Book 6, as he sings of Akhilleus' swift slitting of Lykáôn's throat. Akhilleus scorns the young warrior: "why are you so piteous about [dying]"? Then, after he has killed Lykáôn, he spits out, "Nose down there among the fishes" (21.142). He taunts him: "This way you'll rest. It is rough work / To match yourself with the children of Lord Zeus" (21.214–15). Pursuing Hektor around the walls of Troy, Akhilleus is "bright as that star / in autumn rising, whose unclouded rays / shine out amid a throng of stars at dusk— / the one they call Oríôn's Dog, most brilliant / yes, yet baleful as a sign" (22.31–35). While at the beginning of the poem, human beings feel crushed by the power of the gods, now the human beings feel crushed by a human demi-god.

The fury culminates in Akhilleus' pursuit of Hektor around the walls of Troy. Although Zeus acknowledges that Hektor has burned many thighs for him, he consents to Athêna's bringing aid to Akhilleus. The fury that has been building through several books culminates in the exhilaration of Hektor as he breaches the rampart around the ships and calls for his fellow Trojans to pour in on the Greeks (Book 12). This tumult is recapitulated later in Akhilleus' pursuit of Hektor around the walls of Troy.

Both opposing and supporting the fury of the human beings is the fury of the gods. Their rage starts with Poseidon, who earlier in the poem takes advantage of Zeus's indifference, as the King of the Gods keeps "his shining eyes away from Troy" (13.9). Poseidon's fury is much like that of Akhilleus:

> The god who girdles earth, even as he spoke,
> struck both men with his staff, instilling fury.
> Then upward like a hawk he soared—a hawk
> that, wafted from a rock point sheer and towering
> shoots to strike a bird over the plain. (13.70–75)

The fury of the gods is just as terrifying when it turns to cunning. Hêra overhears Thetis begging for a favor from Zeus. Then, by Book 14, having heard that Zeus has granted the favor, she decides to punish him. She chooses seduction as her means. With steely calculation, she bathes; she oils herself; she puts on perfume, perfume so strong that it "cast fragrance over earth and heaven" (14.188). She does her hair. She chooses a particular dress, earrings for her ears, pretty sandals for her feet. She makes sure to draw attention to her breasts and waist with tasseled jewelry. So outfitted, she makes a request of Aphrôditê: "Lend me longing, lend me desire / by which you bring immortals low / as you do mortal men!" (14.226–28). Then she visits "Sleep, brother of Death" (14.259). As wrath is mixed with sex, the poem moves into a whirlpool of elemental forces. Hêra persuades Sleep with the promise of mistresses. Sleep gets Hêra to swear by "all gods with Krónos in the abyss" (14.310). Zeus's lust overwhelms him: "Desire / for girl or goddess in so wild a flood / never came over me!" (14.355–57). The other gods then hurl themselves into battle. Artistically, this seduction episode repeats the love-making of Paris and Helen in Book 3. But here the love-making of the gods is part of a higher, deeper, more mysterious maelstrom, one that encompasses the whole second half of the poem.

### A Deeper and Wider Ease

The poet uses the middle books to tune our ears to the pattern of fury-followed-by ease in order to prepare us for Book 24. In Book 13, a warrior kills another by "slash[ing] / the vein that runs up the back [and] comes out / along the neck" (13.622–24). Later, death follows a "spear-throw" that went in "low between genitals and navel, there / where pain of war grieves mortal wretches most" (13.647–49). One Trojan's helmet is smacked from his head and rolls along the plain; an arrow just misses Meneláos' chest and goes skittering off the shield. Then, suddenly, the mood changes. In the midst of this turmoil, the poet turns to the daily activities of life:

> On a threshing floor
> one sees how dark-skinned beans or chickpeas leap
> from a broad shovel under a sharp wind
> at the toss of the winnower. (13.668–71)

Gathering chickpeas and beans and seeing them blow in the wind are a reminder that there is a world apart from war. In Book 16, Patróklos declares at a council that he prefers fighting to talk. The mêlée that ensues obscures the body of Sarpêdon, who "lay enwrapped in weapons, dust, and blood. /

Men kept crowding around the corpse." Then the poet turns impassively to a pastoral scene:

> like flies
> that swarm and drone in farmyards round the milk pails
> on spring days when pails are splashed with milk:
> just so they thronged around the corpse. (16.735–38)

These pastoral similes carry a wistfulness. Like the reference to the Trojan women doing their laundry, they are reminders of the simplicity and continuity of daily life at home.

### Third Song: Finality

The third song of the poem is the almost-silent note of finality, when the lyrical ease of elegy ends in the reality that the human condition does not allow for a permanent release from suffering. The first hint of this finality occurs in the opening of the poem:

> Anger be now your song, immortal one,
> Akhilleus' anger, doomed and ruinous,
> that caused the Akhaians loss on bitter loss
> and crowded brave souls into the undergloom,
> leaving so many dead—carrion
> for dogs and birds; and the will of Zeus was done.

It is a brusque opening: the appeal to the goddess, the hammer-blow repetition of anger and its consequences, loss moving to death, the indignity of the fate of bodies abandoned to birds and dogs, and then the end: "and the will of Zeus was done." As has been noted by others, this is the whole poem in brief. It moves with terrifying swiftness over the chain of events that leaves many warriors dead ... and then comes to a stop. The point of the poem will be simply to watch Zeus work out his plan. The Greek word for "plan" is *boule,* and it is ambiguous, meaning either *plan* or *wish.* If the fulfillment is a "plan," then it has a rational content, presumably intelligible to mortals. If it is a "wish," then it is a force, unintelligible to mortals. In the first meaning—"plan"—there is the suggestion that Zeus's reasons can

69

be understood. If it is a "wish," however, then human beings merely watch helplessly as a higher being, more powerful and alien to human life, fulfills its desires. Some readers emphasize "plan" because they see Zeus's oversight of the plot in a "plan" that is ultimately to bring about a just punishment to the Trojans for having abducted Helen. If one emphasizes "wish," however, then the emphasis of the poem falls on the human reaction to any plan that Zeus may have, and that reaction is a different kind of courage, the courage to resign oneself to life's unintelligibility. When toward the end of Book 1, Zeus sternly warns Hêra, who has been complaining about Zeus's private conversation with Thetis, he says:

> If what you say
> is true, you may be sure it pleases me. (1.648–49)

Translated literally, it reads, "If this so, it is likely it is pleasing to me." There could be no more imperious way of stating the case.

In the rest of the poem, Homer makes sure we hear the threat in the somber ninth line of the poem—"and the will of Zeus was done." When Thetis pleads with Zeus in Book 1, she meets a force rarely persuaded. Zeus ponders her request; she takes his knees and asks again; he sits "unmoving for a long time, silent." Finally, he nods is assent:

> He bent his ponderous black brows down, and locks
> ambrosial of his immortal head
> swung over them, as all Olympos trembled. (1.606–608)

When he promises Thetis that his word is trustworthy, the Greek drums with three polysyllabic adjectives to describe his firmness; Thetis should know that no decree of his is *palinagereton* (revocable), *apatelon* (illusory), *ateleuteton* (not brought to an end) (1.526–27).

The will (or plan) of Zeus reverberates in several later places. In Book 7, Poseidon complains about the Greeks' rampart on the shore of Troy, because human beings are forgetting to thank the gods for the gifts bestowed on them. Calling Poseidon a complainer, Zeus promises the ocean god that he can in the future destroy as much as he wishes:

> Come, look ahead! When the Akhaians take
> again to their ships and sail for their own land,
> break up the wall and wash it out to sea,
> envelop the whole shore with sand! That way
> the Akhaian wall may vanish from the earth. (7.549–53)

The view shifts from a localized war to the great changes of geological time. The finality of Zeus's long view renders futile human action and human heroism.

The narration in the later parts repeats this finality. In Book 8, Hêra advises Athêna to withdraw from battle because Zeus will, in the end, determine events. When Hêra complains to Zeus, he, unperturbed by her fury, tells what will happen: Hektor will go into battle, Akhilleus will reenter the conflict, and "in a desperate narrow place, / they [will] fight over Patróklos dead" (8.540–41). When Zeus sends Hektor into battle against the Greeks, pushing the Greek warriors back to the ships in order to "fulfill the special prayer of Thetis" (15.692), Homer is, despite digressions, letting Zeus's will come inexorably to its conclusion. Perhaps the most desperate protest of the poem against the will of Zeus is expressed when Aías, battling Hektor's rout of the Greeks, raises his shout to Olympos:

> O Father Zeus, come, bring our troops from under
> the dustcloud: make clear air: give back our sight!
> Destroy us in daylight—as your pleasure is
> to see us all destroyed! (17.731–34)

The heroic warrior does not ask for escape from death. He asks only that the gods be straightforward.

The poem goes deepest into finality with the death of Zeus' son Sarpêdon. In this passage, Homer capitalizes on the repetitive formulas of the oral tradition. When impassive Zeus comes to the necessary death of his own so he hesitates. First, Homer has Hêra remind Zeus that he cannot change fate. Her question sharply focuses the poem's dread of death:

> A man who is born to die, long destined for it
> would you set free from the unspeakable end? (16.514–15)

71

Then she offers a concession:

> Afterward, when his soul is gone, his lifetime
> ended, Death and sweetest Sleep can bear him
> homeward to the broad domain of Lykia.
> There friends and kin may give him funeral
> with tomb and stone, the trophies of the dead. (16.526–30)

Héra here is not mourning. She is simply reminding Zeus that the dead Sarpêdon will get the customary funeral. Zeus sees what is coming; before Patróklos dies, he will kill Sarpêdon. He does not blink:

> And Zeus
> would never turn his shining eyes away
> from this mêlée, but watched them all and pondered
> long over the slaughter of Patróklos. (16.738–41)

He ponders for another 230 lines; then he accedes to his own will:

> Wipe away the blood mantling Sarpédon;
> Take him up, out of the play of spears,
> a long way off, and wash him in the river,
> anoint him with ambrosia, put ambrosial
> clothing on him. Then have him conveyed
> by those escorting spirits quick as wind,
> sweet Sleep and death, who are twin brothers. These
> will set him down in the rich broad land of Lykia,
> and there his kin and friends may bury him
> with tomb and stone the trophies of the dead. (16.764–73)

The incantations of mourning have the gentleness of the epic similes. It is not Zeus, however, who utters these final lines. It is the epic singer who utters them, putting Sarpêdon to rest, just as in Book 3 he had put Helen's brothers to rest.

In the second passage, the stillness of Sarpêdon's conveyance home is repeated in the weeping of Patróklos' horses. Nature communicates to its own creatures:

> Out of range,
> the horses of Akhilleus, from the time
> they sensed their charioteer down in the dust
> at the hands of deadly Hektor, had been weeping ....
>      Stock-*still*
> as a gravestone, *fixed* above the tomb
> of a dead man or woman, they *stood fast,*
> holding the beautiful war car *still.* (17.478–90; italics added)

The motionlessness of the horses parallels the finality of the mourning for Sarpêdon. Now even creatures of nature feel grief. Zeus addresses the weeping horses:

> Poor things, why did I give you to King Pêleus,
> a mortal, you, who never age nor die,
> to let you ache with men in their hard lot?
> Of all creatures that breathe and move on earth
> none is more to be pitied than a man. (17.497–501)

Zeus's pity, however, is eerily distant. He does not grieve; he merely states a fact. The great decider seems more aloof than ever. But that aloofness is the poem's greatness, its stern refusal of sentimentality.

## 4. The Power of Imagination: Striving toward an Ideal

The description of Akhilleus' shield in Book 18 recapitulates on a large scale the stillness of the horses. In this pageant-like or emblem-like passage, Homer creates the largest moment of ease in the poem, as large as a tapestry of the story of humanity. First, he sounds the notes of doom. Aphrodítê goes to Hêphaistos and mentions again that suffering will be the lot of her son. Hêphaistos says that he wishes he could save Akhilleus from the "black hour of death" when it comes. Then, as the poet begins to describe the shield, he admires the order of the world itself. Hêphaistos

> ... pictured on it earth, heaven, and sea,
> unwearied sun, moon waxing, all the stars

that heaven bears for garland. Plêïadês,
Hyadês, Oríôn in his might,
the Great Bear, too, that some have called the Wain,
pivoting there, attentive to Oríôn
and unbathed ever in the ocean stream. (18.557–63)

Earlier the similes of fishing and grain-gathering and snow and hunting ratified Akhilleus' statement: "Now I think / no riches cannot compare with being alive." Now the singer takes on the role of the protector, evoking the beauty of the eternal patterns of the constellations ("that heaven bears for a garland"). The stars pivot in the same circles as they have for centuries, and the Great Bear, which some have called the Wain, will always be watching to keep these circles moving in order.

The next section continues the circular movement of the stars. First, unreflective custom—the dancing celebrations at a wedding—moves in a circle. Then deliberate custom sits at a trial, while a crowd shouts, restrained by criers. The fury of war is about to break out; the besiegers of a town are deciding if they will destroy the town or accept half of its treasure; the besieged city's warriors, hoping to break the siege, ambush the siege line at a pasture and kill the herdsman; battle breaks out; the dead are dragged away. But at the end of the description, Homer reminds us that the action and its consequences are only a picture: "and all the figures clashed and fought / like living men." The tense is past yet insofar as the figures do not move, it could be the present. Art now does the work of nature in the first section, evoking the eternal.

The circles of the rhythms of life continue in the next section, and again art fixes those repetitions in an endless present. Farmers are ploughing the fields and turning at the end of the row. One ploughman is offered a cup of wine at the turning; he then goes back to his ploughing. Twice Homer uses forms of the Greek verb "to turn," or *strepho*; once he repeats "up and down" (*entha kai entha*), as if he were watching the movement. At the end of the passage he reminds us, however, that nothing, after all, was moving:

They made their turns-around, then up the furrows,
drove again,eager to meet the deep fields' limit'
and the earth looked black behind them, as

74

though turned up by plows. But it was gold,
all gold—a wonder of the artist's craft. (18.629–33)

The black of the dirt, crumbling from the top of the furrow, suddenly becomes fixed. The epic singer's song accomplishes the same effect—movement of the perceived object and then the steady calm of the artist's eye as he works it into a pattern.

The next three sections move from stillness to fury. First, the gleaners are at work, rhythmically swinging their scythes; the children run up to them with their small armfuls; a banquet is being prepared for the workmen; under an oak tree, a king watches contentedly and silently. In the next section, a boy is playing on a harp; he plays a tune of "longing"; others around him, apparently not noticing the longing, are dancing for joy. But in the last of the three sections here, nature's fury breaks out as a mountain lion attacks a bull and tears its guts out, and the hunting dogs can only bark in frustration.

The stillness returns in the bystanders who are "spellbound." Finally, the rim of the shield seems to hold human life in its palms, like the potter:

Then running round the shield, triple ply,
he pictured all the might of the Ocean stream. (18.695–96)

With "all the might of the Ocean stream," the description of the shield has returned to the "earth, heaven, and sea" of its beginning. In a vineyard, youths and maidens are harvesting the grapes

while on a resonant harp a boy among them
played a tune of longing, singing low
with delicate voice *a summer dirge.* (18.656–58, italics added)

The entire shield passage has the lyric quiet of the epic similes. Fitzgerald's paradoxical phrase, "summer dirge"[16] evokes both the plenty of the grapeharvest and the mournfulness of human life.

At the end of the description of the shield, Homer once again combines

16  Greek: λινον, song of Linos.

movement and stillness. The youths are again dancing; Homer imagines them circling among each other. Then the dancers are replaced by a potter, holding the scene in his two hands:

> Trained and adept, they circled there with ease
> the way a potter sitting at his wheel,
> will give it a practice twirl between his palms
> to see it run. (18.687–90)

Here the two planes of the poem—that of the mortals and that of the im-mortals—are held together; the artist, godlike in his imagination, can fix evanescent reality in perfect stillness.

## 5. The Cadence

After the great shield, battle returns. Savagery comes to a climax in the death of Hektor. In Book 24, Hekubê shrieks: "*I could devour the vitals of that man / leeching into his living flesh*" (24.255–56; Fitzgerald's italics). Priam's response is, by contrast, surrender: "if I must die alongside / the ships of the Akhaians in their bronze / I die gladly. May I but hold my son / and spend my grief; then let Akhilleus kill me." Zeus sends out an eagle whose wingspan is like the doorway of a great man of wealth, a comparison that emphasizes Priam's anxiety but also contains it. Then Zeus-who-views-the-wide-world sends down Hermês, the affable god. Panic at the changing of fortune is encased in stillness, as on the shield.

The backing off from life, muffling of noise, and slowing of action con-tinue in the close of Book 24. Book 22's account of the killing of Hektor would seem to be the end of the fury. The athletic games of Book 23 have done the job of ritual, to diffuse the consciousness of loss in forcing attetion onto other actions and other people. Book 24, however, swings between the self-pity of mourning and the impulse to destroy. Akhilleus first wraps the body of Patróklos in the flap of his shield, then turns and stabs the body of Hektor as if he could kill death.

Hermês' words to Priam recapitulate the stories of loss and exile in the earlier part of the song. Calling himself a "young prince," the seventh son of Polyktôr, Hermês tells a tale of his youth and of his memories of seeing

Hektor in battle, just as in Book 3 Helen recalls her brothers, and as Glaukhos in Book 6 recalls the history of the exile of his grandfather Bellérophontês from Argos, and as Phoinix in Book 9 recalls the refuge he finds at the court of Akhilleus' father, Peleus. Quietly, the swirling movements in the telling of Hêra's seduction of Zeus start again, but no resourceful, determined, and well-connected Queen is driving them, only a weak old man and a youthful, solicitous wraith who will not identify himself. In Hermês' speech to Priam, most of the lines are end-stopped rhymed couplets. Fitzgerald thereby decelerates the Homer's rolling hexameters:

> Old father,
> Where do you journey, with your cart and car,
> Where others rest, below the evening star? (437–39)

In the quiet of this episode, it is as if the two of them—Priam and Hermês—had been lifted out of the world altogether. Hermês reassures Akhilleus that the gods are protecting Hektor's body, even if many Greek swords are stabbing it:

> Dear Sir,
> no dogs or birds have yet devoured your son.
> Beside Akhilleus' ship, out of the sun
> he lies in place of shelter....
> The blest immortal ones
> Favor your prince, and care for every limb
> Even in death, as they so cherished him. (489–505)

Then Homer repeats the moment in Book 3 when Helen seems to step away from Priam and the other Trojan elders as she muses about her brothers. Here, addressing Hermês, not knowing who he is, Priam says his son too honored the gods:

> Child, it was well to honor the immortals.
> He never forgot, at home in Ilion–
> Ah, did my son exist? was he a dream?–
> the gods who own Olympos. (24.507–510)

The past of the poem becomes shadowy and weightless; memories that used to be firmly situated in a particular house or on a particular bit of grass or in a particular woods lose their moorings.

The poem's music now changes. Instead of the noise of angry gods or angry heroes, the scene moves in silence, recapitulating the silent gaze at the great shield in Book 18. It is night; the sentries are eating their supper by the fires; Hermês then puts them to sleep. In this silence, the cart carrying Hermês and Priam approaches the dwelling of Akhilleus; Homer pauses to describe how massive it is and how firmly built. Hermês then says he must depart, and rather than promising Priam that Akhilleus will relent he urges Troy's king only to beg earnestly for the body of his son:

> Priam,
> the great king of Troy, passed by the others,
> knelt down, took in his arms Akhilleus' knees,
> and kissed the hands of wrath that killed his sons. (12.569–72)

Here again, as in Book 9, when Akhilleus haughtily answers the pleading of Odysseus and Aías with "nothing can compare with being alive," the poem touches down on the unarguable; when a great king begs mercy from a hostile warrior, a warrior who is to other men almost as powerful as a god, two feelings about life meet each other—the first, that the events of history bat away human dignity with one dismissive flick of the wrist, and the second, that human dignity is its own justification for the human wish that life should not be hard. These two positions stand mute, opposed to each other, as Priam faces the god-like wrath of Akhilleus (the opening of the poem, ("Wrath, goddess, sing"), and Akhilleus-the-god gazes not on an old king so much as on what the wrinkles on the king's upstretched, imploring hands signify—the many years lived, the many battles, the many losses, the sea of memories. The generalizations of a story are the sole means by which the young can understand, dimly, the furrows that the past has put in the hearts of the old and the determination that has enabled the old to go on from one year to the next, loading their memories with ever new losses and griefs.

As Priam begins his plea, he asks Akhilleus to remember his own father, Pêleus, who like Priam "stands upon the fearful doorstep of old age," but who unlike Priam can at least hope that his son will come back from the war. Priam cannot so hope:

> Noble sons
> I fathered here, but scarce one man is left me.
> Fifty I had when the Akhaians came,
> nineteen out of a single belly, others
> born of attendant women. Most are gone.
> Raging Arês cut their knees from under them.
> And he who stood alone among them all,
> their champion, and Troy's, ten days ago
> you killed him, fighting for his land, my prince
> Hektor. (24.592–600)

The poem here gathers the burden of memory as it reaches back into the earlier books in Book 6, Hippólokhos' rehearsal of his family lineage and of his grandfather's exile (Book 6); Phoinix's appeal to Akhilleus, when he remembers that the toddler Akhilleus had hiccupped wine all over him (Book 9); the many passages where Homer tells the history of a shield; and most significantly, Andrómakhê's recollection of Akhilleus' killing of her father, whose body Akhilleus heaved onto the funeral pyre (Book 6).

It is the sorrowing parent who now gets the central focus. The implacable Akhilleus is moved by Priam's imploring him to remember his own grieving father:

> Now in Akhilleus
> the evocation of his father stirred
> new longing and new grief. (24.608–10)

Just as earlier, blind fury was inarticulate in its rage against the having-happened, now mourning is inarticulate in its helplessness before death:

> Then both were overborne as they remembered:
> the old king huddled at Akhilleus'feet
> wept, and wept for Hektor, killer of men,
> while great Akhilleus wept for his own father

79

as for Patróklos once again; and sobbing
filled the room. (24.612–17)

When Akhilleus consoles Priam, it is as if he has taken on the perspective
of a god. In Book 17, Zeus had spoken to Patróklos' horses:

Poor things, why did I give you to King Pêleus
A mortal, you who never age or die,
To let you ache with men in their hard lot?
Of all creatures that breathe and move on earth
None is more to be pitied than a man. (17.497–501)

There, Zeus-who-views-the-wide-world gazed at human life and saw its
wretchedness; the thread of the narrative went slack for just a moment.
Now a similar blow to the chest is even more powerful. Akilleus, the-young-
and-raving-warrior, must remind the old-and-groveling Priam, that suffering is the lot of human beings.

Akhilleus, for a moment free from vindictiveness, gazes on Priam:

Ah, sad and old!
Trouble and pain you've borne, and bear, aplenty.
Only a great will could have brought you here
Among the Akhaian ships, and here alone
before the eyes of one who stripped your sons,
your many sons, in battle. Iron must be
the heart within you. (24.623–29)

While the hatred saturating the air around them is held off, Akhilleus, recalling Priam's words to Helen on the rooftop of Troy in Book 3, invites
Priam to share in mourning:

Come, then, and sit down.
We'll probe our wounds no more but let them rest
though grief lies heavy on us. Tears heal nothing,
drying so stiff and old. This is the way
the gods ordained the destiny of men,

> to bear such burdens in our lives, while they
> feel no affliction. (24.628–34)

The dull tone of voice here recognizes the bitterness of the difference between human and divine lives:

> At the door of Zeus
> are those two urns of good and evil gifts
> that he may choose for us; and one for whom
> the lightning's joyous king dips in both urns
> will have by turns bad and good luck. (12.634–38)

The phrase "the lightning's joyous king" is spoken without irony. It is a fact
that the gods live at ease, and sometimes, more than ease, as they did back
in Book 1 when they laughed at Hêphaistos' clownish story of the day he
was thrown out of heaven. Akhilleus continues:

> But one
> to whom he sends all evil—that man goes
> contemptible by the will of Zeus; ravenous
> hunger drives him over the wondrous earth,
> unresting, without honor from gods or men.
> Mixed fortune came to Pêleus. Shining gifts
> at the gods' hands he had from birth: felicity,
> wealth overflowing, rule of the Myrmidons,
> a bride immortal at his mortal side. (24.638–46)

Akhilleus proceeds with Zeus-like impassivity:

> But then Zeus gave afflictions too—no family
> Of powerful sons grew up for him at home
> but one child, of all seasons and of none.
> Can I stand by him in his age? Far from my country
> I sit at Troy to grieve you and your children.
> You, too, sir, in time past were fortunate,
> we hear men say. From Makar's isle of Lesbos

northward, and south of Phrygia and the Straits,
no one had wealth like yours, or sons like yours.
Then gods out of the sky sent you this bitterness:
the years of siege, the battles and the losses.
Endure it then, and do not mourn forever
for your dear son. There is no remedy.
You will not make him stand again. Rather
await some new misfortune to be suffered. (24.647–61)

The translator Fitzgerald emphasizes Akhilleus' resignation to the will of
Zeus by putting an extra weak stress at the end of many of these lines, which
fall with futility. The Greek verb for "endure" in "Endure it then"—*ane-
cho*—is the same verb used at the end of Book 1 when Hêphaistos laugh-
ingly told Hêra she would have to put up with Zeus's conferences with
Thetis; but now it has a very different resonance.

Even while he is resignedly speaking to Priam, however, the wrath of
Akhilleus does not undergo a catharsis. Priam asks to see the body of Hektor. Akhilleus warns him sternly:

> "Do not vex me, sir," he said.
> "I have intended, in my own good time,
> to yield up Hektor to you
>
> Therefore, *let me be.*
> Sting my sore heart again, and even here,
> under my own roof, suppliant thought you are,
> I may not spare you, sire, but trample on
> the express command of Zeus!" (24.670–84; Fitzgerald's
> italics)

He leaves the room abruptly and begs the soul of the dead Patróklos to forgive him for releasing Hektor's body. He then returns to his tent, offers to
Priam a chair and food. He says that even Niobe, in her grieving for her
children, took something to eat. The image of her grief is as still and as eternal as the image of the shield:

She too, long turned to stone, somewhere broods on
the gall the immortal gods gave her to drink. (24.740–41)

This is the climax of the music of the *Iliad*. The poem reaches its point of
richness in the balance between wrath-just-kept-at-bay and the acceptance
of suffering. Indeed, the beauty of Akhilleus' long speech to Priam about
Zeus's two urns has all the resignation of the poet's own voice about the
destruction of the rampart back in Book 12.

Is there justice in the *Iliad*? Some say yes, some say no. Those who say
yes argue that the Trojans have to pay a price for the abduction of Helen.
The abduction of Helen, however, plays so small a part in the poem that
one could reasonably argue it is inconsequential. Those who say yes, justice
does exist in the poem, also point to the passage in the description of
Akhilleus' shield where there is a council and two parties coming before a
leader for adjudication. But that adjudication, like the abduction of Helen,
has only a small place in the poem, and then it is only a work of the imagination. If there is justice in the *Iliad* it is something hoped for, but its out-
lines are blurry. Perhaps there is something we might call justice in the
suddenly wise tone that Akhilleus takes when he, the younger man, comforts the older man. Here, it seems that savage warriors can put aside their
rage at times, a composure that must underlie human relations for justice
to exist.

But perhaps what the poem is fundamentally about is what great art
does. It sees an ideal but sees also that that imagined ideal may not be realized in this life. The *Iliad* has a dark view of human nature. If Akhilleus
rises in our eyes at the end of the poem, the moment is like that of Book
9, a crystallization in a character of a general feeling in the poem, not a particular character's suddenly coming to maturity. Only the poet can see as
far as Zeus, and then only after he has put together in a whole a poem composed of so many parts. Indeed, perhaps the voice Akhilleus takes on at the
end is really the voice of the sage poet, who feels the summons to see as
widely as does Zeus. Back in Book 12, the poet draws attention to his limitations:

Now there was fighting at the various gates

a difficult thing for me to tell it all,
*as though I were a god.* (12.194–96; italics added)

Still, just before this admission, the poet has indeed talked as much like a god as a human being can. The rampart that the Greeks built as a protection around their ships did not last.

> The immortal gods
> had never willed it, and its time was brief.
> While Hektor lived and while Akhilleus raged,
> and while Lord Priam's town lived on, unsacked,
> so long the Akhaians' rampart stood. But after
> the flower of Troy went down, with many Argives
> fallen or bereft, when Priam's Troy
> was plundered in the tenth year, and the Argives,
> shipped again for their dear homeland—then
> Poseidon and Apollo joined to work
> erosion of the wall by fury of rivers
> borne in flood against it, all that flow
> seaward from Ida: Rhêsos, Heptáporos,
> Karêsos, Rhodíos, Grênikos, Aesêpos
> Skamánder's ancient stream, and Simóeis,
> round which so many shields and crested helms
> had crashed in dust with men who were half gods. (12.9–26)

One follows the action of the poem as if, holding only a flashlight, one followed a road covered in fog, moving forward, but unsure at every moment where the road will turn, what huge tree root will suddenly appear in the path, where a branch has fallen, when the road will move over rocks that will turn out to be the edge of a precipice. Life is never steady.

It has been objected that Homer's world is a world where war is a given, and that human beings should strive to the utmost to escape from such a world. Homer would argue that human beings will never give up fighting. Homer addresses a more fundamental side of war—namely, fighting for a people simply because they are one's own people.

## 6. Teaching Homer in the Modern University

I used to teach Homer in a "great books" class at the University of Pennsylvania where I was an adjunct. One of my best students came to my office to talk about Homer. She was a lovely young woman, and she had a lovely soul. In class, she could quietly hold her own against the most self-confident male undergraduate, articulating her arguments without raising her voice or becoming defensive; could listen carefully without thinking about what she wanted to argue next; could specify what she approved in another's argument and then change her mind; could disagree without waving her hands around in exasperation or garnering support by asking, "Does anyone else think what John said is right?" She did not offer clichés, like Rochefoucauld's "Hypocrisy is the tribute vice pays to virtue," as if such an apothegm settled the matter. She loved poetry and wrote some herself.

Because of a schedule conflict, she asked me would I meet with her in a private tutorial. At our first meeting, I talked for a while about what I considered the heart of Homer. Then I asked her what she would like to talk about. She said what struck her most about Homer was the denigration of women. She pointed out that at the end of Book 1, Hêra is dismissed as a termagant when Hêphaistos gets the gods-at-banquet to laugh at her and that Helen is the cause of the Trojan war and that Aphrodítê is told by Diomêdês that battle is not her place.

As I listened to her talk, I sensed a great weight descend on me. Across from me, in all its dullness (like the immortal Dullness of Alexander Pope), heaving like molten lava, was the failure of the modern university, which has taught many young women that the question to be asked, over and over again, to be: is this story or poem or play sexist? I hear that question, and I inwardly sigh and wonder to myself whether or not I have at this moment the energy for the long discussion, way outside of Homer, that a proper response would require.

She went on to say that literature before the modern era is sexist; we read it so that we can see the same sexist patterns of early literature still in operation today and think to ourselves, well, nothing has changed after all. Hence a certain series on television that in my mind is just plain bad is in her mind an excellent way to see how the patterns between the sexes in the 1950's are still at work.

85

I suggested that there are other more important questions about Homer than whether or not Homer is sexist. She doubted that. I suggested that perhaps a more important question would be what in Homer has moved readers for centuries. She thought, on the contrary, it was necessary, in analyzing all pre-modern authors, to note where they are sexist, for their sexism might be deeply implicated in whatever others had found moving. Still, there were some authors, she admitted, whom she exempted from this analysis. She said Shakespeare was, as is well known, subversive of traditional sexual roles; take *The Taming of the Shrew*. (I noted to myself silently that such a reading of *The Taming of the Shrew* all depends on how you read Katarina's last speech, and I seriously doubted that that speech was meant to be read ironically. But again, a proper response to this observation would require a very long discussion.) Going on, she said, take Rosalind in *As You Like It*. In that play, Rosalind is a woman playing a man. Yes, I said, it is true that Rosalind is saucy and hardheaded when she is dressed as Ganymede, but when she drops the disguise, she is immediately talking like a traditional fainting female. Further, I said, in *King Lear*, Shakespeare borrows the usual stereotypes of women as angels-or-bitches. But even if he does, so what? Isn't the "coming home" of the more or less Prodigal Son story in *King Lear* story more important than Shakespeare's deployment of sexual stereotypes? She did not think so.

Perhaps she was too busy that summer really to give Homer a chance. She had reached for the slicer-and-dicer that had been successful before and hoped it would be successful again. Moreover, I had to admit, she had an argument: Homer says that battle is the opportunity to live life at its fullest; women are not allowed on the battlefield; therefore, Homer does not think women can live life to its fullest. But then the question is, is Homer right about battle being the place where life is lived to the fullest? With that question, we were in for a *really* long discussion. Surely the point of Homer lies in his telling—the defiant fury, the dimly perceived sense of justice, the mourning, the stillness, the ability of Homer-the-singer to modulate so many powerful feelings and balance them, like the potter on Akhilleus' shield, who twirls the pot in his hands.

Still, my student's general point is worth registering. Forty or so years ago, when I was, for a year, a lecturer at Yale (and that was an interesting year!), I was one of several assistant professors who taught a course on, more or less, Chaucer-Shakespeare-Milton. There were several sections of the course, and instructors met regularly when the sections were about to take up a new book. The meeting on Milton started with the chairman of the group saying, affably, that of course with Milton, the woman-question was going to be a problem, and there was no getting around certain lines in *Paradise Lost*, for instance, the line about how women should worship God in their husbands. He raised his hands, palms up, and shrugged a shrug: what is an enlightened modern to do? Milton's failing in this area should be admitted, he said, and the issue then put aside. A sensible enough view, perhaps. At the end of the lively meeting—and those assistant professors at Yale were not lacking in interesting ideas—while the rest of us were gathering our things, the chairman of the meeting strode over to a male colleague and said, "I hear you are taking over my section next semester." He then shook his head back and forth in wonder and emphasis: "You're a lucky man; there are some gorgeous co-eds in that class."

Perhaps in the *Iliad*, women are a symbol of what the battle is for: for beauty that seems immortal (the scene with Helen and Priam), for the continuity of dailyness (the pools where the Trojan women did their washing), but most important, for family life (the scene with Hektor and Andrómakhê and Astýanax in Book 6). As the keeper of the family—the thread that holds together brothers, sisters, fathers, mothers—women are the lodestar for the warrior. When Achilles says he might just pack up and leave this siege-of-Troy business, he does not say he is going to find another city to sack or another general who will appreciate his skill in battle; he says he is going to go home, not to a woman, it is true, because his mother is a goddess, but to his father. Homer made another epic out of that notion—that home guarded by a woman is the warrior's lodestar.

# CHAUCER'S *GENTILLESSE*
# AND THE GOOD HOST

## *1. Judging Tales*

In the course on "The Critical Essay" with Robert Garis, mentioned in my preface, Garis's central question was, "Is this a good play, poem, short story, novel?" One of the books assigned was Doris Lessing's recently published *The Golden Notebook*, a book had received a lot of positive press. Garis had picked a contemporary book because he wished to teach that reading books was more than a pastime; for him, reading books was a time for practice in assessment because it makes a difference what one admires. On my last paper, Garis wrote on my paper, "Read, read a lot. It will help your power of judging."

To that end, Garis expected us to pay attention to the words on the page, their tone of voice, the attitude that tone implied, and finally, and most important, what he called its "tact." In that class, we read a number of very short poems. The first day, we talked for 30 minutes about these four lines:

O western wind, when wilt thou blow?
The small rain down gan rain;
Christ, that my love were in my arms,
And I in my bed again.

For the first paper (suggested length: about two pages), we were to write a critical essay on these 12 lines by one William Collins, a poet of whom I had never heard:

How sleep the brave, who sink to rest
 By all their country's wishes blest;
When Spring, with dewy fingers cold,

Returns to deck their hallow'd mould,
She there shall dress a sweeter sod
Than Fancy's feet have ever trod.

By fairy hands their knell is rung;
By forms unseen their dirge is sung;
There Honour comes, a pilgrim grey,
To bless the turf that wraps their clay;
And Freedom shall awhile repair
To dwell, a weeping hermit, there!

We were to address the question, "Is this a good poem?" Now, 50 years later, I am pondering Garis's question. Indeed, is the poem lacking in tact? Is it cold? Is not all that fancy diction ("hallow'd mould," "sweeter sod," "fairy hands") an ungentle way to talk about those who have died in battle when they were young? Are the valorizing personifications ("Honour," "Freedom") too easy? But then, is there not something properly hesitant about the tone, acknowledging how short-lived grief is? Freedom will be there only for "awhile," and she will be there alone, as a "hermit."

Garis was also interested in movies. When, long after graduation, I had dinner with him in Cambridge, we got into an enthusiastic talk about our favorite black-and-white films— *The Shop Around the Corner, The Philadelphia Story, Top Hat, The Thin Man,* etc., why they worked, why most modern films were pretty bad, and which ones were not so bad. I have heard people say that there are some courses in college you will not appreciate until after you graduate. For me, about no course was that statement as true as about Garis's English 30 in the Fall of 1963 at Wellesley College. The question— is this a good poem?—takes years to think out. But there is no inclination to think it out if someone has not introduced the question to readers when they are young.

A few times in my classes, I have tried to ask that question—does this play, poem, novel "work"? The discussion goes pretty much nowhere. I realize now that answering it takes a lot of practice. One day, before I arrived at my course *Poetry and Politics in Ancient Greece*, the students were vociferously discussing the movie *American Sniper*. The judgments flew thick and fast:

those who objected to snipers (not fair to shoot people who do not know you are there) against those who held that war is war and the point is to kill the enemy; those who thought the hero upon returning to the U.S. on leave should not have stopped in a bar to get himself together, but should have gone straight home to his wife and children, against those who thought a soldier knows all too well that those to whom he is returning have no idea what a war zone is like; those who opposed any American involvement in any armed conflict anywhere in the world, against those who thought that if the United States is not going to police the world, some other more brutal power will. Of course, discussion on these grounds got very heated very soon. Politics always tends to raise the blood pressure.

Movies being the most popular medium these days (along with TV series), judgments of them are the place to start because so many are the moral *koine* for many people. Such a discussion should not be an argument, but a probing of difficulties. Does a work's politics trump its technical and aesthetic success? Is its handling of politics judicious or is it rabble-rousing? Does it touch serious questions seriously, or, if it does claim to deal with serious questions, is it shallow, clichéd? For students, it might be beneficial at least to hear the judgment from someone, "Well, in my view, these shows are not good, and here are my thoughts on why they are not." Teachers shy away from such discussions because they tend to fly off in all directions and because teachers do not want to be in the position of denigrating student culture.

In this chapter, I will talk about Chaucer. People usually like Chaucer because he is funny. But the prologue to *The Canterbury Tales* does not set the tone for enjoying a good laugh. Rather it sets the tone of the long view from a higher plane. It looks down from afar on a group of pilgrims and sees a motley crew. Because of the prologue, we are invited to judge not only the tales the pilgrims tell but the motivation for their choice of tales. Insofar as they are going to visit the grave of a martyr and, allegedly, to thank him for helping them when they were sick, they seem to be motivated at least somewhat by religious devotion, and surely motivation for a story will have some effect on shaping it. When that question comes up, then the listener is led to thinking about the character of the teller. If asking the question, "Is this a good or a bad story?" is the most important question to be asked, then Chaucer's *Canterbury Tales* are practice in that endeavor.

The opening of the prologue sets the tone for judgment. In this passage, Chaucer invites his audience to meditate on the human condition and on human nature. Human beings are like the animals; with the coming of spring, they feel a new zest for life. Unlike the animals, however, they do not throw themselves into mating. Instead, they decide to go on a pilgrimage. Chaucer draws attention to the oddity of this decision by juxtaposing it with the exultation of the birds. In this opening verse paragraph, Chaucer expresses an enchantment with nature's ways, for, as he suggests, in the easy transition from spring fertility to the movement of human hearts, the powers of great creating nature are at work.

Chaucer has the Host provide the criteria, which are not complicated. The tales will be judged for—in Middle English—their best *sentence* and *moost solaas*, that is, for wisdom and solace. *Solaas* in the 14th century could mean either "entertainment" or "consolation," although perhaps the Host means that entertainment can itself be a consolation insofar as it takes the mind off troubles; the Host, after all, is not a deep thinker, and his little formula of *sentence* and *solaas* could be a standard phrase he has given little thought to. Later, the Host's shortcomings as a judge are important in understanding just how much these pilgrims form a company that is truly a group of companions. Because of the Host's contest, Chaucer expects his hearer (these days, his reader) to ponder what in fact makes a good tale. Some acquaintance with the basic questions of moral philosophy is needed to ensure that the criteria are not vapid.

## 2. The Knight's Tale

When we are taught Chaucer in college or high school, we read the tales in linear fashion, one after the other, as separate beads on a string. Time being short, we do not read and then reread the tales, ruminating on one and then another with an eye to understanding what Chaucer means by *sentence and solaas*. Here, I will do that shuttling back and forth among tales in order to show how the terms of measurement become clearer as we move on. Because I assume my audience has not read Chaucer since high school or college, I will summarize *The Knight's Tale* as well as the subsequent tales.[17]

Chaucer sets up *The Knight's Tale* as the tentative standard for a good tale by giving it first place in the narration. In the *General Prologue*, Chaucer praises the Knight for his sense of duty, self-sacrifice, and morality. He is not interested in splendid knightly outfits; indeed, he has come so quickly to the pilgrimage that his tunic is still stained with dirt. Although he has fought all over Europe in defense of the True Faith and has a right to be proud of his valor, he is "modest as a maid." (We may presume that this True Faith is Christianity; the Knight is going on a pilgrimage, but *The Knight's Tale* leaves the matter of the Knight's Christian faith vague.) In sum, he shows "truth, honor, generousness, and courtesy," and is "a true, a perfect gentle-knight." His purpose in going on the pilgrimage is different from the intentions of the other pilgrims, who are seeking the martyr who helped them when they were sick. The Knight, in contrast, is going to pray to the martyr because he wishes to give thanks. Thus, the Knight fights self-lessly for the truth; he has lived a difficult life in order to accomplish this goal; he has not asked for glory as a reward; any success he has achieved he attributes to a power higher than himself. He has, moreover, a great sympathy with the trials that most human beings suffer in this life. Indeed, the central *sentence* of *The Knight's Tale* has to do with a reflection that occurs at some time to everyone—that misfortune occurs without regard to moral justice, that loss leaves one without moorings, that facing life bravely after such a loss seems futile for, as Akhilleus says to Priam at the end of Book 24 in the *Iliad*, "Rather await some new misfortune." One should not expect life to be without suffering, although I have had more than one class where students protested, "Life isn't that bad!" I wonder to myself what the proper response would be to that objection.

In his tale, the Knight uses a subdued romance high style. The *cantus firmus* of the tale is mourning. It starts with a summary of the Duke Theseus' defeat of the Amazons, whose ruler, Hippolyta, had been a "fair courageous queen." On the ride back to Athens, the now-married Theseus and Hippolyta and their entourage meet the women of Thebes, whose husbands

17  The translation is Nevill Coghill's (London and New York: Penguin Books, 1951; revised, 1958).

have been defeated by Creon. After the battle, two young men—Palamon and Arcite—are found alive among the "heaps of slain." The women accompanying Theseus beg him to put these two young men in prison rather than have them killed, and Theseus does so. The second episode of the tale likewise emphasizes suffering. From their prison window, Palamon and Arcite almost simultaneously catch sight of Hippolyta's sister, Emily. Both think they have a right to her. When Arcite is eventually freed from prison, his new liberty is not a boon to him because he can no longer see Emily from his prison window. The Knight gives him a lament:

> Infinite are the harms that come this way;
> We little know the things for which we pray;
> Our ways are drunkard ways—drunk as a mouse;
> …
>
> How eagerly we seek felicity,
> Yet are so often wrong in what we try.

Another lament is given to Palamon because although he can still see Emily, he is in prison:

> O cruel Gods, whose government
> Binds all the world to your eternal bent
> ….
>
> What more is man to you than to behold
> A flock of sheep that cower in the fold?"

The central question of these speeches—is there justice in the universe?—eventually becomes the central question of the entire tale. Whether there is justice or not is less important, however, than the human response to the difficulty of answering that question with solemnity and fortitude. Ultimately, there is reason to believe there is justice in the universe, but that conclusion is hard to maintain with conviction; still, it is part of knightly courage to strive to do so.

The third episode in the tale increases the song of mourning. After

Arcite is freed from prison, Palamon manages to escape. Meeting in Athens and fighting to kill each other, both knights are discovered by Theseus, who insists, with some heat, that they fight in an orderly fashion at a tournament, which Arcite wins. The tale digresses to the grief of the goddess Venus who is unhappy that her knight, Palamon, has lost. The god Saturn assures her that everything will work out to her satisfaction. At the moment of victory, a "furie infernal" causes Arcite's horse to leap to the side. Arcite falls and is badly hurt. On his deathbed he asks, "What is the world? What does man ask to have?" He dies. The tale has reached its nadir. Even the steady and authoritative Theseus is rattled and seeks reassurance from his father Egeus (who seems to have been reading Boethius' fifth-century *Consolation of Philosophy*). Egeus reiterates the theme that life is suffering:

> This world nys but a thurghfare ful of wo,
> And we been pilgrymes, passynge to and fro.
> Deeth is an ende of every worldly soore.

> (This world is but a thoroughfare of woe
> And we are pilgrims passing to and fro;
> Death is the end of every worldly sorrow.)

When, at Arcite's funeral, Theseus offers a consolation to the assembled multitude, he is more hopeful. Death is not the end of every worldly sorrow, he says, because the order of nature teaches that death is part of a greater whole that includes life. Although Theseus' practical solution, that "we must make a virtue of necessity," dilutes any firm confidence that the order of nature is just, human beings must believe that nature's order is just, or life is impossible. Emily then weds Palamon; there is joy at the ceremony. The future of the married couple, however, is not according to the old formula of living "happily ever after." Instead, the ending is subdued: Palamon is said simply to have served Emily with "gentle constancy," or, in Middle English, "And he hire serveth al so gentilly." Human kindness is the best we can do in a world whose justice is not and cannot be obvious to human beings. As Aquinas argued, God is knowable but not by the limited intellect of human beings.

Thus, for the Knight, life's suffering must be endured, by the individual, with acceptance of the limitations of human reason and with something like faith, and, by the group, with *gentillesse,* which is a mixture of humility in one's judgments and forbearance toward the weaknesses of others. When Theseus, enjoying a hunt, comes upon Palamon and Arcite fighting like boars and the ladies accompanying him on the hunt plead with him to spare the two young men, Theseus controls his anger by remembering his own youthful inclinations:

> Though he had quaked with anger at the start,
> He had reflected, having time to pause,
> Upon their trespass and upon its cause,
> And though his anger at their guilt was loth
> To pardon either, reason pardoned both.
> For thus he argued: almost any man
> Will help himself to love, if so he can.

After all, it is human nature, especially with the young, to imagine that romantic love is the fulfillment of life. Maturity brings a generous condescension to the erotic agitations of youth because most adults, at one time or another, have felt these agitations too. *Gentillesse* as forbearance and forgiveness occurs in probably the most famous line in Chaucer, just before this excerpt: "For pitee renneth soone in gentil herte" ("Pity runs swiftly in a noble heart"). That Chaucer intended *The Knight's Tale* to set the standard for the other tales is signaled by the emphasis on pity and *gentillesse* in *The Franklin's Tale* and by the exact repetition of the line in *The Merchant's Tale,* although when uttered by the Merchant, the intention is entirely different from the Knight's.

The telling of *The Knight's Tale* supports its *sentence* that a good human being shows fortitude, self-restraint, and generosity. The Knight uses a subdued high romance, with many repetitions, many metaphors, and many references to the classical gods. Students are quick to note the length of the tale, but that length is part of the Knight's wisdom. First, a serious subject demands grandeur in telling, and grandeur comes from Ciceronian *copia,* a fullness of expression that is appropriate to important questions. Second, the thickness of the Knight's telling allows him to argue that an understanding of human life requires a view stretching far back in time, into worlds that we can know only from history. Any individual human being

95

belongs to the category *humanity*; any individual suffering is part of the suffering that all human beings have endured. Thoughtful people will survey the course of human history and understand that life is not a random collection of individual lives but rather a great river called humankind and that no individual should imagine his suffering is worse or more unjust than the suffering that has occurred in previous eras. Moreover, a good tale has to be long because it must offer a *solaas* that is not dismissive or crudely cheerful. Finally, the consolation must persuade its hearers that we are all in this together.

The tale's grandeur is required to acknowledge the weight of grief. Suffering in the particular instance is terrible, but a good tale will see misery from a distant perspective and portray suffering as the human condition. Grandeur should be aloof. When the tale dips toward the drama of human anger, desperation, or ardor, it steadies itself quickly. For example, near the beginning of the story, Arcite is allowed to leave prison and return to Thebes. At this moment, he is in anguish because he will no longer be able to see Emily from prison. But the knight-the-teller is detached. He prefaces the account of Arcite's misery by turning aside from his story: "But I shall take all day if I repeat / All that he suffered in the first two years." The tale has a way of chronically smoothing ruffled emotional feathers.

The elaborate descriptive passages—of the lists, for instance, where the tournament takes place and of the temples to Venus, Mars, and Diana— also diminish emotional intensity. To the same end function the numerous asides when the Knight tells us how great lengths of time have passed: "Thus, for a year or two, Arcite remained / With Emily the bright, her page-of state"; "Three years went by in happiness and health"; "The summer passes, and long winter nights / Double the miseries and appetites / Of lover in jail and lover free as air"; "But shall I take all day if I repeat / All that he suffered for the first two years"; "In course of time, and after certain years, / Mourning had been accomplished and their tears." The pace is a kind of impassive stateliness; no matter what the excitement, what the joy, what the grief, life will end. The length of this tale is a rejection of the rapidly told solution of escapism or sentimentality (*The Franklin's Tale* and *The Wife's Tale*).

With these remarks, the tale is reminding the hearer that life will go on, as it has for centuries. If the voice of the narrator becomes agitated for a moment, sympathizing with individual characters, it soon rises above the drama. Just before the moment when Duke Theseus becomes the most out-raged, the Knight reminds us that loss of composure is bound to happen, but one should not believe, as the young tend to do, that one life-loss will end the world. When Palamon and Arcite, having met by chance in Athens, are fighting "like boars" till they "were ankle deep in blood," it so happens that Theseus had "a sudden wish to hunt" and comes upon them. This meeting is introduced with the Knight's matter-of-fact narration:

> Now Destiny, that Minister-General
> Who executes on earth and over all
> What God from everlasting has foreseen,
> Is of such strength, that though the world had been
> Sure of the contrary, by Yea and Nay,
> That thing will happen on a certain day,
> Though never again within a thousand years,
> And certainly our appetites and fears,
> Whether in war or peace, in hate or love,
> Are governed by a providence above.

Angered at Palamon's and Arcite's having fallen to blows without a referee, Theseus imposes a means of adjudicating their quarrel. The two hotheads will spend a year (a year!) gathering knights and then fight it out at the tournament.

The tale also diminishes an emotional charge by muting differences of worth. It does not set up a distinction between Palamon and Arcite; both are worthy of Emily (although in my experience, contemporary students, who have succeeded in the meritocracy of the academy, try hard to find a reason why one knight should win her and the other should not). The tale also refuses to debate marriage; marriage and celibacy are both acceptable. Palamon and Arcite both want to win Emily and to marry her; Emily wishes to be exempt from marriage in order to live a life of prayer; neither path is said to be better than the other.

Among students, the ardor for justice inclines them to demand an ac-count; someone or something must be to blame. But for Chaucer, the noble attitude is not to have expected happiness as one's due nor to find someone or something to blame for one's misery. Thus, in the Knight's view, suspense is not good for a story teaching *gentillesse* because it raises the wish for a clearly just ending. In this way, the tale eschews the satisfaction, or perhaps pleasure, of providing a readily identifiable villain. Instead, the even, steady pace of the telling pushes against the arc of a tragedy, which gathers intensity, reaches a climax, and then collapses into acceptance.

Although *The Knight's Tale* eschews the arc of tragedy, however, it does not refuse darkness. Kindness and courtesy will diminish suffering, it is true, but kindness and courtesy will not banish the despair that suffering gives rise to. Human beings mistakenly think that the relief they feel after a crisis will be lasting and steady, and they look for a warrant for these hopes in the gods. But when before the tournament, Palamon, Arcite, and Emily pray to their pagan gods for a good outcome, the gods' signs are ambiguous. After Venus hears Palamon's long prayer, the goddess "shook / And made a sign," which Palamon takes as a happy omen, discounting the "hint" at a "delay." When Emily goes to pray that Arcite and Palamon will give up their passion for her and become friends, the fires at Diana's altar also show ambiguous signs, for when Diana tells Emily that she will be married, the goddess's arrows ominously "clatter" in her quiver. Finally, when Arcite goes to pray, the altar of Mars sends out smoke and fire, and the raspy voice of the god utters "*Victory.*" Arcite gets his victory, but it is not lasting. The subsequent argument among the gods ends with Saturn's dour announcement that he controls events and that human life is death, destruction, and suffering:

> Mine is the prisoner in the darkling pit,
> Mine are both neck and noose that strangles it,
> Mine the rebellion of the serfs astir,
> The murmurings, the privy prisoner;
> And I do vengeance, I send punishment,
> And when I am in Leo it is sent.
> Mine is the ruin of the lofty hall,
> The falling down of tower and of wall
> Of carpenter and mason, I their killer.
> 'Twas I slew Samson when he shook the pillar;
> Mine are the maladies that kill with cold,
> The dark deceits, the stratagems of old.

The endstopped lines and parallelism fairly rumble and growl. Saturn's speech repeats the plaintive cries of Palamon and Arcite earlier in the tale: are men like sheep that cower in the fold? are their ways like the ways of a drunk mouse? Saturn's answer is declarative, not interrogative. The young wonder inquiringly; Saturn makes pronouncements. The tale seems to descend into the dark.

Saturn's view forms the backdrop, then, to Theseus' sermon at the end of Book 4, a sermon borrowed from Boethius' *Consolation of Philosophy*, which in turn depends heavily on ancient Stoicism. The backdrop is necessary to give as much weight as possible to Theseus' sermon, for in Saturn's speech the tale has given full voice to the view that life is controlled by malevolent forces beyond the reach of human beings. When Theseus rises to give his sermon, the tale seems to be holding its breath:

> When all were seated there and hushed the place,
> The noble Duke kept silent for a space
> And ere he spoke the wisdom in his breast
> He let his eyes fall where it pleased him best.

The Duke is silent; he looks around for strength:

> Then with sober visage and the still
> Sound of a sigh, he thus expressed his will:
> "The First Great Cause and Mover of all above
> When first he made the fairest chain of love,
> Great was the consequence and high the intent.
> He well knew why He did and what He meant.
> …
> And that same Prime Mover then," said he,
> "Stablished this wretched world, appointing ways,
> Seasons, durations, certain length of days
> To all that is engendered here below."

There is order, Theseus declares, and there is an intelligence behind it. Still, it is one of the mysteries of this tale that Chaucer does not allow Theseus' sermon to refute Saturn's dark claim. In thinking about suffering, most people remain young, complaining like Palamon and Arcite, or, as the other tales will show, thinking they are grown up when they have moved beyond adolescent indignation to a Saturnish sort of despair. Chaucer has Theseus merely state that nature shows order, not that this order should dispel the human suspicion that life is chaos. The implication is, first, that human beings always live with hope and striving, not with certainty, and second, that a good governor will set an example for the young to imitate. When the tale has Theseus accede to the Theban women's complaint, when he does not put Arcite and Palamon to death, when he allows the two young knights to fight it out in a tournament in which no one will kill the other, and when the tale has the dying Arcite urge Emily to marry Palamon, it is recommending a noble generosity of spirit, not reassurance. He addresses the question that occurs to any thoughtful person and answers it without erasing its difficulties. Moreover, significantly, the Knight does not have a prologue. His *solaas* is a gift of wisdom offered to the pilgrims generally, not an opportunity for pay-back or for grinding an ax. One might say that in this respect, he is a good host.

It is odd that Chaucer's Knight omits from his tale the consolation of the Christian resurrection. Yet perhaps that omission is not so odd. If we are all merely pilgrims on a thoroughfare of woe, as Egeus tells Theseus, then, from the perspective of Chaucer's ideal Christian, no earthly mortal can tell a perfect tale. The word "pilgrimage" in Egeus' speech to Theseus is important: "life is a pilgrimage full of woe." The Knight is doing the best he can in a wretched world; and the best he can do may not be perfect, but it is aiming—pilgriming—toward something higher.

While it is hard to know how the other pilgrims regard the journey to Canterbury, one suspects, from Chaucer's descriptions of them in the General Prologue and from the flaws in some of their tales, that they do not, like Egeus, regard life as a pilgrimage. In the introductory lines, Chaucer had said that spring induces people to go on pilgrimages in order to thank the holy, bliss martyr. But for some of the pilgrims, the journey to Canterbury is a vacation or a business opportunity—a chance to meet eligible men (the Wife), to make some money (the Pardoner), or to take the mind off a bad marriage (the Merchant).

It is unlikely that these pilgrims understand the Knight's *sentence*. It is true, the Knight does not mention the dedication that St. Paul speaks to in, "I have fought the good fight; I have finished my course; I have kept the faith" (2 Timothy 4:7), nor does he mention Paul's line that would be appropriate for a knightly defender of the faith: "Stand therefore, having your loins girt about with truth, and having on the breastplate of righteousness" (Ephesians 6:14). Moreover, the Knight's story lacks the serene hope promised in the gospel of John. Still, the tale is in harmony with the New Testament's emphasis on duty, patience, and love of Christ or love of God's justice. The Knight's Stoicism and his forbearance toward human weakness constitute a secular version of Christian love and Christian patience. Perhaps Chaucer decided to omit a specifically Christian consolation because he wanted his audience to note the omission and to feel something is lacking. Unlike modern novels, *The Knight's Tale* is not about its characters; it is about the love of slow, somber, and dignified traditions that have consoled humanity for centuries. Its *sentence* is stalwart endurance. But in the greater context of Chaucer's long poem, there whispers around this tale the possibilities offered in the New Testament.

### 3. The Miller's Tale

That the other pilgrims do not hear the sentence and solaas of *The Knight's Tale* is implied by the quarrel that breaks out immediately afterward. The Host suggests that a religious figure, the Monk, should go next, as would seem appropriate, for the Knight's secular consolation almost requires a Christian answer. But the drunk Miller loudly insists on being next in line, threatening to leave the "company" if he is not allowed his turn. The Miller's Tale was probably, for some on the pilgrimage, a bit of relief from the sobriety of the Knight's message. Indeed, most people, years after their introduction to Chaucer, remember *The Miller's Tale* much more readily than they do the Knight's.

Artistically, this tale is well told. At the beginning, we are introduced to the carpenter John, his young lodger Nicholas, and his wife Alison, whose physical desirability is appreciated by the menfolk, even in her rebuffs, which are "like a skittish colt / Boxed in frame for shoeing." Absalon too is described with lengthy detail, as is his wooing of Alison and as is Nicholas's plan to make the carpenter believe another flood is coming. Here Cicero's *copia* is used not

101

for rumbling seriousness, as it is in *The Knight's Tale*, but for the sake of inducing forgetfulness. The pacing is excellent. By the time John the carpenter, Alison, and Nicholas are all in their separate tubs and Absalon has wooed Alison rather unsuccessfully (he kisses her bottom, thinking it is her mouth) and has procured a hot poker with which to punish her, the prediction of the flood has been forgotten. When then Nicholas sticks *his* bottom out the window and Absalon burns *that* bottom and when the carpenter hears Nicholas's cry, "Water! Water!" the leisurely told tale suddenly whips forward to the joke.

But perhaps Chaucer is using this tale to invite consideration of the weaknesses of comedy. If *The Knight's Tale* teaches the *gentillesse* that flows from fortitude and generosity of spirit, *The Miller's Tale* teaches the delight of a joke that insults a fellow pilgrim ("John" is a carpenter; the Reeve on the pilgrimage is also a carpenter). *The Miller's Tale* also teaches that elegant poetry is to be mocked; the love-yearning of Absalon surely mocks the love-yearning of Palamon and Arcite. Does it teach *solaas* in the sense of consolation? No. For the Miller, suffering is merely getting in a fix or being made to look ridiculous. Humanity in *The Miller's Tale* is a collection of rascal types scrambling for pleasures, one of which is humiliating others. *The Knight's Tale* rises to magnanimous generalization. The generalization of *The Miller's Tale* is cynical: human beings are beasts and any suffering in life is merely a series of predicaments, tight spots, and jams. (When in class I observe that cynicism as habit leads to a hardening of the moral arteries, most of my students say, quite cheerfully, that my statement may be true, but they nevertheless prefer *The Miller's Tale*.)

## 4. The Clerk's Tale

The four tales in the marriage group—*The Clerk's Tale*, *The Merchant's Tale*, *The Wife's Tale*, and *The Franklin's Tale*—all invite comparisons. *The Clerk's Tale* seems to offer a *sentence* that, like the Knight's, addresses human suffering. A noble, Walter, deciding to marry, chooses a maid from the lower classes. She has a child. Then Walter perplexingly decides to test her, telling her that the child must be killed. After the death of the first child, he tells her he must kill her second child. Then he tells her he is going to marry someone else, and she must leave the kingdom, but not before she decorates the castle for the new bride. In the end, however, Walter decides she has passed the test of obedience, and they live happily together.

The problem with the tale is the Clerk's failure to understand the rhetorical power of the metaphors of allegory. The medieval habit of loaded symbols (Griselda was born in a "barn"; at one point she "draws water from the well"; her father calls her a "pearl") invites interpretation of Griselda as a Christ figure and Walter as the God who causes her suffering. If we take Griselda as the patient Christian before her God, there are passages in the tale that are quite beautiful. For instance, upon Walter's announcement that he wishes to marry her, Griselda says—

> Lord, unworthy though I be
> Of so much honor, so unmerited,
>  If it seems good to you, it is to me.
> And here I promise never willingly
> To disobey indeed or thought or breath
> Though I should die ....

And to make sure that we understand that she would have to be brave so to obey, the Clerk has her add, "though I fear my death." Later, when Walter tells her that he must "dispose" of the child, she says:

> We are all yours and you may spare or kill
> What is your own. Do therefore as you will.

> Nor is there anything, as God may save
> My soul, that pleasing you displeases me,
> Nor is there anything that I should crave
> To have or dread to lose, but you.

In these lines, the submission to a life spent in devotion to God measures negatively the religious devotion of the Prioress, whose solicitude for the weak extends no farther than her pet dogs.

But something is wrong with the artifice of the tale, and that failure is indicative of the weaknesses of the Clerk's moral outlook. Once a reader takes the Clerk's hint that Griselda should be taken as a Christ figure (and the Clerk says as much in the fourth stanza from the end) and that Walter the husband should be taken as God, problems arise; for when the tale is read *without* allegorizing, the question naturally comes up: "What kind of monster husband is this Walter?" Indeed, the Clerk as narrator virtually solicits this outraged response:

> what was the need
> Of heaping trial on her more and more?
> For my part I should say it would succeed
> Only in evil.

Moreover, if Walter is God, what sense does it make for the Clerk to say that Walter "decided to take another wife"? In the Noah story, God is irritated with human beings, but he does not say he is going to make another species.

In Chaucer's *Prologue*, the clerk is as a serious young man, but more important, he is *young*. He has not seen enough of life to understand how most readers would react to the allegorical confusion of his tale, in which they are invited at once to revere Walter and to detest him, to admire Griselda and to be appalled by her. This confusion is a failure in art, whether "art" comes under *sentence* or *solaas*. A successful allegory controls the reader response to a tale's metaphorical machinery. The Clerk elicits sympathy for Griselda as a human figure with a longing to be with God, and then treats her as a semantic chip in an allegory whose tidiness brushes away the conflict between the piety that human beings show to a beloved God and what God, inexplicably, asks them to suffer—the central problem of the Book of Job. The tale is not obviously bad. But there is something wrong deep in the heart of it, and that failure is also a failure of the pious young, who wish to be true to the Lord but who do not or cannot face the consequences of the central paradox of Christianity, that at the same time human beings long to escape the world, they have also been told that life in God's creation is a gift. It is significant that at the end, the Clerk sees no reason to temper the jubilation at the marriage: "For many a year in high prosperity / These two lived on in concord to the close." If Walter is God, however, how else could the tale end?

The *envoi* (send-off) presents problems as well, and these problems too are interesting. Indeed, with its six-line stanzas with repeating rhymes, the *envoi* is so skillful that some have suggested that Chaucer intended to put it elsewhere, for its cavalier tone hardly seems to accord with the piety of the tale. But the motivation for its placement after the Clerk's tale may be one of those mysteries that make great books worth pondering.

The first line of the *envoi* brushes off Griselda's obedience ("Griselda is dead and also her patience / Both together are buried in Italy"), and, rather than urging on wives the patience of Griselda, the subsequent lines urge women to stand up to their husbands and fight back, to eschew humility, and to gossip as much as they please. To justify this change, we might say perhaps that Chaucer makes the Clerk switch to a jaunty tone because he wants the pilgrims to suspect the integrity of the teller. By this interpretation then, the Clerk's is a soul in conflict; the Clerk wishes to please his Lord and also an audience composed of pilgrims who cannot say, as Griselda does to Walter-God, "Do therefore as you will." But by another interpretation, the Clerk is serving not two masters—God and those who want their own will to be done—but three (God, the self-protective, and—the crucial category for young undergraduates–the other clever fellows at university). Just as *The Knight's Tale* shows that all moral considerations must take into account the examples set for the young, *The Clerk's Tale* shows the risk of "loosing" (Polonius' word in *Hamlet*) the young to an Oxford education, which supposedly teaches young clerics to be pious but is much more successful in teaching them to be too clever by half, especially in writing poems with an ingenious rhyme scheme. Perhaps the trouble with the Clerk is his wanting to serve too many masters.

## 5. The Franklin's Tale

Like *The Clerk's Tale*, *The Franklin's Tale* suffers from a misunderstanding of the genre that governs its rhetoric and from a consequent misunderstanding of the fortitude that human life requires. The tale is ostensibly set up as a story imitating the Knight's. It is about the central virtues of the nobility, which are named in *The Knight's Tale* as a *gentilesse* that is composed of "[t]routhe and honour, fredom and curteisye" ("Truth, honor, generousness, and courtesy"). At the end of his tale, the Franklin rings the changes on these words. Aurelius says to Dorigen:

> Thus kan a squier doon a *gentil* dede
> As wel as kan a knyght, withouten drede.

> A squire can do a *generous* thing with grace
> As well as can a knight, in any case.

The magician says to Aurelius:

> But God forbede, for his blisful myght,
> But if a clerk koude doon a *gentil* dede
> As wel as any of yow, it is no drede!

> But God forbid in all his blissful might
> That men of learning should not come as near
> To nobleness as any, have no fear.

And lastly, the Franklin asks his pilgrim-hearers:

> Lordynges, this question, thanne, wol I aske now,
> Which was the mooste *fre*, as thynketh yow?

> My lords, I'll put a question: tell me true,
> Which seemed the finest gentlemen to you?

The plot is set up as a tragedy. The exemplary married couple agrees that in their marriage, Dorigen, the wife, will not have to obey her husband, Averagus, but she will nevertheless respect the truth as much as he does. When Averagus must be absent from her, Dorigen makes a light-hearted pledge to her suitor Aurelius that if he can make the rocks by her castle disappear, she will sleep with him. Aurelius then hires a magician to make the rocks disappear. Upon his return, Averagus tells Dorigen she must be true to her earlier promise to respect the truth and thus must be true to her promise to Aurelius. At this point, the plot is moving slowly and inexorably to a tragic ending, just as does the Knight's. Aurelius, however, forgives Dorigen her promise, and then, fortunately, the magician who made the rocks disappear for Aurelius, forgives Aurelius his debt. When the Franklin asks at the end, "Which was the mooste fre?" (where *fre* means "generous, liberal"), his story suggests that much human suffering could be achieved if both *gentillesse* and an aristocratic nobility underwent democratization; if people would understand that *gentillesse* is not the exclusive possession of the nobility, then human suffering would be relieved.

Thus, the Franklin is a man of the amiable virtues; enjoying life heartily, he wants others to enjoy life too. As a leader, he is more like a genial host than a soldier. The prologue tells us that he is generous; he takes pleasure in feeding troops of people, and his table, open to the whole county, has so many viands on it that it looked as if it had "snowed meat." We know, however, that in the one area in life where he would be called upon to be severe, he has failed; his son is a wastrel. That fact makes us wonder about the connection between parenting and hosting.

The tale has different purposes, then, depending on whether we take it in from the Franklin's point of view, where the good teller is also a good host, or from Chaucer's point of view, where a good tale inspires thoughtfulness in its audience. The Franklin imitates the Knight's tale, but while the Knight confronts the darkness by means of a semi-tragic plot, the Franklin swerves to the wish fulfillment of romance. For him, a good host puts his guests at ease by offering them a tale with just enough sorrow to make the ending sweeter; but to him, virtue is not wisdom but buoyant good spirits. Life is to be enjoyed.

From Chaucer's point of view, then, the tale is shallow. The Franklin's *gentillesse* is that of a man who does not want to be brave and who shrinks from telling others that they have to be brave. But, as with many tales, Chaucer is discreetly silent about any condemnation that a comparison between the two tellers might invite. In some respects, however, the Franklin has a point. The effort to keep the pilgrims together in a "company" is not a despicable motivation, even if it is limited. The Franklin is right about the importance of being a good host; he just needs to think about it a little more.

## 6. The Merchant's Tale

With *The Merchant's Tale*, judgment of a tale becomes much more complex. This tale itself is artistically skillful and frightening. An old Knight, January, wishes to marry, and he wishes to marry a wife who is young. He asks for advice. One counselor, Placebo, tells him to get married because life is short. Another counselor, Justinus, argues against the plan; an old man can never please a young wife. Old January marries anyway, and his bride, May, is very young. January has a house fit for a king and a beautiful garden that allows him to perform *en plein air* anything that he and May "had not done in bed." January's servant Damian gets sick; when, at January's urging, May visits the sick man, he slips her a love note; May, in pity, loves him back. The Merchant then repeats the line from *The Knight's Tale,* this time with icy sarcasm: "Pity flows swiftly in a noble mind." January is stricken with blindness. Damian has sex with May in a pear tree in full sight of the old knight, who is then persuaded by May to think he hallucinated her adultery with Damian.

With *The Merchant's Tale*, a new criterion for judging a tale comes to the fore—the motivation of the teller. As was noted, the Knight did not include a prologue. The Merchant, by contrast, is quite frank about his connection with his tale.

> "Weeping and wailing care and other sorrow,
> I know them well enough by eve and morrow,"
> The Merchant said; "like others I suppose
> That have been married, that's the way it goes;
> I know too well that's how it goes with me.
> I have a wife, the worst that there could be."

This complaint invites the suspicion that the Merchant is going to use the opportunity of an audience to grind an ax. Indeed, very soon one can hear in his tale a personal grievance about to explode, and his tale, full of resentment, scatters bitterness in many directions. This is a soul indisposed to the reflectiveness that *sentence and solaas* require.

The first bitterness is directed toward others. When the tale has January declare that he wants a young wife because old flesh does not please him, one cannot help hearing a scornful indictment of all old men who fail to know themselves, with painful consequences they could have been avoided—and one of those old men is the Merchant himself. He continues in this vein when January asks for advice and prefers the soothing advice of Placebo to the shrewd advice of Justinus. The indictment, then, is directed not only at old men in general but specifically at the Merchant's own stupidity, of which he is all too aware. There is similar self-laceration in January's *aubade* (a love song at dawn) after the wedding night, sitting in bed crowing about his sexual prowess, the skin under his neck flapping back and forth. There is still more self-laceration in the Merchant's decision to paint May's infidelity with vivid realism: he puts January through the indignity of allowing May to stand on his back as she vaults herself into a pear tree to meet Damian, who "[pulled] up her smock at once and in her thrust." Then, apparently taking the Franklin's advice to exercise a self-deluding kind of *gentillesse*, the Merchant allows the Knight to be persuaded by May that he was merely seeing things. Behind these descriptions is bitter satire, directed at himself.

There are, to be sure, moments when the Merchant struggles to exercise philosophical equanimity. After he goes blind, he wishes both he and wife were slain so that he would not have to suffer the suspicion that his wife is having sex with another man. But then he tries to rise above his burning jealousy:

> But in the end, after a month or two,
> His sorrows cooled a little, it is true,
> For when he saw there was no remedy
> He took in patience his adversity....

But then come the next two lines:

> Save that the ineradicable sting
> Of jealousy embittered everything.

In sum, the tale is an indictment of the stupidity of men who were old before they had been wise (the fool's jibe at *King Lear*), of the Merchant's own stupidity, and of sentimental forms of reconciling oneself to life's misfortunes. Had the tale been told without our suspicion of the teller's motives, we might say that, artistically, it shows clever pacing, vivid portrayal of characters, and appropriate punishment for a vain and lecherous old man. If we were medieval listeners, we might give the Merchant some points for the *sentence* in the array of classical quotations that the teller has at his fingertips. We might even appreciate the reference to the Song of Solomon that cements the contrast between the garden in which the adultery is committed and the garden that represents the human delight in marriage.

But from Chaucer's point of view, the whole story is the story-plus-teller. While the Merchant is telling a story (or making a confession), showing how a vain old man was tricked, Chaucer is telling a story about how human vanity leads to self-loathing and also to loathing of traditional institutions, like marriage, which, as the Merchant well knows or else should know, God gave to his human creatures for their happiness. That is, the story is about the Merchant's inability to understand his own story. January's "blindness" is a symbol that ripples with significance; the Merchant is as blind at the end of the tale as January at the end of the story. Spinning in his hatred—of his wife and of women in general, of himself, and of human beings in general—and unable to rise above that hatred, the Merchant writhes in his private hell. Chaucer underlines just how painful that privacy is when he has the thickheaded Host interpret *The Merchant's Tale* as a story about wicked wives:

> "Ey, mercy of God!" our host exclaimed thereat,
> "May God preserve me from a wife like that!"

The doltish Host is deaf to the painful battle in the Merchant's soul. A "gentle" Knight would react with pity to the Merchant's limited understanding of that word. The Host's response, then, brings to the fore the question of the response of listeners to various tales.

## 7. The Wife of Bath's Tale

As *The Merchant's Tale* lines up with other tales in its love triangle, so does it line up even more particularly with *The Wife of Bath's Tale*. Both invite the reader to see the tales as revelations of the teller's philosophical and religious failings. One suspects that the Merchant is not unhappy if his audience thinks he is a fool; after all, at least part of him knows he is a fool, and part of his self-laceration is to put his folly on display before an audience. That the Wife does not know how much she is revealing makes her pitiable also, but for different reasons. One is a lack of moral courage; the other complacent ignorance. Chaucer agrees with Plato on this point; some people do not care to become wiser; they wallow in their ignorance like a pig (*Rep.*, Book 7.535e).

That the Wife is interested in little besides herself is indicated by the sheer length of her prologue, longer than her tale itself and longer than any other pilgrim's prologue. In the extended declaration of her philosophy of life, she may seem at first to be an attractive human type; she is a woman of gusto; she is dismayed by nothing; whatever happens to come her way, she will float to the top. Her idea of marriage is a contest, and she is confident that her track record in this sort of contest is very good. Her prologue is a celebratory song about the many times she has outfoxed one husband after another. She is also content with a fallen world; some may, she says, like bread made with fine flour; she is content to be barley bread. She does not have an excessive reverence for the Good Word; some say the Bible contains moral rules; she holds they are just advice. She is shrewdly provident for the future; married to one husband, she is already thinking about the next. Her idea of *gentillesse* is the use of euphemisms for sex, i.e., she does not like intercourse with "old bacon"; her vagina is her "*belle chose*"; sex is doing one's "nicety"; but the euphemisms are more comic than "gentle." Her vigor, her self-confidence, her acceptance of the future, her cheerful dismissiveness of any criticism, make her a sort of female Falstaff. Like him, she is the essence of comedy. It is, after all, hard not to delight in an indomitable human spirit. Life will go on; there will be moments of dismay but no permanent defeat. Death is unimaginable and not worth even trying to imagine.

Still, the Wife is not as immune to anxiety as she would like her audience to believe. For the most part, Chaucer has her living in a dream world of happy egotism that knows no deflation; she moves with exuberance and conviction from one subject to another. But there are moments when she loses her place:

> Well let me see … what had I to explain?
> Aha! By God, I've got the thread again.

The "thread" turns out to be the next husband. But her question "what had I to explain?" is apt; either she cannot remember that she will need to

111

explain herself before God or she thinks no explanations will be required. Her defense of lechery at the beginning of her prologue will, apparently, be a lead-in to her tale. Its irrelevance to her tale and its length suggests defensiveness; she knows that the Good Word is against her. She sees dimly that she will not be indomitable forever:

> I've had my fruit,
> I've had my world and time, I've had my fling!
> But age that comes to poison everything
> Has taken all my beauty and my pith.
> Well, let it go, the devil go therewith!
> The flour is gone, there is no more to say,
> And I must sell the bran as best I may;
> But still I mean to find my way to fun....
> Now let me tell you of my last but one.

There is nothing she cannot master, except what all human beings eventually must—getting old, dying, and explaining oneself to God. As in *The Merchant's Tale*, there is more to the story than what the teller imagines that he or she is telling.

Tale-telling is the perfect activity for the Wife; it allows her to drift even further than does her prologue into an imaginary world, and the world of her tale is very imaginary—full of fog and sequins and diaphanous fabric. She sets her tale in the time of King Arthur; she introduces an Elf-Queen who rules over a court, and also a hag who has the magic power to turn old people young again. While *The Knight's Tale's* slow pace contributes to the dignity and somberness of its *sentence*, the rapid pace of the Wife's makes hers dismissive: rapes are common, not anything to dwell on. Moreover, rescue from a difficulty is always at hand. Hauled before a royal court, the raping knight does not have to lose his head right away but is given a year by the Queen to find out "what women want."

In the midst of this cantering plot, however, the Wife stops to tell the story of Midas, whose wife could not keep the secret of her husband's donkey ears and who, in desperation, tells it to the water of a nearby swamp. Why does Chaucer have the Wife digress from the initial plot line to tell this apparently irrelevant story?—perhaps because Midas's wife has something on her mind that she must reveal, just as the Wife has something on her mind that she suspects needs some sorting out.

When the loathly lady in the forest tells the knight that she can save him but only if the knight is willing to marry her, the lady includes a long bit of *sentence* on gentility (not attached to wealth and status), poverty (Christ himself was poor), old age (it keeps one chaste). These are the worries that flash into the Wife's prologue at odd moments and then are brushed away. The shallowness of her thinking is apparent in her remarks on old age, which does not bring wisdom but merely removes desire. After the sermon and after the old hag has posed a choice to the Knight—he can have her young and beautiful but unfaithful, or old and haggish but faithful—and after the knight allows the hag herself to make the choice, the Wife has the hag give the knight everything—a wife both beautiful and faithful. In middle age, the Wife is trying to sort out the connection between selflessness and happiness; perhaps faithfulness in marriage was what she wanted all along, not mastery in perpetual marital combat. She has, however, always led a self-protective life, and she cannot give it up.

Again, at the end of *The Wife's Tale*, Chaucer emphasizes the Wife's mode of thinking as part reverie, part lusty bragging, part combat with Christian morality. First, the Wife ends her tale with cheerful, dreamy banality:

> So they lived ever after to the end
> In perfect bliss.

This ending contrasts with the end of *The Knight's Tale* where Palamon is said to have treated his wife Emily with "constancy," not with the Wife's fairy-tale "perfect bliss." Then, awaking from her reverie and suspecting she has shown weakness before her audience, the wife reverts to her old lusty, armored self:

> and may Christ Jesus send
> Us husbands meek and young and fresh in bed,
> And grace to overbid them when we wed.
> And—Jesu, hear my prayer—cut short the lives
> Of those who won't be governed by their wives

And all old angry niggards of their pence.
God send them soon a very pestilence!

While the Merchant's bitterness overwhelms his shame at self-revelation, the Wife lacks the awareness of an audience that shame would imply. In her prologue, she shows that, for her, life is not a bitter bargain but an exciting contest.

Her tale reveals even more—that her soul is struggling with combatants she can barely see and can never defeat—getting old and self-delusion. Despite her apparently cheerful zest for the world of Becoming (in the Middle English version, "experience" is the first word of her Prologue), she has a vague—very vague—idea of the world of Being. In the midst of the loathly lady's sermon on *gentillesse*, there occurs this odd passage:

Take fire and carry it to the darkest house
Between this kingdom and the Caucasus,
And shut the doors on it and leave it there,
It will burn on, and it will burn as fair
As if ten thousand men were there to see,
For fire will keep its nature and degree,
I can assure you, sir, until it dies.

Here Chaucer shows the pathos of the Wife's confusion. She has an image of *gentillesse* as a fire that will burn forever, connected somehow to Being rather than Becoming. The metaphor for its continued vigor, however, is an audience ("as if ten thousand men were there to see"), and, we may presume, the guarantee for the Wife's eternal youth would be such an admiring male audience. She does not know that her Aristotelian-sounding physics do not lend support to her confidence that *gentillesse* is eternal: a fire will "keep its nature," she announces, "until it dies," a bathetic contradiction. That the passage ends with the death of the essence of the fire, of the four elements the one most likely to "rise," is Chaucer's signal that the Wife has not thought about the paramount question of the fate of the human soul after death. The Wife's good spirits do not wholly disguise her struggling to face spiritual difficulties which, to her credit, she half perceives. The Miller, after all, does not perceive any such difficulties. Her tale, at least, is just on the edge of prayer.

Hardly has one seen the parallel between *The Wife's* and *The Merchant's* tales when the question arises: are we meant to see self-revelation in other tales, an indication that all human beings betray their failings but also that, somewhere in their confused souls, they long for clarity of judgment, and failing clarity, then fellowship and the Good? Even the bitter and vindictive Merchant has moments when he can emerge from his wrath at those around him to see that for him, some self-criticism might be in order:

> He rubbed his cheek against her tender cheek,
> And said, "Alas, alas that I should seek
> To trespass—yet I must—and to offend
> You greatly, too, my spouse, ere I descend.
> Nevertheless, consider this," said he.
> "No workman, whatsoever he may be,
> Can do his work both well, and in a flurry;
> This shall be done in perfect ease, no hurry.
> It's of no consequence how long we play,
> We are in holy wedlock, and we may,
> And blessed be the yoke that we are in,
> For nothing that we do will count as sin."

For January, the advantage of marriage is removing any charge of bestiality. Still, if it is himself whom the Merchant is mocking, he is showing a modicum of self-awareness. In another passage, the Merchant can, just for a moment, conceive of what the world looks like to someone not caught in his own personal rage. He has January sitting up in bed with the "slack of his skin about his neck … shaking." Then the narration switches to January's young wife: "God knows what May was thinking in her heart." Somewhere in the Merchant's prison of self-pitying vindictiveness, he has enough dispassion for reflection on his own grotesque bragging and also on the reaction of another soul.

Even the Miller, habituated to cynicism as he is, can nevertheless imagine another view besides coarse raillery, a world where people are kind and friendly to each other. When Nicholas induces the carpenter to prepare for a second Flood, he foresees an aqueous utopia:

After the mighty shower has gone away,
You'll float as merrily as merrily, I undertake,
As any lily-white duck behind her drake,
And I'll call out, "Hey, Alison! Hey, John!
Cheer yourselves up! The flood will soon be gone."
And you'll shout back, "Hail, master Nicolay!
Good morning! I can see you well. It's day!"
We shall be lords for all the rest of life
Of all the world, like Noah and his wife.

Somewhere in his adolescent, joking, spiteful soul, Nicholas (and the Miller) can at least imagine good fellowship or "company." Chaucer's giving both the Merchant and the Wife moments of self-knowledge urges forbearance in assessing these tellers.

## 8. The Pardoner's Tale

With the subject of self-indulgence, we come to the most troubling of the tales, the Pardoner's, for this one seems to outdo all the others in its cynicism. The tale is well-paced, coming as it does to the logical conclusion of the proverb, "Thieves cannot be true to one another," and ending in three deaths, which the Pardoner sees no reason to lament. Three young rioters get drunk in a bar and boast that they dare to meet a figure called Death, who by means of the plague has been scattering corpses all over the village. They swear they will find him and give him his due punishment. They meet an old man who is longing to die. The rioters insult him, calling him a spy for a "certain traitor Death," who has been killing young people. They want to know where this Death fellow is so that they can kill him. The old man impassively tells them Death is over there near that oak tree. Under said oak tree, the rioters find gold and draw straws to select the one of them who will go to town to get provisions while the other two guard the gold. The one who gets the short stick goes to town, buys a bottle of wine, and pours poison into it. Upon his return, the two other louts kill him (dividing two ways is more profitable than dividing three ways), drink the wine in celebration, and then die themselves. The plot is tight, the ending swift, the atmosphere full of the grim satisfaction of another proverb fulfilled: "Do not look for death, for he will find you."

With *The Pardoner's Tale,* Chaucer gets the reader audience to consider the responses of the pilgrims. After all, to the Pardoner, his audience is composed of lambs for the fleecing, and his audience cannot fail to notice that assessment of them. To him, there is no such thing as justice but merely the necessity for all human beings to scramble for a living; those who have even a little bit of cleverness are justified in taking advantage of the credulous, and the Pardoner assumes the members of his pilgrim-audience are very credulous. His prologue is an orgy of cynicism: he has been successful, he says, in getting his hearers to believe that the old sheep bones he carries around in bottles are the bones of saints; that one of the bones, if dipped in a well, will cure cattle of a disease; that the special mitten he is offering to sell will increase the harvest. He boasts about telling "a hundred lying mockeries"; he admits that he "spits [his] venom forth"; he admits that he preaches against the very avarice by which he makes his living … and so on. Then he launches into his well-shaped tale. While his audience, the "yokels" as he himself calls them, around him are in the stunned state that a well-told tale will induce, musing on the deadly mysteries of life, the Pardoner takes advantage of their bewilderment, warns them that death could occur at any minute, and solicits purchasers. To take advantage of an audience through the magic spell of tales is a violation of the unstated agreements of storytelling: the storyteller is a host who wishes to be generous. Only in advertising is one expected to buy.

Then comes a response that is not at all tentative. The first pilgrim the Pardoner solicits is the Host, and in doing so he is publicly insinuating that the Host is the most gullible of the party, and the one thing Harry Bailey, that *boffo* man-of-the-world, does not want to be called, is naïve. He retorts with outrage: "I wish I had your bollocks in my hand" (the Middle English for "bollocks" is "coillons"—testicles); he would have them "shrined in a hog's turd." Other tales elicit boorish responses, but those responses have been short and inconsequential and confined to one or two pilgrims. No response is as vulgar as the Host's response to the Pardoner.

For Chaucer, a good teller should be a good host, someone who welcomes strangers, oversees the general good will of the company, and provides moral nourishment for the individual members. The awareness of the limits of secular "good company" and the ideal that measures those limits depend so much on intuition that it cannot be reduced to an art with rules.

What are the rules for well-chosen words that express understanding without saying too much? As Plato argues in *The Statesman,* the great statesman simply knows—in a way he is not fully able to make precise—human nature, and even more particularly, the state of harmony in individual souls, how the parts of a soul are balanced in relationship to the practical business of staying alive and in relationship to the more important business of striving for a transcendent goal (294e). Like the art of punishment in the individual case, the art of judging tales cannot be articulated. Chaucer resorts to simple manners to restore the "company"; he has the Knight insist that the Pardoner and Host exchange a kiss.

Chaucer is generous where Plato is stern. When Plato makes a distinction between the many and the few, he regards the (unintelligent) many as a political problem to be assessed. For Chaucer, a good host should *appreciate* what strengths his listeners may have. Chaucer is not alone in his consideration of the storyteller's responsibility to be a good host. As Henry James also says, when reflecting on Turgenev: "We hold to the good old belief that the presumption, in life, is in favor of the brighter side, and we deem it, in art, an indispensable condition of our interest in a depressed observer that he should have at least tried his best to be cheerful."

# PROBLEMS IN TEACHING SHAKESPEARE

## *1. Shakespeare and Novelistic Characters*

Once in class we were discussing the problems of leadership in connection with Pericles as presented in *The Peloponnesian Wars* of Thucydides. I said, "Those of you who are English majors know that Shakespeare addresses this subject in *The Tempest*." One student said, no, he had not read *The Tempest*, that Shakespeare was no longer required for the English major, and, moreover, he knew from high school that he did not "respond to Shakespeare." I was struck by the suavity of this statement, most students having the street-wisdom to know one does not say such a thing to a professor of English, in a tone that suggests that everybody knows that not responding to Shakespeare is the same thing as not liking spinach. On another occasion, I heard a student confidently state that Plato was wrong in thinking that an art that appealed to the ear was higher than an art that appealed to the taste buds. We all have preferences, he maintained, and preferences cannot be debated.

But these arguments are not true. You may not be able to use arguments to persuade someone not to dislike spinach, but those who know something about music can persuade others to see virtues in pieces of music they once did not respond to. There is also taste, and taste has to do with thoughtfulness. As I said in the introduction, we would not say that the judgments of a woman in her forties who still liked Barbie dolls should be taken seriously.

Perhaps the student who did not respond to Shakespeare was tired of the argument that Shakespeare was an author every educated person should know. After 1970 or so, it was not uncommon for Shakespeare to be referred to in a phrase in apposition, as in "Shakespeare, that great cultural icon," uttered with irony; for the tide had changed, and Shakespeare was no longer an old master, the star in the once great firmament of the canon, the notion of a "canon" having been debunked. Decades ago, I gave a hearing to that idea—that "the canon" must go—when I taught Shakespeare by "demystifying" him. It was unsatisfyingly easy to do. One of the students from a small town in North Carolina who, in coming to Chapel Hill, thought he was entering to the world of important ideas, burst out in class, "Why are we talking about Shakespeare and all this discourses-of-power-stuff! Of course there is power talk! The question is, what is it being used for?" He was a kind of student I saw not infrequently at the University of North Carolina—the eager undergraduate from a small town, who, hungry for ideas, wanted his professors to spread the feast on the table. The memory of him helped me to assess the "narratives," as they say, of literary criticism, which can surely be themselves a discourse of power and whose goal is worth pondering. His earnestness, his drive, and his exasperation have for decades reminded me of something important.

Perhaps the student who did not respond to Shakespeare meant that Shakespeare addressed conflicts that were no longer important in the modern world because the matters have been settled. Women should be able to do, and can in fact do, whatever men can do. That view now reigns as a truth; the scholarship—or whatever it is that determines these things—is settled. But Shakespeare had another view. Women preserved a morality that helped to tie together a polity. Once upon a time, the line between the public life and the private was not sharp; courtesy softened human negotiations in both spheres. With the establishment of commercial republics, negotiations in the public sphere became what is called professionalism. It then became the contribution of women to keep alive in the private sphere the old gracefulness and courtesy. That seems to be the view of Henry James in *The Portrait of a Lady*, when the wise old man of the beginning of the novel, Mr. Touchett, remarks that changes are coming and that "the ladies will save us." Later it became the common conviction that James's view was benighted. But the old Shakespeare—the one who used to be a cultural icon—taught the value of courtesy to any polity. One might consider his arguments in this sphere, for his notion of courtesy stretches from simple goodhearted politeness at one pole to justice at the other.

But the largest stumbling block for moderns became Shakespeare's belief in a transcendent world. With the secularization of morality in the eighteenth century, there arose the virtue of a gentleman, for which a transcendent world was not necessary. Manners were not connected to Christian charity; they were simply the formalities of an aristocratic class. Then such formalities themselves came to be regarded as empty formulas, nowhere near as successful as ordinary good-heartedness in restraining the potential wildness of human nature. But one may wonder if good-heartedness is altogether reliable. Perhaps people need an unwritten law they feel they have to answer to.

The transcendent used to be reference point. If one did not want to go the way of religion, one could go the way of Plato. That is, reason assumes an ideal standard that we may not know in this life, but which inquiry and thoughtfulness can get us closer to. When I put the question to my students, "If there is no belief in a standard, where then is the measure between good and bad or at least between acceptable and better?" they usually say, as they had learned to say, "There are no universals." I then put another question to them, "How are we to regard Shakespeare's distinction between good characters and bad?" There was silence. "So, then, Shakespeare is just working us up with emotion-laden terms that have no meaning?" Silence. "So, in *Hamlet*, when the new king patronizes his nephew, who has suddenly become his stepson, and the stepson, Hamlet, replies with a caustic pun that communicates his resentment at being patronized by his new father, it is just for the sake of dramatic tension, not because there is something repellant in this new King's manner and that the stepson is right to resent being so addressed?"

During my last semester at the University of Pennsylvania, I taught a course called "Shakespeare and the Bible," and I anticipated resistance. The first class started with my saying that the course was misnamed, because there are only a few instances in Shakespeare where knowing the particular passage in the Bible counts for interpretation of the plays. All one has to know is the general idea that human beings are basically good with a strong inclination to evil, and that there is a transcendent world toward which most human beings aspire; the ones who do not are usually the villains. Still, it might alter one's interpretation of *A Midsummer Night's Dream*, for instance, to know that Bottom's speech at the end of Act 4 is a mangled quotation from St. Paul, more or less about how human beings cannot know what God intends for them. But I admitted that there are plays for which invoking Christianity would make no sense—*Antony and Cleopatra* and *Julius Caesar*, for instance, and perhaps *Troilus and Cressida*.

I soon discovered that I had a much more fundamental difficulty on my hands. Interpretation by the motivation of individual characters is an approach to reading ingrained by the novel. By "character," moderns mean "the more or less realistic figures who act according to psychological plausibility." In the modern, realistic novel, there is nothing more real than the individual trying to figure out his or her social situation. To combat this mode by saying, "these are not characters; they are highly articulated symbols" is not persuasive. It does not help that the figures in Shakespeare's plays are routinely called "characters" by almost everyone who writes about Shakespeare. I myself cannot think of a substitute. (It is to be noted that Tolstoy, like my student, could not respond to Shakespeare, because the characters did not act in a manner that was psychologically plausible.)

Characters in Shakespeare are placed in the hierarchies of a moral world. In *The Merchant of Venice*, Bassanio and Antonio inhabit a city called "Venice," where live also a community of Non-Believers. These Non-Believers are not the particular kind of Jews who make their living in the particular way Venetian Jews did in sixteenth-century Venice but rather the archetypical, cruel, money-lending Jew of Christian iconography. Antonio is melancholic not because he is losing his friend or worried about his investments. He is melancholic because Shakespeare is making an argument, through Antonio, about a noble soul's calm about worldly possessions as well as being prudent about money. Solario and Solanio are in the play because their giddy manner of speaking emphasizes, by contrast, the music of Antonio's speech. The play is headed toward the fifth act, where Jessica and Lorenzo are gently teasing each other and where Lorenzo speaks about the power of music to tune the soul to the harmony of the angels and where Portia, who has shown how the written law can deal out justice in an unangelic world, arrives to show how courtesy can restore friendships. Gratiano is present in this group because even in the high world of Belmont, there will always be someone who does not know how to reach for a still higher world. In this play, the music of the timbres of speech pulls together in a community. The "characters" are highly articulated symbols of states of soul.

In *A Midsummer Night's Dream*, the characters are types. The young women are female adolescents, rhapsodizing about friendship solid or friendship betrayed, love requited or love unrequited. The young men are male adolescents—eager for sex, eager for combat. The generalizing is harder to see when we turn to the figures in other plays because, as has been pointed out many times, the distinctive power of Shakespeare is his creation of characters who seem "real." In a novel, it would be the author's responsibility to offer a good reason why someone like Helena in *A Midsummer Night's Dream* loves Demetrius; in Shakespeare, she just does, partly because she is female youth, which loves-to-be-loving, and partly because it is the nature of human beings, young or old, to act irrationally.

Psychological probing is seductive. The power of the novel to individualize a life invites living vicariously; when the formerly cold beloved suddenly turns warm, the reader feels her own temperature rise. When we watch a character come to realize that being selfish, being ambitious, having unrealistic expectations about life will not achieve happiness, the reader gets a short course in growing up; for the truth in such a novel is coming to terms with the conflict between a given social situation and an individual's strengths and weaknesses. This is the appealing plot line of most success stories as told in the modern world.

It was the tendency of living-another-life-through-the-novel that Flaubert was fighting in his remark that an author should write "without love or hate for any of the characters." Plato's complaint with literature— that it is too emotional—is worth considering. When students come to college and say they "love literature," what they generally mean is they love or hate individual characters. The more a reader concentrates on the amiability of the character, however, the less likely she will see the abstract argument that a great novel is aiming at, how complex that argument is, how much it acknowledges the other side of the argument, how fair it is in its judgments.

Especially in coming to understand Shakespeare, the tendency to identify with characters has to be combatted, for the question should not be, "Why does Helena love Demetrius if he is so mean to her?" but rather "What is Shakespeare aiming at that requires this exaggeratedly whiney character?" Shakespeare needs this morose type for two reasons. Helena forms a contrast with the enormously self-confident Hermia. At the beginning of the play, he needs Helena's outsized gloom and Hermia's outsized self-confidence in order to establish a clear contrast with the emotional calm of these two women at the end of the play—because that emotional calm and its connection with a transcendent world is where he is headed.

Similarly, in *Twelfth Night,* the question is not, "Why does Olivia refuse the suit of Count Orsino?" but rather, "Why does Shakespeare decide that *Twelfth Night* should start with the Countess Olivia resisting Count Orsino's protestations of love?" That is, in order to understand why the playwright has characters do the things they do, a reader must pay attention to the general argument about human life the playwright is trying to put together.

The shorthand for this view of Shakespeare's idea of a character is to say that behind each play of Shakespeare, there is a fable, and what governs the figure we call a "character" are the various arguments that make up the fable. One could use the word *theme* instead of fable, but *theme* runs the risk of reducing the play to a wise saying: "do not let jealousy lead your imagination astray," or "do not let ambition lead you astray," or "do not let a false love keep you from your natural happiness," or some such. A fable is a hypothesis about human life, like a parable in the Bible, a story that is obviously a fiction and yet contains the shadow of a truth that only those who understand the mysteries of life will see. Like a parable, the fable insists upon a vague suggestiveness. The simplicity of the fable's language is oracular without being ghostly. In *A Midsummer Night's Dream*, the presentation of the fable has three surfaces sliding over each other: the folk language of an agricultural civilization, the heraldic language of court, and the wisdom of a world not seen. To articulate the wisdom of the fable is to dull its wonder or its pain. But the fable is more than whatever terrible or wonderful successes or failures came to this or that character-who-is-also-a-person.

Here Spenser's preface to *Fairie Queene* is helpful. When Spenser talks about a theme being "cloudily enwrapped in allegorical devices,"[18] the metaphor of clouds points to a higher world, or, in that odd word in the King James Version of Genesis, a "firmament." The clouds are the first step out of the sensuous reality of this world and the mysterious world of God, whose deep truths are beyond human articulation. In many plays of Shakespeare, that higher world—God, Being, Truth—generates the characters. What makes Shakespeare still marvelous (marvelous to some) is his subtlety in opening the clouds for a momentary illumination of what lies beyond

---

18   "*A Letter of the Author's,* in *Spenser: The Faerie Queene*, ed. by A. C. Hamilton (London and New York: Longman's, 1977). p.737, spelling modernized.

the firmament. In an uncharacteristically perceptive moment near the beginning of *A Midsummer Night's Dream*, Lysander puts the matter well. The
course of true love never did run smooth, he says—a thought that certainly
lacks originality. But he goes on. True love is

> momentary as a sound,
> Swift as a shadow, short as any dream,
> Brief as the lightning in the collied night;
> That, in a spleen, unfolds both heaven and earth,
> And ere a man hath power to say "Behold!"
> The jaws of darkness do devour it up.
> So quick bright things come to confusion.[19]

True love is a vision of brightness and permanence in an unstable world.
In many of Shakespeare's plays, an extraterrestrial world hovers at the edges.
We fail to see it, because, as Lorenzo says to Jessica near the end of *The Merchant of Venice*, "the reason is, your spirits are attentive."[20] We are overly attentive to the myriad particulars of the sensible world. To see the world as
far as the firmament, we have to be in a state of receiving, not in a state of
exercising attentiveness. To anyone with some religious leanings, this is not
a foreign idea.

When a character is constituted by the world beyond the firmament,
he does what he does because Shakespeare needs to reveal an order that derives from Nature. In most of Shakespeare's plays, maturity is coming to
understand that higher perspective. Consider the case of the Countess
Olivia in *Twelfth Night*, a fairly secular play. It would not be inappropriate
to say that Shakespeare has Olivia act the way she does simply to set up a
good comic turn; after all, the play starts with the ever so slightly exaggerated languor of Orsino, by which we are primed for a comic take-down of

19  *A Midsummer Night's Dream*, 1.1.141–49), ed. by Wolfgang Clemen, in *William
    Shakespeare: Four Great Comedies,* introduction by Sylvan Barnet (New York:
    Signet Classics, 1998). All citations to *A Midsummer Night's Dream* are to this
    edition.
20  *The Merchant of Venice*, 5.1.70, ed. by Kenneth Myrick, in *William Shakespeare,
    The Merchant of Venice,* general editor, Sylvan Barnet (New York: Signet Clas-
    sics, 1998). All citations to *The Merchant of Venice* are to this edition.

an aristocrat who is overdoing the fineness of his sensibilities. Olivia too seems to be overdoing her aristocratic fineness in her exaggerated mourning for her brother. Then, in Act 1, Scene 5, Shakespeare, with the figure of Viola-Cesario, thrusts a breath of fresh air into the choking atmosphere of Olivia's grief. Coming from the sea like a magical spirit, Viola-Cesario does not understand the formalities of aristocrats. The Countess Olivia brushes her-him off as more than a bit impertinent. But then, because Olivia is intelligent and hence curious, she cannot resist asking this strange sea-creature Cesario how she-he might woo, at which point Cesario puffs out her-his chest like a robin just cruising in from the south and landing on a lawn somewhere in the north:

> Make me a willow cabin at your gate
> And call upon my soul within the house.
> Write loyal cantons of contemned love
> And sing them loud even in the dead of night.
> Halloo your name to the reverberate hills
> And make the babbling gossip of the air
> Cry out "Olivia!" Oh, you should not rest
> Between the elements of air and earth,
> But you should pity me.[21]

Viola, with her high-temperature ardor, naturally accents the first syllable of the pentameter line. To this outburst, the stunned but still composed Olivia replies, "You might do much." She is at the top of the waterfall, about to be swept over. She controls herself with her usual self-discipline, for her question "What is your parentage?" is a prudent inquiry into the appropriateness of Viola-Cesario as marriage material. So far, we are still within the earthly bounds of the novel or of Roman comedy. Shakespeare is getting us to delight in watching an icily composed aristocrat discover that love can lead her to something "that unfolds both heaven and earth," in Lysander's formulation. Later in the

---

21 *Twelfth Night*, 1.5.269–77, ed. by Herschel Baker, in *William Shakespeare: Four Great Comedies*, introduction by Sylvan Barnet (New York: Signet Classics:, 1998). All citations to *Twelfth Night* are to this edition.

play, Shakespeare uses other characters to expand Olivia's rather circumscribed vision even farther.

Here let me digress to *A Midsummer Night's Dream*. At the end of Act 4 in that play, the four lovers wake from their dream-filled night; a veil is lifted. Each seems to know, quite suddenly, who his or her proper mate should be. They have been stripped of their self-satisfied and passionate desire to get a lover in the great competition for lovers, and rise to a moment when wonder at a higher world de-individualizes them:

> *Demetrius*: These things seem small and undistinguishable,
> Like far off mountains turned into clouds.

> *Hermia*: Methinks I see things with parted eye,
> When everything seems double.

> *Helena*: So methinks:
> And I have found Demetrius like a jewel,
> Mine own, and not mine own. (4.1.189–95)

Gone is the manic combativeness, self-confidence, whine, and possessiveness of teenagers; the characters have learned the composure in the soul that makes it possible to say, "mine own, and not mine own." When Theseus, Hippolyta, and Egeus stumble upon the awakened lovers and Egeus repeats his diatribe against Lysander, Demetrius answers like one who has seen a vision:

> *Demetrius*: *(to Theseus:)* My lord, fair Helen told me of their stealth,
> Of this their purpose hither to this wood,
> And I in fury hither followed them,
> Fair Helena in fancy following me.
> But, my good lord, I wot not by what power—
> But by some power it is—my love to Hermia,
> Melted as the snow, seems to me now
> As the remembrance of an idle gaud,
> Which in my childhood I did dote upon;
> And all the faith, the virtue of my heart,

The object and the pleasure of mine eye,
 Is only Helena. To her, my lord,
Was I betrothed ere I saw Hermia:
But like in sickness did I loathe this food;
But, as in health, come to my natural taste,
Now I do wish it, love it, long for it,
And will for evermore be true to it. (4.1.163–79)

The reader-of-novels will interpret these lines as a sign that Demetrius has matured beyond adolescent swaggering. But tone of voice is everything. Demetrius says, with wonder, that a benign mysterious force ("I wot not by what power") changed his affections and brought him to his "natural taste." He has been in touch with a higher Nature.

Shakespeare adds another "waking-up speech." In this one, Bottom emphasizes the vision of the firmament, not getting a sexual mate. He starts with his characteristic enthusiasm; he is virtual five-year-old on the playground:

> *Bottom*: *(waking)* When my cue comes, call me, and I will answer. My next is, "Most fair Pyramus." Heigh-ho! Peter Quince? Flute the bellows-mender? Snout the tinker? Starveling?

Puzzled, he pauses and looks around for his companions:

> God's my life, stol'n hence, and left me asleep? (4.1.203–207)

Then, forgetting his companions entirely, he remembers his dream and contemplates it. His tone is mystified and amazed:

> I have had a most rare vision. I have had a dream, past the wit of man to say what dream it was. Man is but an ass, if he go about to expound this dream. Methought I was—there is no man can tell what. Methought I was, and methought I had but man is but a patched fool if he will offer to say what methought I had. (1.4.207–214)

As he reaches for something that he cannot wholly understand, the words that come to him would be familiar to his audience:

> The eye of man hath not heard, the ear of man hath not seen, man's hand is not able to taste, his tongue to conceive, nor his heart to report, what my dream was. I will get Peter Quince to write a ballad of this dream. It shall be called "Bottom's Dream," because it hath no bottom; and I will sing it in the latter end of a play before the Duke. Peradventure, to make it the more gracious, I shall sing it at her death. (4.1.214–22)

These words would be familiar to the audience because they are St. Paul's:

> But as it is written, eye hath not seen, neither ear hath heard, neither came into man's heart, the things which God hath prepared for them that love him.
> (1 Corinthians 2:9, Geneva Bible, 1560)

Shakespeare's shows artistic tact. If he had had Bottom quote Paul accurately, the passage would have a jarring note of solemnity, and Bottom would seem to have acquired a staff and cowl. By making Bottom mangle the quotation, we behold—if that is not too strong a word—the bestowal of the most exalted language in the play on the stupidest and most self-involved character.

The clouds of glory that trail from the words of St. Paul rearrange all the earlier incidents in the play. We were not watching individuals as they worked out their courtships but rather the world of "man" as the Bible thinks of "man," that creature whose life is like grass, which grows up in the morning and, in the evening, is cut down. The rules of classical decorum, separating the intelligent high from the unintelligent low, operating in the early part of the play in the distinction between blank verse and prose, dissipate. We are, for a moment, taken out of an Ovid-Plautus-Terence world into the world of *The Second Shepherd's Play.* The fairy realm, whose comedy seemed straight out of a Roman screwball comedy ("ill met by moonlight, proud Titania") now ripples with the promises of God's solicitude for human beings, whose lives are beheld by guardians in a higher realm, distributing mercy and rescue in equal dole. The implausibility we conceded when, at the beginning, we heard that the play would be a comedy (because, after all, we know what it is to keep decorum), balances against a voice that will brook no skepticism. Paul is invoked, and the truth he speaks suddenly stabilizes the play. And yet that truth is kept tentative. Why does Shakespeare have Bottom echo St. Paul in comic terms? Because the play is, one minute, holding St. Paul at bay by the rules of classical decorum and by an awareness of fiction, and the next minute, it is holding classical decorum and fictionality at bay, by invoking, however comically and however briefly, the True Word.

There is a crucial figure in this move from darkness and confusion to light and clarity. That figure is Puck, who, as an unmarried male, is above the world of growing into sexuality; there is, after all, no Mrs. Puck. In this way, Puck is like Bottom; there is no Mrs. Bottom either. In the exemption of both of these characters from the turbulence of sexuality, they share something with the vestal-virgin friend of Titania and also with the "fair vestal thronèd by the west" whom Oberon saved from "Cupid's fiery shaft." They share another characteristic. Like Oberon, they are protector figures. Puck is a comic version of a guardian angel; he will see to it that the lovers get paired off rightly. Bottom protects his fellow rude mechanicals from the potential displeasure of Theseus or Hippolyta ("we must leave the killing out"; "look to the ladies"). In this way, all three share something with the mermaid on a dolphin's back, whose "dulcet and harmonious breath" made "the rude sea [grow] civil at her song" (2.1.151–52). They bring harmony. When we ask, why does Shakespeare give Bottom an apparently religious transformation ("Oh, Bless, thee, Bottom! Bless thee! Thou art translated!" [3.1.119–20]), the answer is not, as it might be in the novel, "Bottom has grown, matured." The answer is Shakespeare wants to suggest that a semi-divine power can work through simpletons.

Let us go back to *Twelfth Night*. As in *A Midsummer Night' Dream*, Shakespeare uses different characters to evoke another world and thereby expand the vision of characters whose vision needs some expanding, so does he also in this play. In *Twelfth Night* the figure parallel to Bottom is Feste, who also is sexless and who also stands outside the action, casting a dubious glance on both aristocrats and wastrels. His version of a transcendent world is called Nature. For him, Nature is a world distinct from naval fights between dukedoms and struggles of rascal dolts, like Sir Toby and Sir Andrew, an independence that helps Feste keep a foothold in a great house without being a part of it. Maria scolds Feste for having been absent without leave:

> *Maria*: Yet you will be hanged for being so long absent, or to be turned away. Is not that as good as a hanging to you? (1.5.16–18)

To this warning, Feste shrugs:

> Many a good hanging prevents a bad marriage, and for turning away, let summer bear it out. (1.5.19–20)

Nature brings summer; and summer's warm weather will take care of him; for him Nature is what it is for Ariel in *The Tempest*.

Like Bottom, Feste has some special semi-religious wisdom. He corrects the lady Olivia's grief by catechizing her.

> *Feste*: Good Madonna. Give me leave to prove you a fool.
> *Olivia*: Can you do it?
> *Feste*: Dexteriously, good madonna.
> *Olivia*: Make your proof.
> *Feste*: I must catechize you for it, Madonna. Good my mouse of virtue, answer me.
> *Olivia*: Well, sir, for want of other idleness, I'll bide your proof.
> *Feste:* Good madonna, why mourn'st thou?
> *Olivia*: Good fool, for my brother's death.
> *Feste*: I think his soul is in hell, madonna.
> *Olivia*: I know his soul is in heaven, fool.
> *Feste*: The more fool, madonna, to mourn for your brother's soul, being in heaven. Take away the fool, gentlemen. (1.5.56–71)

Olivia approves:

*Olivia*: What think you of this fool, Malvolio? Doth he not mend? (1.5.72–73)

Feste is not to be regarded as a whole-hearted believer, for later in the play he seems to mock the catechism when, as Sir Topas, he schools Malvolio. But here, in this exchange with Olivia, he is endorsing the notion of an afterlife, and the Lady Olivia takes his reproof. It is agreed between them that confidence in a life after death is more important than the proprieties of mourning. Again, Shakespeare shows his artistic tact. He keeps the interchange sprightly; the wit wards off a solemnity that would be jarring.

In this way, Shakespeare uses Feste to emphasize an alliance with Viola, who is a also a natural force, emerging from the sea and ready to "sing to the reverberate hills." Shakespeare underlines this alliance by giving Feste a scene alone with Viola, in which she notes the shrewdness of his observations (3.1.58–66). Both contrast with Olivia's wish to control the world, as when she says to Viola, "I would you were as I would have you be" (3.1.144). Both of them teach gratitude: Feste is grateful for summer; Viola tells Olivia that she should be grateful for Orsino's adoration. When, then, Olivia cannot help being attracted to Viola, Shakespeare is pushing her out of a punctilious world of good manners into one that requires humility, not as a gentlemanly, decorous humility, but as one that bows before the law of Nature. As Sebastian wryly remarks to Olivia at the end of the play: "So comes it, lady, that you have been mistook / But nature to her bias drew in that" (5.1.259–60).

Thus, through Feste, *Twelfth Night* expands its emotional register. In Illyria, people get excited; in Feste-land, people do not, and the reason has to do with religious equanimity that chimes with the equanimity of an old man who knows that "a great while ago the world began." Feste's other world reminds those with too much pride that humility is the foundation of love and that it engenders gratitude for whatever happiness human beings are allowed.

Of course, to hear that music at all, one must be attuned to its tenor. One *can* be deaf to it, as one can be deaf or blind to elegance. For most students, the stiffness and formality of authority deserves mockery. Modern performances of Shakespeare usually play to these democratic judgments, arranging the stage action to draw hearty laughs or warm feelings; often the audience laughs where it was not meant to. Perhaps Ben Jonson was wrong when he said that Shakespeare "was not for an age but for all time."

But we can see the problem a different way. Perhaps Shakespeare is not "for all time" only for those whose interpretive templates are dominated by modern allegiances to excitement and sentimentality. They miss what the playwright, with artistic grace, keeps subtle—alas, perhaps too subtle. Indeed, for those who find lively characters pleasing, the loss of that higher world is not a diminution to be lamented. Then we are entering a much larger discussion.

## 2. Novelistic Characters and Authority

As I suggested at the beginning of this chapter, Shakespeare's courtesy is also connected to justice, and with justice comes authority and power. While characters in the novel tend to inhabit a coming-of-age-story, in Shakespeare, authority figures are already of age. Their job is not to find love but to consider what institutions tear communities apart and what institutions hold them together. If the goal is to make the polity stable and to establish harmony within it, then moderation must be encouraged.

Students tend not to see this reciprocity between moderation in a governor and stability in a state. Lady Olivia of *Twelfth Night* seems to them merely "cold." They ignore the fact that Olivia is in charge of a large house full of dependents. With good reason, then, does she talk about "my people," among whom there are more rascal types than sober ones. For students, Malvolio's insistence on order *needs* to be rattled, and Lady Olivia's dependence on his stewardship ("I would not have him miscarry for the half of my dowry" [3.4.65–66]) can be ignored.

Similarly, in *All's Well that Ends Well*. A weak or sick older generation is struggling to keep in line a willful younger generation. The one who most definitely needs his willfulness checked—Bertram—is inclined to favor a man who is a bag of words—Parolles. After his cowardice and lying are revealed, Parolles considers:

> If my heart were great
> It would burst at this. Captain I will be no more,
> But I will eat and drink and sleep as soft

As captain shall. Simply the thing I am
Shall make me live. Who knows himself a braggart,
Let him fear this; for it will come to pass
That every braggart shall be found an ass.
Rust, sword; cool, blushes: and Parolles live
Safest in shame! Being fooled, by fool'ry thrive!
There's a place and means for every man alive.
I'll after them.

The soliloquy starts with a shrug (along the lines of "status demands that I toe the line, and I have had enough of such line-toeing") and ends with vitality. When in *King Lear*, Shakespeare needed a villain, he deepened the colors of the Parolles-type to create Edmund. What attitude toward Parolles does Shakespeare expect? Disgust? Perhaps. Amusement? Perhaps. Or perhaps a mixture of amusement and melancholy, for although Parolles is right—there is a place for every man alive—that, in the context of *All's Well that Ends Well*, is not altogether a happy fact.[22]

Shakespeare may, however, expect Parolles' philosophy of life to be assessed. The same requirement arises with Falstaff in the *Henry IV* plays. A suavely dark interpretation, popular in the days when I was teaching, held that Shakespeare uses an exuberant and childlike Falstaff to cast suspicion on the moral character of Hal, who, it was claimed, represents the crafty politician who has read his Machiavelli and has polished a charming amiability for political gain. But perhaps Falstaff is not simply a comic life force; perhaps he is used in the play to show how hard it is to resist the pleasure of just enjoying life, for comedy certainly lifts the spirits.

### 3. Measure for Measure *and the Problem of Allegory*

With *Measure for Measure*, the problem of a prejudice against order and discipline becomes especially difficult. Students' dissatisfaction with the play is vocalized most vigorously at the ending; how in the world could any of these marriages work? But the theme—or the fable—of the play is

---

22  *All's Well That Ends Well*, 4.3.344–54, in *Signet Classic Shakespeare*, ed. by Sylvan Barnet (New York: Penguin, 2005).

announced in the first line: "The properties of government to unfold." The representative of the properties of good government inevitably seems stiff. In *I Henry IV*, Hal's easy amiability with his Eastcheap companions softens his clear-eyed moral assessment of them. But in *Measure for Measure*, Duke Vincentio is not surrounded by a band of good Eastcheap lads. Instead, Shakespeare emphasizes his solitude. If some are disappointed when Hal assesses with clarity his own moral stature and the moral stature of others, they positively shudder when the Duke makes his pronouncements.

When I say in class, "we are supposed to take the Duke more or less allegorically," there is an outcry. The outcry is based on two grounds. First, students say that if the city (Vienna) was corrupt, it was the Duke's own fault, as he himself admits when he says he had been too lenient with his subjects ("The baby beats the nurse, and quite all athwart / Goes all decorum"[23]). An appeal to the characteristic opening of New Testament parables, "a king went into a far country," does not help to rescue him. Second, students are horrified by the Duke's marriage to Isabella. For them, Isabella is a plucky young woman who had a goal in life—to become a nun—and the pompous and emotionally flat Duke pretty much forces marriage on her. A man is explaining life to a woman! She does not get to choose her life course! How could this young and vibrant woman ever be happy with this prematurely aged stuffed shirt?

Although the play ends in marriage, the play is not about what makes a happy couple. It is about just what the first line said it was about—the properties of *government*. We should try what Flaubert suggested—consider the artistic difficulties facing a playwright in writing a play (with a plot, of course) about politics. In this play, Shakespeare tried to combine two very different genres—a treatise and a comedy. A treatise *considers* political questions; drama, however, requires characters to *do* something, and the conflicts that arise in *doing something* have to be resolved. The marriage of Isabella to the Duke is the representation of two opposing forms of government: firmness in upholding the law and equity in the particular case. When the plot devolves into a standard happy ending, with couples nicely paired off, the playwright was perhaps counting on his audience to remember the line from

---

23 *Measure for Measure*, 1.3.30–31, ed. by S. Nagarajan for Signet Classic Shakespeare, general editor Sylvan Barnet (New York: Signet Classics: 1998).

the Psalms, "Mercy and truth are met together; righteousness and peace have kissed each other" (Psalm 85:10). From the novelistic point of view, the marriage is bound to fail; but from the point of view of an allegory, it might make sense.

As the good governor, the Duke surveys the various questions it is his duty to think about: first, his own morality; second, the morality of his people and his role in bringing them to a proper understanding of a good Christian life; third, the morality of his counselors and seconds-in-command; fourth, the resistance of human nature to being governed and the accompanying conviction that perfect justice can and ought to be fulfilled, even in a fallen world. While individual characters are thinking about their ambitions and their happiness, the Good Governor always has on his mind what is on the other wall, a picture of Bad Government, as in Pietro Lorenzetti's fresco in Siena. Only in some kind of tableau of reconciliation, which marriage is insofar as it brings families together, can one forget that other bad world and imagine, for a time, that good government can be permanent. Like Feste, then, the Duke sees more than do the individual characters. One must be alert to the generic sources on which Shakespeare draws to make this complex character.

But there is another problem besides how an audience understands the Duke generically. That problem is appreciating Shakespeare's thoughtfulness in considering political difficulties. Unfortunately, colleges compartmentalize learning: literature belongs in language departments, logic in philosophy departments, political philosophy in Poli-Sci departments. Students entering a Shakespeare class will expect to talk about metaphor and feelings and character development and character psychology, not about political theory. If they have encountered any political theory, it will have been in an introductory Poli-Sci class, where Plato's political thought was presented as a list of "key ideas in Plato," before the class moved on to "key ideas in Aristotle," and thence to "key ideas in Hobbes, Locke, Marx." This teaching of political theory rarely addresses what problems a political thinker confronts, how he solves them, *whether* he solves them, his view of human nature, his views of the fundamental principles on which the state must be founded, the concessions he has to make, the tensions he resolves, and the tensions he may not be able to resolve.

Let us take up another problem—authority—not the householding authority of Lady Olivia but political authority. For Aristotle, politics is friendship-between-rational-people writ large; therefore, the judgments that influence the choice of a friend resemble the judgments of a ruler. A person in authority should have knowledge, moral character, and experience. Further, his goal should be both to make good citizens and to preserve the state. For contemporary citizens of a commercial republic, the political community is a contract writ large. The ruler's job is to oversee the enforcement of those contracts—that is, to oversee the functioning of the law. For Shakespeare, the ruler is a nurturing father. His job is to preserve the state, to make his subjects orderly citizens, and *also* to save their souls. As has been pointed out many times, the Christian ruler always has difficulty in reconciling his allegiance to a polity located in this world and also to a heavenly community in the next. The first requires firmness in enforcing the earthly law and the second requires obedience to a heavenly law.

When Shakespeare has Duke Vincentio admit that he has been lax in enforcing the law, the point is not that all corruption in Vienna has been the result of the Duke's failure as a governor but rather that the Duke is rightly acknowledging his own moral failures as a nurturing father and vowing to do something about them. The burden on the Duke as a moral leader is far greater than the burden on an administrative leader of a commercial republic.

The Duke's opening speech to Escalus serves to highlight the Duke as a leader conscious of the difficulties of his position. He compliments Escalus on his "science" (knowledge) about "the nature of our people"; the city's "institutions"; and the "terms for common justice" (1.1.1–11). When the Duke then converses with Angelo, Shakespeare lets us know that the Duke is aware that that a governor's moral virtues have political force, and it is his responsibility to use them ("for if our virtues / Did not go forth of us, 'twere all alike / As if we had them not" [1.1.33–35]). The Duke knows that that a good governor should reflect on human nature: "What figure of us, think you, he [Angelo] will bear?" (1.1.16). He acknowledges his own withdrawn, impassive temperament ("I do not relish well / Their [the people's] loud applause and aves vehement" [1.1.69–70]). If a modern reader does not hear this speech rightly, that is, as the prelude to a consideration of an abstract problem, he will say the Duke is cold and stiff.

The street scenes that follow are often regarded as a refreshing alternative to the Duke's chilly severity. In Act 1, Scene 2, the young bucks of

Vienna exchange political jokes about the Duke's negotiations with his rivals, about religion, about the diseases that follow upon sexual license; they conclude with the cynical view that all men are infected scoundrels. Lucio is distinguished from this group only by his concern when he hears that his friend Claudio is being taken to prison. Then enter the sex-mongers, Mistress Overdone, a madam concerned about her trade, and Pompey, her laconic and shrugging handyman, who assures her that her business is not going to wilt because city officials can always be bribed. These characters should not be regarded as refreshing alternatives to the Duke's life-killing strictures. Rather they show what a ruler must deal with; there will always be a class of human beings that knows how to thrive off human weakness.

But besides the marriage ending, besides the remote, impassive demeanor of the Duke, besides the problem with any figure who represents authority and disapproval of license, there is the problem of the preparation-for-death speech that the Duke addresses to Claudio in 3.1. I once saw a performance where the director, in order to save the speech from being a dead spot in the play, decided that the Duke should be a version of Polonius, the old fussbudget in *Hamlet*. In that performance, the Duke seemed to be trying out rabbinical (or priestly) solutions to a problem he regards as merely rhetorical, as if, "maybe if I take this tack, it will sound good? or perhaps I should go with that one?"[24] But if the Duke is portrayed this way, then the marriage at the end of the play *really* does not make any sense. Moreover, the director forgoes an opportunity to introduce solemnity about death, and reconciling Claudio to death is one of the nurturing father-governor's duties. His parallelisms characterizing death ("a breath thou art," "thou art death's fool," "[t]hou art not noble," "[t]hou'rt by no means valiant," "[h]appy thou art not," "[t]hou are not certain"), the steadiness in the short sentences, and the unperturbed dismissiveness are all reminiscent of the rhythms of Ecclesiastes.

As it turns out, the Duke's speech is ineffective, for in Act 3, Claudio's fear of death has taken over his imagination: "Aye, but to die, and go we know not where. / To lie in cold obstruction and to rot, / This sensible warm motion to become / A kneaded clod" (3.1.118–21), and he implores Isabella, "Sweet sister, let me live!" Shakespeare's decision to have Claudio

24  The director was Mark Rylance, and he himself played the Duke.

fail here is not meant to show that the Duke uttered ineffective platitudes; rather, Shakespeare is showing what in human nature, the law—secular or Christian—must contend with. Sympathy with human weakness inclines us to protest against the law. But sympathy with human weakness does not make the law wrong.

## 4. Allegory and Realism

At the extreme, the complaint with allegory is with the notion of evil itself. I once had a student argue that there is no such thing as evil; then the question becomes: which is worse, using stereotypes for the representation of evil, thereby risking a template that casts suspicion on readily identifiable types, or giving up the representation of evil altogether? But even more fundamental is the question: is justice merely the statutory law as it stands at any given time, but which can change tomorrow?

Allegory is also said to be a bad genre because it does not face the complexity of human character. Literature without allegory acknowledges that complexity and thereby teaches empathy. Oddly, however, when students read *Measure for Measure*, they have little empathy for Angelo, who at the end of 2.2 and beginning of 2.4, shows remarkable self-knowledge, which is, perhaps, meant to be contrasted with Isabella's self-righteousness at the end of the play. Moreover, it might be that Shakespeare recognizes the tendency of allegory to make contrasts that are too sharp ("Angelo, bad; Isabel, good") and is trying to temper them.

The proponent of allegory would concede that if one reduces literature to "messages," those messages are often trite. She would also concede that in order to speak to the unphilosophical soul, literature needs sensuousness. But she would also argue that the very means by which literature inveigles interest and emotion are risky because they undermine both restraint and clear thought. Plato would say that it is a miscalculation of the relation of parts of the human soul to each other to think that pleasure will allow reason to govern. Samuel Johnson himself was dubious about modern realism:

> Many writers, for the sake of following nature, so mingle good
> and bad qualities in their principal personages, that they are

both equally conspicuous; and as we accompany them through
their adventures with delight, and are led by degrees to interest
ourselves in their favour, we lose the abhorrence of their faults,
because they do not hinder our pleasure, or, perhaps, regard
them with some kindness for being united with so much merit.
(Rambler #4)

In short, just as Plato warned, literature is exciting, and in a state of
excitement the soul cannot judge wisely. Allegory is, by comparison,
clear, or at least clear*er* than realism. It rises above the claims of the
particular on the sympathetic imagination, all too ready to feel compassion.

Because in *Measure for Measure*, moral reason is invited to do its work,
it moves from one consideration in the central argument to another—the
Duke's knowledge of human nature, Angelo's divided soul, the panic of
Claudio's fear of death, the fury of Isabella's contempt for Claudio's weakness, the clever sleaze of Lucio, the half-witted sleaze of Mistress Overdone
and Pompey—all the time, weighing and measuring the emotional claims
of these figures. By means of these characters, the playwright can show
human mistakes—namely, thinking that strong feeling makes one right,
that the law is a nuisance, that mercy is a right. In the play, these mistakes
are concessions to the very human desire that there should be some way
not to have to suffer. The counterweight to these desires is the firmness of
the Duke. If human beings receive mercy, it is the gift of God. Behind the
play is Augustine's warning in the *City of God* that one should not expect
perfect justice in the Earthly City.

The artistic difficulties in making such an argument necessitate Shakespeare's introduction of two puzzling characters. Escalus and the Provost
seem extraneous to *Measure for Measure*. When we concentrate on the play
as a skillfully presented allegory, we can see that Shakespeare needs voices
that would mediate the sternness of the Duke. Escalus and the Provost are
soft-spoken, deliberate, reflective characters who contribute to the music
of pondering. They see both sides of the question, that the law causes pain
and yet it is necessary.

This paradox justifies the oft repeated word *remedy* in this play. Elbow
uses it when he arrests Pompey for being a pimp:

140

Nay, if there be no remedy for it, but that you will needs buy
and sell men and women like beasts, we shall have all the world
drink brown and white bastard. (3.2.1–3)

By "remedy," Elbow seems to mean merely, "your solution for the problem
of how to make a living." Isabella, on the other hand, uses "remedy" when
she imagines that redemption should be readily available to human beings.
In Act 2, she cries to Angelo:

> Alas, alas!
> Why, all the souls that were forfeit once;
> And He that might the vantage best have took
> *Found out the remedy*. How would you be,
> If He, which is the top of judgment, should
> But judge you as you are? O, think on that;
> And mercy then will breathe within your lips,
> Like man new made. (2.2.72–79; italics added)

But as a mere human being, Angelo cannot, in any event, offer the forgiveness of Christ. Elbow's tone is jocularly practical, Angelo's one of intransi-
gence, Claudio's one of a desperate hope that justice can be evaded, and
Isabella's a false expectation that human beings judge like Christ.

Shakespeare prepares the significance of "remedy" through Escalus'
lines to Angelo at the beginning of the play. First, Escalus is given lines that
establish his humility:

> and it concerns me
> To look into the bottom of my place.
> A pow'r I have, but of what strength and nature,
> I am not yet instructed. (1.1.75–80)

Then later, when Escalus hears Angelo deny his plea for Claudio, he is given
a choric generalization:

> Well, Heaven forgive him, and forgive us all.
> Some rise by sin and some by virtue fall:

Some run from breaks of ice, and answer none
And some condemned for a fault alone. (2.1.37–40)

The point of Escalus' subsequent interchanges with Pompey, Elbow, and Froth in the same scene is to make us hear the earnest search for clarity and the earnest effort to fight sentimentality, both frustrated. Shakespeare uses the Provost to give a choric argument for mercy:

*Provost*: Alas,
He [Claudio] hath but as offended in a dream!
All sects, all ages smack of this vice; and he
To die for't! (2.2.3–5)

Just eight lines before, Shakespeare had used Escalus to voice the heart of the dilemma:

*Escalus*: It grieves me for the death of Claudio,
*But there's no remedy.*
*Justice*: Lord Angelo is severe.
*Escalus*: It is but needful:
Mercy is not itself, that oft looks so;
Pardon is still the nurse of second woe.
But yet—poor Claudio! *There is no remedy.*
(2.1.280–86; italics added)

Here is the best defense of allegory. It can examine an issue like justice and then divide it into parts. We should not be concentrating on the difficulties of individual characters. We should instead be watching how the play analyzes an idea here, the difficulty of administering the law. With Shakespeare's great tragedies, we might use allegory to see *behind* the character to see what these complex plays are groping toward.

Escalus's line "There is no remedy" is also the utterance of the exhausted Akhilleus as he gazes at the old man Priam at the end of the *Iliad*. In that work, what Akhilleus sees is the unintelligibility of life, without hope. In *Measure for Measure*, there is hope, but it will require human beings to submit to their status as fallen creatures, a submission that very few are capable of. Shakespeare wrote a searching and painful play. If we disregard the allegorical formality and the various inflections of "remedy," it remains painful and the ending is entirely unsatisfactory. We protest—comedy is supposed to reconcile, heal, make joyous!

But perhaps when at the end of the play, Shakespeare brings out all the traditional comic moves—marriages, reluctant husbands—we are expected to hear this ending as the cadential material at the end of a symphony. The play is not working for comic freedom but for "measure." Thus the elegiac music subdues the exuberance of the comic formulas. Comedy's wish for happiness can never be realized in this life. The Renaissance poet Thomas Campion got the tone right.

> Now winter nights enlarge
> The number of their hours;
> And clouds their storms discharge
> Upon the airy towers.
> Let now the chimneys blaze
> And cups o'erflow with wine,
> Let well-turned words amaze
> With harmony divine.
> Now yellow waxen lights
> Shall wait on honey love
> While youthful revels, masques, and courtly sights
> Sleep's leaden spells remove.
>
> This time doth well dispense
> With lovers' long discourse;
> Much speech hath some defense,
> Though beauty no remorse.
> All do not all things well;
> Some measures comely tread,
> Some knotted riddles tell,
> Some poems smoothly read.
> The summer hath his joys,
> And winter his delights;
> Though love and all his pleasures are but toys,
> They shorten tedious nights.

Little pleasures do not amount to happiness, but they do soften our disappointments.

Why is it necessary to consider all these matters in reading Shakespeare—the fabula, the allegorical structure, the strictures of the law, the invocation of a world above this one, a wryness that is both a secular and a Christian recognition of the imperfections of the world? Because the plays offer wisdom, and to assess that wisdom fairly requires getting beyond the prejudices of modernity—namely, interpretive prejudices (allegory is bad) and philosophical prejudices (aristocratic self-restraint is bad; religion's appeal to a higher, more perfect world is a delusion). We read great books because they make us see our prejudices.

The wisdom of the past—easy to say, harder to teach, the views of the present being so much more exciting. I once was outside the English department at Penn, fiddling with my recalcitrant bike lock, and a student ambled over to tell me he was going to drop my course because he found the reading useless. As I recognized his voice, I raised myself from a stooped-over position to hear what he had to say. It was a nice afternoon in late fall—crisp air, leaves turning color, bright blue sky—the autumn fireworks. Ortega y Gasset's argument in The Revolt of the Masses, the student said, were those of an old man, and every older generation has felt that the world is going to the dogs. My shoulders dropped; I looked past his face to the orange of the autumn leaves, putting on their show, against the blue sky. I thought to myself, "Yes, and every younger generation thinks the older generation clings to the past out of weakness." "Well," I said, "civilizations do crumble—slowly, maybe, but they do crumble." "Oh, come on," he said, "that's a little dramatic." I paused and then looked past him at autumn shining in its somber way. The Scotch-Irish in me started talking inside my head. Oh, my young lad, you don't know how much your confidence puts me in a state of melancholy. The world is all before you, you think. How fortunate you are to have figured out so much at your young age, and you scarce out of breeches! Your civilization may be collapsing around you as we speak!

# SHAKESPEARE'S *TEMPEST*

## *1. Teaching the Play*

In the previous chapter, I mentioned a former student who said he did not respond to Shakespeare. Some students will admit they agree with him, especially when it comes to *The Tempest*. The characters, they say, are thin; the lovers are unbelievable, ("Who talks like that?"); Prospero is stiff; the comic characters are silly. For them, the highlight of the play is Shakespeare's supposed farewell to the theater in Prospero's lines at the end of the play. In those lines lies a good drama because anything that can be read biographically has the intensity of "real life." Finally, Prospero's age is definitely a drawback because, except perhaps for the aged Kind Lear, old people do not have the stake in the future that youth does. If one has the luck to live to three-score-years-and-ten, however, one knows that there are still things that need some musing on.

At the end of my last semester of teaching, I thought I would give myself a treat and teach *The Tempest*. Right away, I could see that I would have much work. A very bright young woman remarked that in a previous class it had been *demonstrated* that *The Tempest* was a colonialist document (Prospero colonizes Caliban's island). Someone else had heard, and she thought what she had heard was true, that the play showed both colonialist oppression *and* racism; Alonso's court begged him not to send his daughter to Africa to marry an African prince.[25] Others pointed out that in the first act, Shakespeare goes out of his way to make Prospero unlikeable. He is cranky with Miranda when, like the petulant old man that he is, he insists that she listen to his life story and is cross with her for not paying strict enough

---

25  *The Tempest*, 2.1.127–32, in *Four Great Comedies*, ed. by Robert Langbaum, introduction by Sylvan Barnet, Signet Classics (New York: Penguin Books, New York, 1998).

attention. He is harsh to Ariel. He is also harsh to Caliban, a charming innocent, whom he has enslaved. Ferdinand is dislikeable too. He is a cipher; no self-respecting male lover grovels before his beloved in the way this prince does. Furthermore, Miranda and Ferdinand cannot really love each other because Prospero has merely engineered their courtship. In sum, the characters are remote, and the play whispers of evil things.

It was, to be sure, late in the semester; students were tired; a few had not read the play at all; several sensed my irritation with these latter; some had received bad grades on a diagnostic short paper. One student, who actually was quite bright, had received a bad grade because his paper had offered an argument too true to be good. Feeling combative, this student asked me what the difference was, after all, between Caliban's wanting to rape Miranda after he had been thwarted in his first attempt and Ferdinand's "wanting" her (wanting her sexually, that is). I paused for a moment, then sighed and said, looking out the window, "My, what cynicism! And also bit tone-deaf." The young woman sitting next to him winced. She thought I was being too harsh. This student was, as I say, bright, and it wasn't really tone deafness that was the problem. It was a failure of moral discrimination. I should have been more alert to the necessity for confronting that difficulty. But how far back can a teacher go?

As for the colonialism—perhaps parts of *The Tempest* have something to do with the justification of colonialism—maybe—but that judgment depends on whether one reads the play as realism or as an allegory. As for the charge of racism, it is to be noted that the character who accuses Alonso of "loos[ing] his daughter to an African" (2.1.130) is Sebastian, Alonso's brother, that would-be murderer; he is the racist one, not Alonso; he is, as the audience finds out later, quite the operator. As for the reverential adoration of one's beloved—perhaps that is in a register students cannot hear. In Ferdinand's lines, Shakespeare borrowed the wonder, worship, and gratitude of Renaissance love poetry, but most students are not acquainted with that because their teachers are teaching them other things. Moreover, one might wonder if there is a deeper cultural reason why students regard desire restrained as no different from assault thwarted.

Then, too, *The Tempest* is a masque, and a masque requires adjustment to the genre. The story is stylized, as in a ballet. It has allegory's strong moral themes, and as a result, more than in other of Shakespeare's plays, the characters are representative types. The play presents, for the most part, a Judaeo-Christian view of the great world—human beings are fallen; fallen human life can never be perfect; good people suffer; the young are charming in their ready belief that human nature is good; redemption is possible; wisdom begins in reason and fear of a higher-than-human power; freedom, which all human beings long for, is fulfilled at the highest level in contemplation of divine powers that made the earth beautiful; and, finally, in love of humankind. The play shows human despair, human comforts, the unfulfillable human longing for a world without work or suffering, and trust in the existence of another, higher and happier world—happy, that is, in the sense of serene. But this love is not presented without a glance at the other side of the coin; some parts of earthly life and some human beings are not so loveable. The wonder of the play is Shakespeare's having found the various "local habitation[s] and a name" for an abstract idea with many complicated parts.

Perhaps readers might get farther in understanding this play if they were to regard it as a reshaping of *Measure for Measure*. Whereas the side plots of *Measure for Measure* have an intensity that makes the play wobble (and that makes a comic denouement awkward), in *The Tempest* Shakespeare has steadied the wobbling, chiefly by connecting the subplots more firmly to a center. This center figure is a governor with something of the detachment of the Duke in *Measure for Measure*; but while Duke Vincentio's disguise forces a greater detachment from the characters around him, Prospero engages with the characters on his little island; his detachment is expressed chiefly in wry asides. He comments dryly on Ferdinand's assumption that he is now King of Naples (1.2.430–37), and when near the end of the play, Miranda exclaims, "Oh brave new world / That hath such people in it," Prospero checks her naïve enthusiasm with, "'Tis new to thee" (5.1.183–84).

Moreover, Shakespeare develops a complex inner life for Prospero. He is a governor who is also a servant of the divine and, as such, has thought philosophically about Nature as the great orderer of things. Nature is in part his assistant in bringing characters to their knees but also a friend, almost a confidante, who brings the beauties of the earth to his visions. Finally, unlike Vincentio, Prospero's inner life is complicated by emotions not wholly under his control—resentment of his brother and impatience with schemers.

Significantly, an important word that ties *Measure for Measure* and *The Tempest* together has been changed. In *Measure for Measure*, the word is "government," announced in the opening line with somewhat heraldic formality: "Of government the properties to unfold." In *The Tempest*, the important word is "authority." In many ways the two overlap, but in important ways they do not. In substituting "authority" for "government," Shakespeare extends the play's philosophical considerations. This governor has a different relationship with those he governs. In part, they are his subjects, but they could become his friends. Why some could be and why some could not explore the tenor of friendship, and because it is rare, how precious it is.

In this regard, it is important to note that at the end of the play, not everyone has come to a fuller understanding. Notably, Antonio and Sebastian are silent. Shakespeare's purpose in keeping them silent is to emphasize the intractability of some human souls and therefore the size of the task Prospero faces. In *Measure for Measure* the Duke manages rather easily the release of his subjects from fear of death, from prison, from pimphood, from abandonment, from indignation at the world's injustice. Prospero, on the other hand, must deal with souls that may or may not be awakened to knowledge. For this task he must be shown to be aware of what methods are appropriate for different souls.

More important, however, in giving Prospero a complicated inner life, Shakespeare includes this governor-type in the play's movement toward a general "sea change." If his subjects are to be his friends, he must learn to forgive. In his long narration of past events, Prospero's irritation with Miranda emphasizes by contrast his agitation and resentment at the beginning of the play and his philosophical calm at the end.

## 2. Authority

The key word "authority" is uttered in the play's first scene, in the midst of accusations and ripostes by desperate characters. On first reading, the word flies by the audience. At the moment of the storm, the Master of the ship calls for the Boatswain. The Boatswain is ready to serve. He passes the orders of the Master on to the sailors, urging them to their duties and, significantly, to "listen to the master." The aristocrats from Milan and

Naples come from below deck and reprimand the Boatswain for shouting and remind him that there is a king on board. He brusquely presents them with a choice:

> *Boatswain*: You are a counselor, if you can command these elements to silence, and work the peace of the present we will not hand a rope more; *use your authority*: if you cannot, give thanks you have lived so long, and make yourself ready in your cabin for the mischance of the hour, if it so hap. Cheerly, good hearts! Out of our way, I say. (1.1.21–24; italics added)

If the aristocrats can do something to save their lives at this moment, they should do it; if not, they should look to their prayers: "use your authority" is a shout of exasperation from a member of the ship's staff, who himself has accepted master's orders to "fall to yarely" (1.1. 2–3). On second reading, this word "authority" resounds with the rest of the play. The Boatswain is, in this situation, the man with authority because he knows seamanship. Later, Prospero has even greater authority because he has a higher knowledge. Here, however, Shakespeare concedes, as does Plato, that in certain situations, the man to be obeyed is the one with appropriate skills.

As the play sifts the question of authority, it hearkens back to other words and phrases spoken in this first scene. Who or what should be the "master"? The Boatswain asks, "Do you not hear him?" He could mean the captain of the ship, but he could also mean Nature, who controls the storm. As the play broadens its scope, there is a still higher master to be listened to.

Moreover, insofar as all human beings are imperfect, they have a duty to encourage each other: "Cheerly, cheerly, my hearts," calls the Boatswain to the sailors. Gonzalo remarks about him: "I take comfort from this fellow; methinks he hath no drowning mark upon him." Since in this life calamities are likely to happen, people should not blame each other when those calamities do occur. Gonzalo admonishes the Boatswain: "You do assist the storm," and later, "Nay good, be patient." Since the gods control human events, one must submit to his wisdom; Gonzalo begins a prayer with ,"The wills above be done!" On the other hand, since the gods love human creatures, they will forgive their little scruples, as with Gonzalo's admission that he has a preference for leaving this life standing on land: "but I would fain die a dry death." The whole of this short opening scene is a prologue to the rest of the play. To appreciate Shakespeare's artistry here, of course, the play has to be read at least one more time to see how the play moves from agitation to patience.

Almost all the characters in the play feel trapped. Ariel wants his freedom from service. Caliban wants freedom from slavery. Ferdinand says he happily submits to log-carrying, but Miranda wants for him freedom from such ignominy. Antonio wants freedom from a barren island. Alonso wants freedom from his grief. Prospero alone knows, however, that except for Ariel's, the other characters' ideas of freedom are deficient. True freedom is presented in the marriage pageant of Act 4. Then Prospero calms his agitation by watching his project come to fulfillment, as he gazes at the masque-within-a-masque as if he had forgotten earthly life altogether. This is what human beings, if they had knowledge of the highest human freedom, would wish for, to lose oneself in admiration of the beauties of the universe or, to put the matter in Plato's terms, in erotic love of Beauty and Goodness.

Thus, the wisest longing for freedom in the play belongs to Prospero. Shakespeare starts the play with the Boatswain's exasperation with human nature. With Prospero, that exasperation is deepened. All of Prospero's recalcitrant minions have earlier been talking about the slavery they have to endure and the freedom they think they deserve, some more petulantly than others. But it is Prospero who has been the most nettled—netted—one, because, as a ruler, he is duty-bound to tend to people who do not have his knowledge (recall Socrates' weariness in his conversation with Crito). In the masque with Iris, Ceres, and Juno, however, he can float into a higher realm. The higher realm is the overarching theme that the play muses on, how much human beings are exasperated, in one form or another, by the limits of human life, and how little they recognize that their freedom will come from recognizing the authority of a better master. Ultimately, the need for a full recognition of a true master applies to Prospero himself.

The exasperated (and exasperating) human types fall into three categories. The first category is the unaristocratic and unintelligent. The only reason that Stephano and Trinculo fail in Caliban's plot to murder Prospero is their stupidity. Once in Prospero's chamber, they are distracted from their goal by trying on his fancy clothes. Trinculo, on the other hand, has just enough self-awareness to have some doubt about the wisdom that comes with their inebriated state. Shakespeare gives him a wonderfully comic line: "They say there's but five upon this isle; we are three of them. If th'other two be brained like us, the state totters" (3.2.5–7).

The further glory of the line is its pertinence to the central question of the play—good governing—but reinflected in a comic mode. When it comes to ransacking Prospero's wardrobe, Caliban is the only who can keep his eye on the goal. Nevertheless, he too is a slave to false masters. Despite his training (as opposed to education) in talking good Bible ("how to name the bigger light, and how the less" [1.3.35]), he is still a slave to love of power, and his love of power competes with his love of pleasure; he cannot resist the liquor that Trinculo freely offers him. Still, Caliban is the only one of the drunken trio who, at the end of the play, asks for pardon, and he is the only one of the three who hears, however dimly, a higher music.

The second group are the aristocratic and selfish, who are introduced in the first scene as self-important grievance mongers. In 2.1, they entertain each other with acid jokes about Gonzalo's efforts to cheer them up. When Antonio tries to persuade Sebastian to kill Alonso, we are watching men always on the lookout for the main chance, and their vigilance in this regard is chilling. When at the end of 2.1, Sebastian is, in Antonio's devising mind, too slothful in seizing the opportunity when it presents itself, Antonio urges him take hold of the moment:

*Sebastian*: Well, I am standing water.

*Antonio*: I'll teach you how to flow. (2.1.225–26)

Here he means, to follow Machiavelli's advice and seize an opportunity. When at the end of the play, these two are offered forgiveness, they say nothing.

Alonso is an exception in this group; he realizes that the death of his son Ferdinand is punishment for his plot against Prospero. Some readers are unsatisfied that the play does not have a happy ending embracing everyone. In not bringing Sebastian and Antonio into the fold, however, Shakespeare looks hard at the reality of human nature and human life generally; not everyone is educable, and this being so, human life is a somewhat melancholy affair.

The third group is not so obviously destructive; its human aspiration is charming but not thoughtful. It is represented by Gonzalo, who is a good man and does his best to keep up the spirits of those who have lost hope. But his speech is Shakespeare's warning against idle utopianism:

> In th' commonwealth I would be contraries
> Execute all things. For no kind of traffic
> Would I admit; no name of magistrate;
> Letters should not be known; riches, poverty
> And use of service, none; contract, succession,
> Bourn, bound of land, tilth, vineyard, none;
> No use of metal, corn, or wine, or oil;
> No occupation; all men idle, all;
> And women too, but innocent and pure.

And then the next crucial line:

> No sovereignty. (2.1.152–16)

Here, Shakespeare is using Gonzalo as a version of the "hum" that Caliban hears with wonder and delight later in the play (3.2.143). When he imagines a perfect and impossible society, Gonzalo is dreaming in verse:

> All things in common nature should produce
> Without sweat or endeavor. Treason, felony,
> Sword, pike, knife, gun, or need of any engine
> Would I not have; but nature should bring forth
> Out of it[s] own kind, all foison, all abundance,
> To feed my innocent people. (2.1.164–69)

The sweet and loyal counselor fills his dream-city with generous affection for human beings. His subjects, he muses, would not have to work hard; they would not be subject to the law's command. True, he is trying to cheer his comrades, but his idle generosity underlines the point about the exclusions at the end of the play. The good ruler's knowledge does not rely on daydreams but on the realities of earthly life. Since the fall, human nature is not innocent; the governor has a duty to punish evil subjects.

Although Prospero's means of punishment terrifies Miranda, who does not want to see anyone drowned, his purpose is to induce characters to recognize a higher master. With Alonso, Prospero's method is effective; Alonso responds with fear and guilt:

> O, it is monstrous, monstrous!
> Methought the billows spoke and told me of it;
> The winds did sing it to me; and the thunder,
> That deep and dreadful organ pipe, pronounced
> The name of Prosper; it did bass my trespass.
> Therefore my son i' th' ooze is bedded; and
> I'll seek him deeper than e're plummet sounded
> And with him there lie mudded. (3.3.95–102)

Here, Shakespeare allows some pity for Alonso; he does, after all, love his son. Similarly, Shakespeare treats with affection Gonzalo's pastoral vision of a happy community. He assumes his audience is sympathetic enough with religion's longing for peace on earth to find Gonzalo loveable and to find Antonio and Sebastian, those sarcastic jokesters, repellant.

In managing the various characters around him, however, Prospero does not find it easy to be tactful, and the antiphonal back and forth between his own irritation and the voices of those in need of correction is an important part of the play's music. In the first scene with Miranda, Prospero's practical wisdom seems cranky because it is played against Miranda's easily aroused compassion. She is all worry and pity. He must soothe her, with a voice-in-charge ("I have with such provision in mine art / So safely ordered..." [1.2.28–29]). Prospero also must also check Caliban's wild exclamations and demands, reminding him, forcefully, of what Caliban owes him and of Caliban's misdeeds. After the interchange with Caliban, the music switches to the register of the tentative-divine: "This is no mortal business" (Ferdinand, 1.2.407); "It carries a brave form. But 'tis a spirit" (1.2.412); "I might call him / A thing divine" (Miranda, 1.2.418–19). But the lovers' admiration for each other is played against Prospero's harsh insistence on respect for authority: "My foot my tutor? Put up thy sword, traitor!" (1.2.469). The good ruler cannot afford to be too amiable.

### 3. Freedom

In Prospero's interchange with Ariel, the music switches to release from duties and eagerness for freedom: "Spirit, fine spirit, I'll free thee / Within two days for this." But Prospero's generosity is short-lived. Smarting under his obligations, Ariel reminds Prospero of a promise:

> *Ariel*: Since thou dost give me pains,
> Let me remember thee what thou hast promised,
> Which is not yet perform'd me.
>
> *Prospero*: How now? moody?
> What is't thou canst demand?
>
> *Ariel*: My liberty. (1.2.242–45)

The anticipation of his escape from service is like a bird batting its wings against the bars of its cage. Indeed, Prospero later calls Ariel his "bird" (4.1.18 ). The anticipation of freedom rings like a refrain in the play:

> *Prospero*: Thou shalt be as free
> As mountain winds. (1.2.499–500)
>
> *Caliban*: Freedom, high day! High day, freedom! Freedom, high day, Freedom! (2.2.194–95)
>
> *Ferdinand*: Ay, with a heart as willing
> As bondage e'er of freedom. (3.1.87–88)
>
> *Prospero:* And thou
> Shalt have the air at freedom. (4.1.265)
>
> *Prospero*: Thou shalt ere long be free. (5.1.87)
> *Prospero*: But yet thou shalt have freedom. (5.1.96)

*Prospero*: Bravely, my diligence.
Thou shalt be free. (5.1.240–241)

In Act 5, the promise of Ariel's freedom is finally fulfilled. In the scenes with Ferdinand and Miranda, the expectation of release from duty chimes like a bell. Ferdinand claims that he has space enough in his prison of log-carrying, but Miranda does not share his somewhat hallucinatory state; she wants him to be free. The play suggests the regretful view that life is in some ways a prison, with only short spells of happiness. At the end, in melancholy tones, Prospero himself asks to be set free.

The music of confinement and obligation plays antiphonally against the voices of reassurance. After Prospero's rehearsal of his and Miranda's history in Milan, the musical register of consolation is taken up by Ariel, Prospero's almost-angelic messenger. As Ferdinand mourns the loss of his father (1.2.388ff.), Ariel's steady tetrameter lines offer a promise that echoes St. Paul:

> Full fathom five thy father lies;
>     Of his bones are coral made;
> Those are pearls that were his eyes;
>     Nothing of him that doth fade
> But doth suffer a sea change
>     Into something rich and strange. (1.2.397–402)

The line in Paul is I Corinthians 15.51: "Behold, I show you a mystery; we shall not all sleep, but we shall all be changed." The first scene of the play establishes fear, anxiety, the expectation of liberation, and the fulfillment of hope. Then the second scene plays the fugal answer: fear is replaced by reassurance (Miranda), anxiety is replaced by wonder (Ferdinand), and restlessness (Ariel) is replaced by dutiful patience and promise of liberation (Prospero).

In Act 2, Scene 1, Shakespeare plays cheerfulness against scheming. In this scene, in which Sebastian, Alonso, and Antonio are grumbling about being washed up on a barren island, Gonzalo takes over the role of Miranda in the previous scene—namely, as the voice of gratitude and wonder. The stony sarcasm of the two plotters plays against Gonzalo's blithe refusal to be brought into their circle of cynicism. As Alonso takes on the voice of despair, Sebastian and Antonio become the parodies of purposeful authority figures (Sebastian at least *treats* Antonio as if Antonio were more intelligent than himself and hence the authority figure). Antonio is the man of purpose, a free-lance Machiavellian prince, ready to stir up some action ("my spirits are nimble" [line 206]; "to perform an act / Whereof what's past is prologue, what to come, / In yours and my discharge" [lines 256–59]). His plotting parodies the calm preparations of Prospero as the wise leader. Finally, when these two use the word "hope," it is only opportunism. Antonio says to Sebastian of Ferdinand's possible death—

> O, out of that no hope
> What great hope have you! No hope that way is
> Another way so high a hope that even
> Ambition cannot pierce beyond a wink beyond
> But doubt discovery there. (2.1.243–47)

For him, everything is steering ambition to its goal. Antonio's idea of ruling is having subordinates: "My brother's servants / Were then my fellows; now they are my men" (277–78). Having "fellows" comes back later in the play at a more abstract level.

The three comic figures—Caliban, Stephano, and Trinculo—also participate in a fugal parody. In 3.1, Caliban's anticipation of freedom parodies Ariel's eagerness for it at the end of 1.2. Stephano's comfort, a bottle of liquor, parodies the comfort Gonzalo finds in the Boatswain ("I have great comfort from this fellow. Methinks he has no drowning mark upon him" [1.1.29–3]). Caliban's wonder at Stephano ("Hast thou not dropped from heaven?" [2.2.142]) parodies Miranda's instant admiration for Ferdinand ("There's nothing ill can dwell in such a temple" [1.2.458]). Caliban's enthusiastic promise to bring the isle's abundance to his two fellows ("I'll show thee the best springs; I'll pluck thee berries" [2.2.168]) and Stephano's absurd confidence "that we shall inherit here," parody Ferdinand's searching wonder: "This music crept by me upon the waters, / Allaying both their fury and my passion / With its sweet air" (1.2.392–95). Caliban's slavish adoration of Stephano ("I will kiss thy foot" [2.2.156]) parodies Ferdinand's noble acceptance of service ("[F]or your sake / Am I this patient log-man" [3.1.66–67]). Both Stephano's angry growling at the voice he takes to be a devil and Trinculo's instinct for self-preservation in his last-minute repentance ("O, forgive me my sins!" [3.2.135]) parody Ferdinand's intimation of a higher realm ("This is no mortal business, nor no sound / That the earth owes" [1.2.407–08]). Some are hopeless because they are bereft of hope (Alonso), but others are hopeless because, sweet though they may be, they cannot keep their minds on the goal, let alone consider the worthiness of that goal.

Caliban is the special case in this Stephano-Trinculo-Caliban trio, and his distinction points to the play's argument about harmony. He is different from Stephano, the brain-rattled Machiavellian, and from Trinculo, the loveable dope, in his delight in the life of the body, except of course when he is punished with "stripes." He is excited by the life of the senses and responds to its stimulations with alacrity. He is also liberal in offering that life to his two new friends. Finally, he is a Bottom-figure from *A Midsummer Night's Dream*, the protective clown who is confident that the world of his imagination will bring health and happiness to everyone:

> Be not afeard; the isle is full of noises;
> Sounds and sweet airs that give delight and hurt not. (3.3.141)

These communications from a higher world bring to Caliban sleep, dreams, and the delusion of great riches. His vivid imagination shows a soul that can aim steadily at nothing, one minute praising the beauty of the isle and the next minute cursing and imagining putting a nail through Prospero's head. Although Caliban loves the particulars of nature, and although his enthusiasm for them is infectious, he does not understand the link between nature as freshets, nuts, and berries, and Nature as the great "master" to whom the Boatswain appeals in the first scene. For him, happiness is not evidence of something higher but a series of titillations. Music is for him "noises" and "humming."

A higher harmony for a happy human life is represented by Miranda and Ferdinand, who do not crow about or even anticipate freedom but rather accept the constraints put upon them. Before freedom, one endures bondage, but the goal being something superior, the bondage feels like freedom: "This my mean task / Would be as heavy to me as odious, but / The mistress which I serve quickens what's dead / And makes my labors pleasures" (3.1.4–7). Ferdinand has his hierarchy straight. Labor for a superior being is not burdensome. He says to Miranda, "But you, O you, / So perfect and so peerless are created / Of every creature best" (3.1.46–48). The scenes with Ferdinand and Miranda float over all the nastiness, crudeness, and exasperation of the other characters. If they unwarrantedly imagine that all of nature is happy with them, their delusion is forgivable because they are young. In the idiocy (in the ancient Greek sense of "being thoroughly private") of youthful passion, they cannot reflect on life in general. They lack Prospero's experience.

Ariel is Caliban's counterpart. In himself, he is like Aristotle's fire, the only one of the four elements who wishes to rise in the way fire "wishes" to rise to its proper place. Caliban, on the other hand, is nature as purely bestial sensuousness, and as such he must be contained. With that containment comes resentment. Ariel is also Puck from *A Midsummer Night's Dream,* whose folk wisdom ("Jack shall have his Jill") is here reinflected as angelic delight gracefully dancing even as it serves. Only near the end of the play, when Prospero announces his imminent release ("Thou shalt ere long be free" [5.1.87]), does Shakespeare give his audience a sense of what Ariel considers his home. Significantly, that information is conveyed in a song, and the song is in the present tense:

> Where the bee sucks, there suck I:
> In a cowslip's bell I lie;
> There I couch when owls do cry.
> On the bat's back I do fly
> After summer merrily.
> Merrily, merrily shall I live now
> Under the blossom that hangs on the bough. (5.1.88–94)

Like Feste in *Twelfth Night,* Ariel's home is summer, the shorthand for nature. Human beings may wistfully imagine a life without cares, but they cannot live in Ariel's eternally pleasant summer, where Nature bestows perfect ease on her favorite. Prospero says he will miss the music of Ariel's serenely cheerful freedom: "Why, that's my dainty Ariel! I shall miss thee / But yet thou shalt have freedom" (5.1.95–96). When Prospero decides to burn his books, he accepts the inevitable constraints of an earthly existence until death gives him release.

Now we come to the masque of Act 4, which at first seems so odd a diversion from the play's apparent goal; but it is important for understanding the wider philosophical themes of the play. Shakespeare spends Act 2 and the first two scenes of Act 3 showing the human resistance to the authority that would bring happiness. Then, at the masque in Act 4, Prospero is given center stage as he watches the gods' blessing of Miranda's and Ferdinand's wedding. The action stops. Prospero's little "vanity" (i.e., an empty nothing [4.1.41]) is an oratorio in poetry. Here are gathered together the protectors of female virtue, the guardians of agriculture, and the source of Gonzalo's "all foison, all abundance." Here too are echoed the earlier references to earth's comforts: "long heath, brown furze" (Gonzalo in the first scene), the beauty of the island and every fertile inch of it, the sweet air, and the music, humming, and singing. The disorder that Venus and Cupid hoped to wreak on the marriage parodies both the cunningly planned disorder of Sebastian-Antonio and the haplessly planned disorder of Caliban-Stephano-Trinculo. "Be not afraid," says Iris (4.1.92), echoing, but in a more solemn mode, Caliban's earlier "Be not afraid, the isle is full of noises." The tetrameter lines of Ceres' blessing song, lilting with weak stresses at the end of the line, hush the moment:

Honor, riches, marriage, blessing,
Long continuance, and increasing,
Juno sings her blessings on you,
Earth's increase, foison plenty,
Barns and garners never empty,
Vines with clust'ring bunches growing,
 Plants with goodly burden bowing,
Spring come to you at the farthest
In the very end of harvest.
Scarcity and want shall shun you
Ceres' blessing so is on you. (4.1.106–17)

This is Nature's counterpart to Gonzalo's wished-for utopia. Ferdinand responds with breathless admiration:

Let me live here ever!
So rare and wond'red father and a wise
Makes this place Paradise. (4.1.122–24)

Iris's lines that follow shift the focus from an imagined paradise to rural joviality, in which "sicklemen" get to meet "nymphs." The pageant offers an imagined landscape for a soul in harmony with nature. It is the counterpart to Ariel's home, "where the bee sucks," and, like Ariel, has a service to perform "until the time be out" (1.2.246).

## 4. The Highest Freedom

At this point, however, the pageant breaks off abruptly because disharmony is about to break out, not in a tempest on the sea but in Prospero's soul. Although *The Tempest*'s governor figure is knowing and firm, he too is human, rattled by the imperfections of human life:

I had forgot that foul conspiracy
Of the beast Caliban and his confederates
Against my life. (4.1.139–41)

Shakespeare uses Ferdinand to call attention to Prospero's vexation. He says to Miranda, "Your father's in some passion / That moves him strongly." Like Gonzalo, Prospero would prefer to dwell with what he himself called the "vanity" of the marriage pageant. He knows it is an escape from more intractable matters almost as much as a dream utopia was for Gonzalo. As Prospero says to Ariel:

Shortly shall my labors end, and thou
Shalt have the air at freedom. (4.1.264–65)

And a few lines later:

They being penitent,
The sole drift of my purpose shall extend
Not a frown further. (5.1.28–30)

160

Renouncing his "rough magic," he will also renounce expectation of a political harmony that is not possible in this life.

The composure that Shakespeare has Prospero struggle to achieve changes him from the great orderer to the great consoler. He now speaks with deliberate calm, as if it had been Ferdinand who was rattled, not he himself. He repeats the Boatswain's encouragement from Act 1.

> You do look, my son, in a moved sort,
> As if you were dismayed; be cheerful, sir. (4.1.146–47)

He then echoes Iris's adjuration in the masque: "Be not afraid" (4.1.92) with the dignified balance of soul appropriate to a leader whose duty is to protect the young from "dismay." The "vanities" must cease. The gods will not come to earth:

> Our revels now are ended. These our actors,
> As I foretold you, were all spirits, and
> Are melted into air, into thin air;
> And, like the baseless fabric of this vision,
> The cloud-capped towers, the gorgeous palaces,
> The solemn temples, the great globe itself,
> Yea, all which it inherit, shall dissolve,
> And like this insubstantial pageant faded,
> Leave not a rack behind. (4.1.148–56)

Shakespeare has skillfully set up these lines: first, the rapt gazing on the harmony between human life and a transcendent world, then the vexed impatience with reality, then the effort at self-control, and finally the rueful dismissal of life, as in the Book of Revelation, as only an "insubstantial pageant." Veneration ("cloud-capped towers, the gorgeous palaces, the solemn temples") is mixed with acknowledgment of idle dreaming ("baseless fabric of this vision" and "insubstantial pageant"). Visions are lovely, but they are not stable. Anticipating death, Prospero is reminding both himself and his audience of the wisdom of age: the earth is beautiful and to be treasured, but it will give way to a higher realm that is even more beautiful. Even the wisest human soul must defer to the most authoritative master, who has so set up his huge creation that human life is merely a small part.

Only by reference to this higher world can human life be redeemed and only under special circumstances, and only on this island can a leader bring scapegraces to their better selves. In the real and fallen world, salvation for a shipwrecked soul is not possible. Prospero on the island has been bestowed, for a time, the power of "rough magic." The time has come to renounce it ("But this rough magic I must now abjure" [5.1.51]). As with *A Midsummer Night's Dream,* in which the reminder of death hovers around the gentle protections of comedy, here the reminders of duty hover around the imagined release from duty. Prospero must go back to Milan.

The play is groping for a more complete understanding of human nature, but also a fuller understanding of human beings' standing in the world. It is human nature to long for freedom, but the freedom of some is constrained by the ambitions of those who want to win more than they want freedom, by the laziness of those who do not want to work to gain it, and by impatience of the intelligent with the necessity to contain those would-be champions and the sloths, and finally by the elusiveness of Nature's apparent promises of ease.

### 5. Reflections on Imagination

The change in Prospero's disposition is not a question of a misanthrope becoming a kinder man, as the much-emphasized lines near the beginning of Act 5 suggest:

> *Ariel.* Your charm so strongly works 'em,
> That if you now beheld them, your
> affections Would become tender.
>
> *Prospero.* Doest thou think so, spirit?
> *Ariel.* Mine would, sir, were I human. (5.1.17–20)

"Affections" here does not mean "fondness"; it means "passions." Shakespeare is invoking the traditional view of the soul, inherited from the ancients, in which reason must rule the passions in order for the soul to flourish at its highest capacity. He invokes the traditional view in Ariel's speech as he watches the desperate aristocrats:

> Their understanding
> Begins to swell and the approaching tide
> Will shortly fill the *reasonable* shore
> That now lies foul and muddy. (5.1.79–82; italics added)

The "rich and strange" sea change of Ariel's lyric in 1.3 promises that Alonso will undergo a change. For the ancients, the highest flourishing of the soul is the freedom from the passions in order to find and then contemplate the truth; in a Christian dispensation, it is the freedom to love, or forgive, and to be grateful to the creator. When Ariel urges Prospero to forgive Caliban, he is reminding Prospero that his greatest longing is for freedom from the prison of the desire for vengeance, a worse prison even than having to do one's duty.

The serenity of loving and forgiving requires something else besides reason. That "something" is not imagination in the modern sense, which might be defined as "considering other possibilities." In the Renaissance, however, with its philosophical terms learned from Aquinas (who learned them from Aristotle), the imagination's job is to report sense impressions to the soul. Shakespeare assumes this definition when he gives Caliban an enthusiastic speech in which he seems to be talking about imagination, although he does not use that word:

> Be not afeard; the isle is full of noises,
> Sounds and sweet airs that give delight and hurt not.
> Sometimes a thousand twangling instruments
> Will hum about mine ears; and sometimes voices,
> That, if I then had waked after long sleep,
> Will make me sleep again; and then, in dreaming,
> The clouds methought would open and show riches
> Ready to drop upon me, that, when I waked,
> I cried to dream again. (3.2.140–48)

The point of this speech is not to show that Caliban is a visionary creature after all and that Prospero was unduly harsh to him. It is instead to prompt thought about the faculty of imagination.

The trouble with imagination as messenger of sense impressions is, of course, the instances where it makes mistakes and is therefore untrustworthy. It is also, however, a bringer of unfulfillable dreams or deceitful evil dreams or evil dreams. When Caliban remembers trying to rape Miranda, he immediately imagines the act with relish: "O ho! Would't had been done!" (1.2.349). It is noteworthy that Caliban's evocation of the music on the island mentions a plenitude of sound (noises, twangling instruments, humming) but not harmony. In his case, imagination both rivets the soul's attention but also distracts it, thereby obscuring higher things.

When, in *The Merchant of Venice*, Bassanio stands before the caskets, he calls the imagination "fancy." His song addresses two kinds: "Tell me where is fancy bred, / In the heart or in the head?"[26] The opposition between heart and head suggests a clear alternative between the two. When imagination is bred in the heart, it is one kind of "fancy," and, presumably, the untrustworthy one. Alternatively, the fancy that is bred in the head is fancy that is allied with reason. When Prospero asks Ariel to present the masque and suggests getting a "corollary" (4.1.57) of spirits rather than lack a single one, he seems to be invoking imagination as the reliable sort of fancy.

But if there is a higher fancy, a fancy that is reason's assistant, it might be the power in the soul that, instead of scattering the soul's will, concentrates it and *moves* the soul to will the path to the good. That inclination is fostered by imagining a power that governs with solicitude the entire universe and human lives. Shakespeare suggests this connection when Prospero summons his "nobler reason" against "fury":

And mine shall.
Hast thou, which art but air, a touch, a feeling
Of their afflictions, and shall not myself,

26  *The Merchant of Venice*, (3.2.63–64) ed. by Kenneth Myrick for Signet Classics, General Editor Sylvan Barnet (New York: Signet Classics, Division of the Penguin Group, 1998).

> One of their kind, that relish all as sharply,
> Passion as they, be kindlier moved than thou art?
> Though with their high wrongs I am struck to the quick
> Yet with my nobler reason 'gainst my fury
>  Do I take part. (5.1.21–27)

Prospero does not say he is convinced by Ariel's rational arguments. He says he will imitate Ariel's "feeling / Of their afflictions." He is *moved* by Ariel's statement: "shall not myself … be kindlier *moved* than thou art?" That is what the sea change in Ariel's song in Act I ("but doth suffer a sea change, / Into something rich and strange") brings about. The goal of freedom is not only to reason more sharply but to become part of the human fellowship that Antonio dismissed and that Alonso has come to appreciate (2.1.277–78). The higher fancy moves the soul toward this fellowship. For Socrates, freedom is happiness of the solitary, inquiring state of the philosopher. For Shakespeare, in this play, it is the capacity for friendship, or fellowship. Chaucer had implied as much in *The Canterbury Tales*, but Shakespeare here has worked out a fuller articulation of it.

The two versions of imagination are suggested in Act 5 of *A Midsummer Night's Dream.* In Act 5, when Theseus dismisses imagination, he seems to be referring to mere "fancy":

> The lunatic, the lover and the poet
> Are of imagination all compact.
> One sees more devils than vast hell can hold,
> That is the madman. The lover, all as frantic,
> Sees Helen's beauty in a brow of Egypt.
> The poet's eye, in fine frenzy rolling,
> Doth glance from heaven to earth, from earth to heaven;
> And as imagination bodies forth
> The forms of things unknown, the poet's pen
> Turns them to shapes, and gives to airy nothing
> A local habitation and a name.
> Such tricks hath strong imagination,
> That if it would but apprehend some joy;
> It comprehends some bringer of that joy. (5.1.21)

165

Theseus sounds worldly-wise. In his view, poetic imagination merely makes "airy nothing" seem real; human beings should stick with reality. Shakespeare seems to be denigrating his own work.

Hippolyta has another view. The imagination can reach for the something steady and dependable:

> But all the story of the night told over,
> And all their minds transfigured so together,
> More witnesseth than fancy's images,
> And grows to something of great constancy;
> But, howsoever, strange and admirable. (5.1.23–27)

The strange and admirable and constant thing can, possibly, bring a change that might be called "transfiguration," or, as Bottom's friends call, it "translation," as in "O Bottom, thou art translated!" (See Hebrews 11.5)

*The Tempest* ends on a similar reflection—that change in the soul from excitement, whether of appreciation or of judgment, promotes psychic order. The irascible Prospero might be said to be "transfigured" into a benevolent father-governor. The release from the desire for punishment is Prospero's freedom. Then he can let Ariel go:

> Then to the elements
> Be free, and fare thou well! (5.1.18–19)

And, in his last lines, he asks for his own freedom:

> And my ending is despair
> Unless I be relieved by prayer....
>
> As you from crimes would pardoned me,
> Let your indulgence set me free.

The music of this ending should be appreciated. The tetrameter repeats Ariel's songs, in both "Full fathom five thy father lies," and also in "Where the bee sucks, there suck I." The tone moves from dismay to admission of faults, and finally to an appeal to mutual forgiveness. The note is appropriately quiet for a man who is expects that his death is not far off.

I once heard a graduate student dismiss *King Lear* and *The Tempest* as the plays of an "old man." At the time I was astounded by the remark—that someone so young could so confidently assume that only the soul-troubles of the young were interesting. In Shakespeare's view at least, a serious person is still trying to understand life even in old age.

If students shrink from Prospero's irritability and sternness, the reason is perhaps their not yet having entered into parenthood. For a parent, whose years have made her aware of the accidents of living, there are many things to worry about, both within her control and things not in her control. The greatest worry is not knowing what *is* the best path to the highest happiness. A parent's view on that matter can change a great deal between the time of the rearing of small children and the time of old age. For the members of Shakespeare's audience, however, Prospero's irritability in having to bring wrongdoers to their better selves would not have been so puzzling. They would have been accustomed to the abstractions of allegory and to the story of the wise god who disciplines those he loves with fear, as with Jacob, who was made afraid at Bethel as part of some soul-training necessary before he became the father of Israel (Genesis 28), or as with Jesus and the rich young man who is confident that he can follow his Lord without having to give anything up (Matthew 19). Students who do not know the Bible construe the relationship between Prospero and Miranda in terms they are accustomed to—family comedies on television. In family comedies on television, fathers are an affable sort, rarely stern. Prospero is not an affable sort—or perhaps one should say, the highest wisdom is not of an affable sort.

The person who taught me Shakespeare at Wellesley College was Beverly Layman, who, when he retired, moved back to a farm in West Virginia. Layman was not a favorite among my fellow undergraduates. They regarded him as boring. It was true, he did not encourage class discussion; the hour and fifteen minutes of class time were silent except for his voice. Nor was he what people like to call "a charismatic lecturer," or the kind who walks around the classroom gesticulating, changing his voice from a whisper to a shout, throwing out first one hand and then the other to make an "on one side *this* and on the other *that*" point, the kind of lecturer that Thomas Mann parodies in the portrait of Kumpf in *Doktor Faustus*. His Shakespeare classes were not exciting in that way. Being a shy man, Layman felt keenly students' impatience with him.

I sat in Layman's class rapt. I still have my Shakespeare book from that year with many marginal notes in pencil. In the margin of the 4th Act of *King Lear*, I have written, "Today he is tense, reaching for something." This reflection is in relation to Lear's saying to Gloucester who has a bloody bandage around his eyes, "Doest thou squiny at me? [squint at me]? No, no blind Cupid, I'll not love," when of course the blinded Gloucester is not squinting as if he were shooting an arrow, nor does his old, wrinkled, and beaten face look like Cupid's. As I listened to Layman, I was watching a subtle mind "search" the play and then "collect" it, gathering resonant bits and listening carefully to the harmony or disharmony of their timbres, somehow bringing to our ears the extraordinary harmonizing of ideas and feelings.

After my years in graduate school, the culture of college changed. It became important for classes to be entertaining. Evaluations allowed students to make youth's desire for excitement an important criterion for good teaching, and a professor who was said to be good could persuade a class that his ideas were, indeed, *really exciting*. (Why this enthusiasm should be a requirement for good teaching was a mystery to me and still is. My physics teacher in college was never excited or exciting, but class was riveting.) Part of the excitement was supposed to stem from class participation; students should contribute their views; it was good for them. Professors started putting on their syllabi, "class participation is required." Students who were streetwise in academia figured out how to fulfill this requirement by discovering comments that had only a tangential relationship to the discussion at hand, heard from another professor or read on Wikipedia the night before. After all, discussions can often be like ping-pong matches, which are, to be sure, entertaining; one player rears back from the table and, using his whole arm, smacks the ball with so much overspin that, after it bounces on the opponent's side of the net, it loops in a high arc out of reach; the point is over and the conclusiveness is satisfying. Then the talk goes on to something completely different. It is hard to teach these clever ones how to slow down, to proceed carefully from one idea to another, to attend to the course of an argument and to be fair to the positions agreed upon up to that point, but most important keeping the discussion on track. Those who do want to follow the argument, who want to feel their way through a work, tend to be quiet; it is difficult for a teacher to clear a space for them when the others have so quickly and emphatically made up their minds. As Plato's Socratic dialogues show, good teaching is difficult and rare. But then it is also true that patient and thoughtful students are rare. The ones I have known have provided me with wonderful conversations.

# *PARADISE LOST*: THE FALLEN STATE

## *1. A Fugue with Three Voices*

If, after a first time through Paradise Lost, one were asked what it is about, the answer would probably be, it is about the Fall and the promise of redemption. But if one reads it again, the answer is not so easy. One starts hearing things—repetitions, parallels, reverberations. Then Milton's phrase in Book 11—"resonant fugue"—suddenly seems a curiously apt description of the poem. It is a fugue with three themes. The first is a fall into excessive confidence in one's own power. The second is complaining that one's lot is unfair. The third is giving one's soul up to a higher power. The third song is the hardest to hear, for it is the middle voice, and, like all middle voices, it is overpowered by the higher and lower registers. At first, its strain is faint; and then it falls into dissonance; finally it becomes the cadence, indeed, a surprisingly quiet cadence. At that point, the five invocations of the poem, which on first reading seemed like interludes separate from the main plot, suddenly seem to be the crucial chord progression of the poem's resonant fugue. As it turns out, the poem is less about the Fall than the state of fallenness.

Milton's poetry, as we all know, is difficult. He says in his preface that he chose blank verse because long lines could draw out the sense. The long sentences give Milton two advantages. They emphasize a short line by contrast, as in Book 9's climactic: "[s]he plucked, she eat." They can also take a full survey of the great variety of the earth's geography and various events of human history. But most important, they create artistic grandeur, displeasing to many readers, beautiful to others.

It might be good to consider why Milton chose to write in such an ornate idiom. Perhaps the poet deliberately wanted his audience looking in two directions, first, toward the unfolding of events and, second, toward the detached view of the artist, who, while telling his tale, is also hinting at a whole larger than any particular part. Then, too, the story of Adam's and

Eve's Fall risks sentimentality. In the Old Testament, the oracular spareness in the telling diminishes the problem. An epic, however, cannot be spare. Milton could have extended his poem by including lots of detail about the original parents' daily life. But that solution would introduce a sweetness that Milton wants to limit. The note he searches for combines wonder and pity and regret with submission. It occurs most quietly and yet most richly in the ending of the poem. Part of that richness is its simplicity, contrasting with the grand idiom the poem uses almost throughout.

Thomas Mann considered the problem of sentimentality. In the short story *Tonio Kröger*, the titular character gives instructions on how to read a truly great work. There is a difference between art and great art, Mann has Kröger say to his artist friend, defending his detachment:

> "For so it is … feeling, warm, heartfelt feeling, is always banal and futile; only the irritations and icy ecstasies of the artist's corrupted nervous system are artistic. The artist must be unhuman, extra-human; he must stand in a queer aloof relationship to our humanity; only then is he in a position, I ought to say *only* so would he be tempted, to represent it, to present it, to portray it to good effect…. For sound natural feeling, say what you like, has no taste." Thomas Mann, *Tonio Kröger*

In *Paradise Lost,* one ear of the reader is on the unfolding of a plot, which, because it is full of sorrow, could easily become sentimental. The other ear is appreciating Milton's artistic deftness in solving the difficulties he had to overcome.

The divided hearing of the poem—now on the tale, now on the telling—has another advantage. It emphasizes the shift in keys when the narration moves from the central story to the four invocations in body of the poem. In *The Reason of Church Government*, Milton apologizes for referring to his own life.[27] One wonders then, why in these invocations,

---

27  John Milton, *Areopagtica and Other Writings,* ed. John Poole. "Perhaps I might seem too profuse to give any certain account of what the mind at home in the spacious circuits of her musing hath liberty to propose to herself, though of highest hope, and hardest attempting…" (p. 28). (Hereafter cited as *Other Writings.*)

Milton risks the especially grievous sentimentality of dwelling on his own spiritual struggle. But in fact these invocations resonate fugally with the goal of the whole epic: to define "what gives heroic name / To person or to poem" (Invocation, Book 9). As it turns out, artistic detachment merges into the long and high view of the Almighty as he looks down on man.

Because the subject of the poem is less the Fall than fallenness, its unity is hard to grasp. For some readers, the point lies in the human or human-like events of Books 1 and 2, Books 4 and 5, and Books 8, 9 and 10, because the human figures in those books can be construed as they would be in a novel. Thus, Satan is a strong and defiant revolutionary, punished unjustly by a tyrannical ruler. Adam is a good man tied to a rebellious wife. Eve is an energetic woman stifled by both God and by Adam.

At the beginning of the poem, Milton asks his muse to tell of "man's first disobedience / And the fruit, of that forbidden tree." On first reading, "fruit" is understood as the apple of the Tree of Knowledge, but on second reading, one wonders if "fruit" also means "consequences." In the fallen state, pride—or self-satisfaction, or desire to be admired, or unwillingness to accept authority, or self-pity—whatever one calls it—entangles human beings in futile efforts to find a clear path. Paradise is a painful memory of what might have been. If before the fall, God would send down one of his winged tutors to set the soul on the right path, now human beings are on their own, and the visits of God's messengers are few. The invocations take place not in the time of incidents leading up to the Fall, but in present—fallen—time, the time of the writing of the epic.

Because Adam's central mistake in eating the apple was a failure to understand that "reason is [the soul's] being" (5.487), Milton must get the reader to think in abstractions about what God, or the Godhead, or Being-with-God, means. In Book 3, God announces his plan for the course of human history, and also justifies it. Then in Books 5, 6, and 7, God shows what divine power means. He is almighty, as he must be, for only through his ultimate power can the human creature be confident that evil in the universe will be defeated. He is Being in the sense of an order that guarantees the balance and beauty of the material world; but He is also Being in the sense of the power to generate (Book 7), for a creation that can itself produce beauty will inspire gratitude. But most important are God's logically consistent principles, for only through consistency can He be reliable.

For Milton, "just seeing" the argument of a tale, as Conrad phrased it, has a dangerous vagueness because it lacks rational articulation. Milton makes sure to be explicit. God said that if Man disobeyed Him, He would put Man to death; Man did disobey him; therefore, God must stand by his principles: "Die he, or justice must" (3.210).

Having presented these principles, Milton then offers Book 8's more approachable Godhead or a more comfortable Being-with-God. Adam's conversation with Raphael is a Being-with-God in a genial "celestial colloquy" (8.455) between a generous tutor and a willing pupil. In the poem, the central metaphor for this colloquy is "Being-in-a-Garden." But because the metaphor of the garden concentrates on the immediate loveliness of Paradise, Milton must show, as he does in Book 7, that that loveliness is secondary to the miracle of the creation itself—its variety, mutual dependence, and self-sustaining order.

Intellectual principles also apply with Adam and Eve. Adam is a loving husband, but he is also the Rational Creature as opposed to the animals. For the Rational Creature, discipline of the soul requires living up to the distinction between human beings and beasts. Man is free; he is free because he can reason. Rationality is the basis of authority. Authority demands from Adam a sternness that is an imitation of God's. Human rationality, however, is not as consistent as God's. Being a lesser version of God in a world of marvelous beauty, Adam will misjudge his highest good; he does so when he calls Eve "the last and best / Of all God's works" (9.890). It is a hard truth for human beings that love generates the impulse to gratify; it is difficult for the human of superior reason to enforce his will with a beloved.

Eve is an allegorical figure as well as young woman who gardens. She is Beauty itself, Beauty as proportion and grace, the Christian version of Lucretius's *alma Venus,* "nurturing Venus." Eve moving through the garden tending her flowers governs their coming to maturity, in both their biology and the development of their souls. It is no surprise that when Satan beholds Eve in the garden, he stands "stupidly good" (9.465). His adoration of Beauty seems as justified as all the Petrarchan poetry of the Renaissance argued it was. But the order of the universe is a hierarchy. Adam's fate touches on the inevitable and painful choice in human love between devotion to God and devotion to a human beloved.

Although Plato's Truth, Beauty, and Good are all synonymous, Beauty is the one most likely to threaten the stability of that triangle. The human instinct to respond to the evocations of Beauty can be a danger because it speaks to intuitive understanding rather than rational understanding. Although beauty evokes a transcendent world, it is not capable of "giving an account," as Plato would have it. The two words, "stupidly good" that describe Satan's reaction to the sight of Eve suggest not only beauty's power to "draw the soul to good," in a phrase of one of Sidney's sonnets, but also its unsteadiness.

It is often said that Milton starts the poem with the fall of Satan because he was following the epic formula: begin in the middle of things. But Milton begins with Satan's "sense of injured merit" (1.98) because Satan is, from the start, in a state of confusion; it is not for nothing associates Satan with "mist" later in the poem (9.75, 180). Satan's confusion is stubbornly holding to his defiance of God because, in his mind, his outrage is justified. In a fugal echo, Adam voices to God a similar complaint: "Inexplicable / Thy justice seems" (10. 754–55). In the bonds of the wish for mercy without justice—claiming one is entitled to it—the soul is not thinking clearly.

The devils in hell *seem* like the kind of beings who can find the way out of their predicament; they are strong, confident, and brave. Showing contempt for those who, in their eyes, are sluggish and anxious, they think that a full life is holding power and basking in the admiration that it inspires. For the reader, it is hard to resist the bravery of the devils. Heroic defiance of a mightier power always rivets the attention. If at a later point in life, we read again Books 1 and 2, we reconsider those lines that earlier were so invigorating: "Fallen cherub, to be weak is miserable," "preferring / Hard liberty before the easy yoke / Of servile pomp"; "Better to reign in hell than serve in heaven." Then we understand that Milton started the poem with the devils loudly orating in hell because their state of mind is the worst kind of fallenness—the thrill of defiance without rational assessment of the goal.

Here, Milton is examining "Christian Humanism" that is so often invoked by intellectual historians to characterize the period of the Renaissance. For the classical tradition, the greatest human beings show wisdom and courage, and the human polity holds together because those with wisdom and courage hold positions of authority, which is most signaled by martial valor and political leadership. In the *Nicomachean Ethics*, Aristotle's great-souled man is confident of his right to be proud. This view of great-souledness is not in easy harmony with the Christian view. In the Christian tradition, human beings reach their fulfillment in obedience to God's command. The human polity holds together because its members agree to live by God's laws. Obedience to God might seem to be easier than becoming a man of classical virtue because obedience does not require the same courage and drive. On the other hand, obedience may be harder, for it requires self-denial and most important, humility. Great-souled men regard humility as degrading, as Satan's pronouncements in Books 1 and 2 of *Paradise Lost* show. To Satan, humility is groveling.

In the invocations of *Paradise Lost*, Milton is examining this fault line in the two parts of Christian Humanism, the classical separation of the intelligent and courageous from the unintelligent and cowardly, and a Christian embrace of each human being as an Everyman. When he wrote *Paradise Lost*, he, like Satan, was "in dubious battle" (1.401). In his early prose works, Milton shows a clear contempt for lack of intelligence. He could not decide who was more thickheaded, the English populace or the officials who governed them. He was also contemptuous of some of his readers: But this is got by throwing pearl to hogs," (Sonnet 12); "A book was writ of late called Tetrachordon ... some in file / Stand spelling false" (Sonnet 11); poems are often "waste from the pen of some vulgar amorist, or the trencher fury of a riming parasite" (*Of Education*); he feels disdain to be forced to leave his studies "to the club quotations with men whose learning and belief lies in marginal stuffings"[28]; he feels exasperated that "England hath had her noble achievements made small by the unskillful handling of monks and mechanics" (*Reason of Church Government*, Book 2).

With courage and contempt comes ambition, and the young Milton was also ambitious. While in his thirties and writing the *Areopagitica*, Milton thought God would bestow his praise on him for teaching the English people to awake to a new age in God's church. But at least some part of him knew that being a great spitter of tacks was not in harmony with Christian humility. In the *Areopagitica*, Milton admitted that his thoughts might have an "adventurous edge,"[29] and in the first invocation to *Paradise Lost*,

28  *Reason of Church Government*, in *Other Writings*, pp. 31–32.
29  *Areopagitica*, in *Other Writings*, p. 122.

he calls his poem an "adventurous song." In the *Areopagitica,* he admitted that he could also be accused of seeking fame. Further, in *Of Education,* Milton says that the goal of education is to make young men "brave and worthy patriots," "renowned and matchless men," and "famous to all ages."[30] All of these statements show admiration for the classical great-souled man.

About poetry, Milton is also divided. In *The Reason of Church Government,* he sees poetry's purpose as more or less Aristotelian therapy, to "allay the perturbations of the mind,[31] and set the affections in right tune" (where "affections" means "passions"). This description sounds like Aristotle's view that tragedy should arouse pity and fear and, through catharsis, purge the soul of these emotions; that is, tragedy should bring the spectators' souls to the great-souled man's calm. But, interestingly, in the same work, Milton says that poetry's purpose is descriptive, not therapeutic; it should give a psychological account, that is, describing the "wily subtleties and refluxes of man's thought" in evading self-knowledge and indulging self-justifying pride. In that description, the purpose of poetry is to show the movement of the mind as it struggles to see its confusion. This is what Milton sought to do in his invocations.

Milton's struggle between defiance and submission appears early in his poem *Lycidas,* an elegy for a classmate of Milton at Cambridge. About eighty years ago, John Crowe Ransome, in an influential essay, considered the liabilities in writing an elegy that calls attention to the poet himself. In Ransome's view, in doing so a poet does not keep decorum. The classical elegy, he argued, is a public statement of mourning that expresses the grief felt by all the mourners. When Milton should have been concentrating on the death of Edward Phillips, he was thinking about his career as a poet. Ransome had a point. Early in *Lycidas,* Milton worries about his own death ("So may some gentle Muse / With lucky words favor my destined urn" [line 20]), worries about his literary success in the world ("Fame is the goal that the clear spirit doth raise / That last infirmity of noble mind / To scorn delights and live laborious days" [lines 70–72]). He rails against the corruption of the false shepherds of the church ("What recks it them? What

30  *Of Education,* in *Other Writings,* p. 90.
31  *Reason of Church Government,* in *Other Writings,* p. 29.

need they? They are sped…. The hungry sheep look up and are not fed" [lines 122, 125]). When in the last eight lines, the poet switches to the third person ("Thus sang the uncouth swain to the oaks and rills" [line 188]), the speaker has a new composure ("Tomorrow to fresh woods and pastures new" [line 193]). But for Ransome, this change does not help; the poem is too personal, when, to keep decorum, it should be a public poem of consolation. (His is an interesting observation, for when modern students complain about Milton, it is the stylization that bothers them. For Ransome on *Lycidas*, the poem should have been *more* stylized.)

In the invocations to *Paradise Lost*, Milton seems to make the same error. He presents a struggle that is particular to him. The invocations to Books 3 and 7 are about his blindness, and Milton did in fact go blind. In Book 7's invocation, he talks about being "with darkness and with dangers round / And solitude," and in 1659 Milton was put on a proscription list for several months and had to be moved by his friends from house to house. Milton, however, expects us to distinguish between Milton-the-Poet and Milton-the-Pilgrim. Milton-the-Poet is regenerate; he is looking back at himself in an earlier stage, when he was the unregenerate Milton-the-Pilgrim, suffering from confusion in the soul. In making this distinction, Milton-the-Poet could create a story about Protestant Everyman's struggle to be a good Christian. He could dramatize a state of mind that, at the time of the epic's narration, the poet had outgrown. One might wonder, however, if the ending of the poem shows that the pilgrim-poet has resolved the struggle.

## 2. Resonant Forms

To mute the indecorous personal voice in the invocations, which risks the sentimentality of portraying his misery ("on evil days though fallen and on evil tongues"), Milton draws on other poetic forms that his readers would have known well, poetic forms that stylize personal feeling.

Perhaps the most loved poetic form of Milton's time was the sonnet. In Philip Sidney's sonnet sequence, Sidney calls himself Astrophil and the woman he addresses is Stella—that is, "star-lover" and "star." Stella was in fact an actual woman, one Penelope Devereux. We moderns, raised on the marriage novel, tend to particularize the "I" of these sonnets as a real individual man who loved a real individual woman, and our hearts tremble for a real, live love story (too many novels.) The classicization of the names diffuses the biographical reference. Sidney's story, then, depicts not his personal experience but rather the general story of unrewarded devotion. Romeo and Juliet are also stylized versions of a young couple in love; they do what youth always does—imagine that love guarantees a force field that will overcome obstacles. The pleasure in reading this poetry is appreciation of the clever alterations of the traditional story of love's anxiety, despondency, devotion, and loss.

In the last sonnet of Sidney's sequence, number 107, this stylization of feeling expresses precisely the emotions Milton, in the invocation to Book 3, also wants to express: admission of failure and longing.

> Stella, since thou so right a princess art
> Of all the powers which life bestows on me,
> That ere by them aught undertaken be
> They first resort unto that sovereign part;
> Sweet, for a while give respite to my heart,
> Which pants as though it still should leap to thee,
> And on my thoughts give thy lieutenancy
> To this great cause, which needs both use and art;
> And as a queen, who from her presence sends
> Whom she employs, dismiss from thee my wit,
> Till it hath wrought what thy own will attends.
> On servant's shame oft master's blame doth sit;
> Oh let not fools in me thy works reprove,
> And scorning say, "See what it is to love."

In this sonnet, the speaker addresses the beloved, asserting that the lady is his center of gravity, as a religious person would say to his God. The poem is only two sentences long, one eleven lines, the other three lines. The length of these sentences contributes to the feeling of resignation to the beloved's dismissal combined with a barely controlled longing to be near her. The charm of the poem is the stylization of the woe of loss and the woe of not being a better person.

For stylized emotion, Milton also draws on the Psalms, just as Sidney drew on the arc of feeling of Psalm 22. Sidney's line, "Which pants as though it still should leap to thee" echoes the thirsty soul of Psalm 42:

> As the hart brayeth for the rivers of the waters, so panteth my soul after thee, O God.
> 
> [2] My soul thirsteth for God, even for the living God: when shall I come and appear before the presence God?
> 
> [3] My tears have been my meat day and night, while they daily say unto me, Where is thy God?
> 
> [4] When I remembered these things, I poured out my very heart: for I had with the multitude, and led them into the house of God with the voice of singing and praise went with them to the house of God, as the multitude keepeth that feast.
> 
> [5] Why art thou cast down, O my soul, and inquiet within me? Wait on God: for I will yet give him thanks for the help of his presence.
> 
> [6] O my God, my soul is cast down within me, because I remember thee; therefore will I remember thee from the land of Jordan, and of the Hermonites, and from the hill Mizar.
> 
> [7] One deep calleth another deep by the noise of thy waterspouts: all thy waves and thy floods are gone over me.
> 
> [8] Yet the LORD will grant his loving kindness in the day, and in the night will I sing of him; even a prayer unto the God of my life.
> 
> [9] I will say unto God which is my rock, Why hast thou forgotten me? why go I mourning when the enemy oppresseth me?
> 
> [10] My bones are cut asunder while my enemies reproach, saying daily unto me, Where is thy God?
> 
> [11] Why art thou cast down, my soul? and why art thou disquieted within me? Wait on God, for I will give him thanks; he is my present help and my God.
> 
> (Geneva Bible, 1560)

The speaker here is asking for help from the greatest teacher, the "deep" or the "god which is my rock." His voice is the generalized voice of the "believer in despair," or "the believer needing spiritual assistance," or "the believer seeking acceptance."

In Sonnet 19, Milton follows again the psalmodic tradition. The poem has the same arc of feeling and the same generalized voice.

> When I consider how my light is spent,
> Ere half my days in this dark world and wide,
> And that one talent which is death to hide
> Lodged with me useless, though my soul more bent
> To serve therewith my Maker, and present
>  "Doth God exact day-labor, light denied?"
> I fondly ask. But Patience, to prevent
> That murmur, soon replies, "God doth not need
> Either man's work or His own gifts. Who best
> Bear His mild yoke, they serve Him best. His state
> Is kingly: thousands at His bidding speed,
> And post o'er land and ocean without rest;
> They also serve who only stand and wait."

In the octet of the sonnet, Milton has given grandeur to his complaint by casting it into a periodic sentence and then ending it with the querulous demand: "Doth God exact day labor, light denied," with all of the accusatory emphasis on "exact." When, in the sestet, he gets to the Christian answer to the octet's problem, Patience speaks out of the blue, chastising him in the simplest of sentences. The resemblance of her pronouncement to the stern voice of a Greek or Roman god reminds us of another genre that stylizes the voice—classical epic.

The generalized desolate worshiper of Psalm 22 belongs to a tradition with a very long ancestry—pastoral. Psalm 22 is a religious complaint poem that might be called "anti-pastoral."

> My God, my God, why hast thou forsaken me, and art so far
> from my health and from the words of my roaring?
> [2] O my God, I cry by day, but thou hearest not; and in the
> night, but have no audience.
> [3] But thou art holy, and doest inhabit the praises of Israel….

⁶ But I am a worm, and not a man; a shame of men, and the contempt of the people.

⁷ All they that see me have me in derision: they make a mowe [purse their lips] and nod the head, saying,

⁸ He trusted in the LORD that let him deliver him; let him save him, seeing he loveth him. . . .

¹² Many young bulls have compassed me: mighty bulls of Bashan have closed me about.

¹³ They gape upon me with their mouths, as a ramping and a roaring lion.

¹⁴ I am like water poured out, and all my bones are out of joint: my heart is like wax; it is molten in the midst of my bowels.

¹⁵ My strength is dried up like a potsherd; and my tongue cleaveth to my jaws; and you have brought me into the dust of death.

¹⁶ For dogs have compassed me: the assembly of the wicked have enclosed me: they pierced mine hands and my feet.

¹⁷ I may tell all my bones: yet they behold and look upon me. . . .

¹⁹ Be not thou far off, O LORD, my strength; hasten thee to help me.

²⁰ Deliver my soul from the sword; my desolate soul from the power of the dog.

²¹ Save me from the lion's mouth: and answer me in saving me from the horns of the unicorns. . . .

Feeling surrounded, besieged, attacked—Milton pours these reactions into his description of the devils in Book 1. The images of "water" and "wax"— or, not having a firm shape—characterize the devils in Book 2, insofar as they have no clear idea of how they should go forward: should we fight defiantly (Moloch)? Should we find a way to get used to our pain (Belial)? Should we act like Hobbesian man and "compose our present evils" (Mammon)?

What is the common balm for this desolation? A garden, of course, the happy fields and ease of pastoral, the imagery of which plays such an important part in Isaiah and in the Song of Solomon, and likewise in the very next psalm after Psalm 22:

WHERE THE MUSES STILL HAUNT

The LORD is my shepherd; I shall not want.

² He maketh me to rest in green pastures, and leadeth me by the still waters.

³ He restoreth my soul and leadeth me in the paths of righteousness for his name's sake.

⁴ Yea, though I should walk through the valley of the shadow of death, I will fear no evil: for thou art with me; thy rod and thy staff they comfort me.

⁵ Thou doest prepare a table before me in the presence of mine adversaries: thou doest anoint mine head with oil, and my cup runneth over.

⁶ Doubtless kindness and mercy shall follow me all the days of my life: and I shall remain a long season in the house of the Lord.

In the shift from Psalm 22 to Psalm 23, Milton sees an artistic problem. One minute the speaker is in a state of isolation and fear. In the next, he feels protected. An epic, however, cannot express the change in the soul by inserting a blank space on the page and simply starting over again with a new poem. In his epic, Milton had to consider how he was going to manage this transition.

### 3. Invocation to Book 1—The Pilgrim and the Poet

In the first invocation, the signals that Milton is imitating classical epic are quite clear. When he addresses the Muse ("Sing, heavenly Muse"), he is recalling the opening line of the *Iliad*. The first 16 lines of the poem, which summarize the action of the whole, imitate Virgil's opening to the *Aeneid*, which likewise summarizes the action of that epic. The first note is one of energy and confidence in warrior greatness. First, he announces that his project is bold; he says he "intends to *soar* above the Aonian mount," and he is going to do something "*unattempted* yet in prose or rhyme." Then, too, the last line—"And justify the ways of God to man"— has all the grand decisiveness of the classical maker of epics.

On first reading, one might say the first part of Book I's invocation is a good example of Renaissance ease in mixing a classical and Christian tradition. But then comes something entirely unclassical. Besides the Muse, Milton also calls on the "Spirit who doest prefer / Before all temples th'upright heart and pure." After the declaration of the theme in the rolling pentameter line of the 16-line sentence, the sentences suddenly become very short, and the lines are cut up with caesuras and uneven rhythm: "What in me is dark, illumine; what is low / Raise and support." Earlier, the poet intended to "soar / Above the Aonian mount"; now he asks to be "raised." "[D]ark" here is premonitory, for when we enter the plot of the poem itself, it is in the midst of darkness with Satan. Oddly, however, in the last lines, the poet is once again bold: "That to the *height* of this *great argument*" has the ring of the classical hero's ambition and his confidence. He hopes to "*assert* eternal providence," and, drawing on the a stately regular meter in the last line, he plans to "justify the ways of God to man"

Only on second reading does the inconsistency register, and we understand that the poetic voice is divided between Milton-the-Pilgrim and Milton-the-Poet. The first is a divided soul; the second is presiding over the confusions of that divided soul.

> Of man's first disobedience, and the fruit
> Of that forbidden tree, whose mortal taste
> Brought death into the world and all our woe
> With loss of Eden, till one greater man
> Restore us, and regain the blissful seat
> Sing, heavenly muse, that on the secret top
> Of Oreb, or of Sinai, didst inspire
> That Shepherd, who first taught the chosen seed
> In the beginning how the heavens and earth
> Rose out of chaos; or if Sion hill
> Delight thee more, and Siloa's brook that flowed
> Fast by the Oracle of God, I thence
> Invoke thy aid to my adventurous song,
> That with no middle flight intends to soar
> Above the Aonian mount, while it pursues
> Things unattempted yet in prose or rhyme,
> And chiefly Thou, O spirit, that dost prefer
> Before all temples the upright heart and pure,

Instruct me, for thou know'st; thou from the first
Wast present, and with mighty wings outspread
Dove-like satst brooding on the vast abyss
And mad'st it pregnant: What in me is dark
Illumine, what is low raise and support,
That to the height of this great argument
I may assert eternal providence,
And justify the ways of God to men.

Milton-the-Pilgrim shows bravado: he will "soar with no middle flight." At the end of Book 2 and at the end of Book 4, soaring is what Satan says the God's angels are too timid to do.

When he boasts that he going to write something that has been "unattempted yet in prose or rhyme," Milton is echoing a line in the second stanza of the introduction to Ariosto's *Orlando Furioso*.

Dirò d'Orlando in un medesmo tratto
cosa non detta in prosa mai, né in rima:

I will tell of Orlando at the same time, *things not before said in prose or rhyme.*" Significantly, for the ordinary "said" (*detta*) of Ariosto, Milton substitutes "attempted": "things *unattempted* yet in prose or rhyme." In the change from *said* to *attempted,* Milton introduces the laden word *tempt,* and later in Book 1, Milton practically forces the association with Satan when he has Satan say that God "tempted our attempt" (line 642).

Once when I was teaching Milton, a student who had been silent for a while, gazing out the window, turned his head and blurted out, "Who does Milton think he is, 'justifying the ways of God to man'?" Indeed, how could a mere mortal ever explain God? This student led me to much reflection on the poem.

## 4. Invocation to Book 3

In the invocation to Book 3, Milton-the-Poet clarifies matters. In the first invocation, he had mixed genres to show that the speaker, Milton-the-Pilgrim, is in a state of confusion. From the point of view of Milton-the-Poet, however, his poem is an "adventure" in mixing genres in order to describe what he called in the *Reason of Church Government* the "wily subtleties and the refluxes of man's thought." His former self was confused between a classical and Christian ethos. He is still confused in the invocation to Book 3. Lacking a firm shape, it falls from adoration to boasting and then to complaining.[32] While the first invocation announced an ambitious project, here the launch into a novel kind of art form wobbles unsteadily. This one begins as a prayer with the ecstatic longing of some of the Psalms and of Petrarchan sonnets:

> Hail holy light, offspring of Heaven firstborn,
> Or of the eternal coeternal beam
> May I express thee unblamed, since God is light,
> And never but in unapproached light
> Dwelt from eternity, dwelt then in thee,
> Bright effluence of bright essence increate?
> Or hear'st thou rather pure ethereal stream,
> Whose fountain who shall tell? before the Sun,
> Before the heavens thou wert, and at the voice
> Of God, as with a Mantle didst invest
> The rising world of waters dark and deep,
> Won from the void and formless infinite.

Like Psalm 42 and like some Petrarchan sonnets, the invocation starts with the poet barely able to breathe with wonder, and then on that breathless plane, muses about his definitions; is God light or the Word? The lines chant repetitions: "light ... light ... light," "dwelt ... dwelt," "bright ... bright." Then "dark," both as a sound and as an idea, starts to repeat, "waters dark and deep ... Stygian pool ... obscure sojourn ... through utter and through middle darkness ... dark descent ...." Then the speaker feels his confidence returning; he was in hell, but he managed to climb out of it, borrowing a virtual quotation from Virgil: "hoc opus, hic labor est" (translated literally, "this is the work, this is the labor").

---

32  Milton, *The Reason of Church Government*, in *Areopagitica and Other Writings*, op. cit., p. 29.

> Thee I revisit now with bolder wing,
> Escaped the Stygian pool, though long detained
> In that obscure sojourn, while in my flight
> Through utter and through middle darkness borne
> With other notes then to the Orphean lyre
> I sung of chaos and eternal night,
> Taught by the heavenly muse to venture down
> The dark descent, and up to reascend,
> *Though hard and rare.* (Italics added)

Back in Book I, Milton called his song "adventurous" (1.17); later in the poem, after Eve has eaten the fruit, Adam will call Eve "adventurous" (9.921); Satan is referred to by the devils in hell as "their great adventurer" (10.440). The ambiguity in "venture"—perhaps an undertaking entered into with trepidation, but perhaps an invigorating challenge—suggests the confusion in the pilgrim's soul. On the one hand, the pilgrim talks as if his escape from the "Stygian pool" was his own devising and that he was as brave and steady as Aeneas in accomplishing it. On the other hand, he falls almost immediately afterward. Adventures are risky.

In the second section of the invocation, the pilgrim at first seems to be satisfied with his new location above ground. He feels the warmth of a sun that nurtures human beings and has dinner with their earth ("at ev'n / Sups with the ocean" [5.425–26]). Calmly, he "revisits" the holy light, once "with bolder wing" and a second time "safe." But hardly does the poet sound grateful—"Thee I revisit safe / And feel thy sov'ran vital lamp"—when an emotional wave hits him. He wanders—or errs, or falls—as uncontrollable thoughts catch him unawares:

> Thee I revisit safe, but thou
> Revisit'st not these eyes, that roll in vain
> To find thy piercing ray and find no dawn;
> So thick a drop serene hath quenched their orbs,
> Or dim suffusion veiled.

Although the pilgrim has used his imagination to pull himself out of the darkness, he has not escaped feeling unjustly treated. He reminds himself that he has consolations:

> Yet not the more
> Cease I to wander where the Muses haunt
> Clear spring, or shady grove, or sunny hill,
> Smit with the love of sacred song, but chief
> Thee, Sion, and the flowery brooks beneath
> That wash thy hallowed feet, and warbling flow,
> Nightly I visit....

The landscape he wanders through promises comfort ("or shady grove or sunny hill"), but then the old ambition for fame returns:

> nor sometimes forget
> Those other two equaled with me in fate,
> So were I equaled with them in renown,
> Blind Thamyris and blind Maeonides,
> And Tiresias and Phineus, prophets old.
> Then feed on thoughts, that voluntary move
> Harmonious numbers, as the wakeful bird
> Sings darkling and, in shadiest covert hid,
> Tunes her nocturnal note.

Others were blind also, but they gained "renown." He too may gain renown. He renews his song. "[I]n shadiest covert hid" is this invocation's version of Psalm 23's "thou preparest a table before me in the presence of mine enemies," but without Psalm 23's serenity. Indeed, the poet has exchanged his "bolder wing" for singing in the dark.

The emotional instability continues. For the briefest moment, he is content: "Thus with the year/ Seasons return...." But again, despair attacks. He may feel the change in the seasons, but he cannot feel the change from dark to light:

> Thus with the year
> Seasons return, but not to me returns
> Day, or the sweet approach of ev'n or morn,
> Or sight of vernal bloom or summer's rose,
> Or flocks, or herds, or human face divine,

> But cloud instead, and ever-during dark
> Surrounds me, from the cheerful ways of men
> Cut off, and for the Book of knowledge fair
> Presented with a Universal blank
> Of Nature's works to me expunged and razed,
> And wisdom at one entrance quite shut out.

In these lines, the poet's "fall" lands with a cry on "Day." Its placement as the first syllable in the line forces a contrast with "seasons" in the previous line. The change of seasons he could sense without being able to see, but the ordinary changing of the light between day and night is denied. The repetitions of "or" in "[o]r sight of vernal bloom or summer's rose / Or flocks or herds or human face divine" signal not delight, rather a helpless collapse. He then implores the light, as he did earlier, but this time gratefully, mixing pastoral and vision in the resonant phrase "plant eyes."

> So much the rather thou celestial light
> Shine inward, and the mind through all her powers
> Irradiate; there plant eyes, all mist from thence
> Purge and disperse, that I may see and tell
> Of things invisible to mortal sight.

The word *mist* rings ominously because we are on our second reading and we know that in Book 9, in which Satan tempts Eve, he "involved himself in a mist." Milton, the fallen wayfarer, may be in a mist here as well, indulging in the human tendency to imagine that one has mastered the darkness on one's own ("thee I revisit now / with bolder wing"), when in fact the surest safety can only be bestowed.

This invocation fugally resonates with the ending of Book 9, where Adam and Eve bitterly lament their fates and accuse each other. Adam, like Milton-the-Pilgrim of Book 3's invocation, wants to live "in some glade / Obscured." He accuses Eve of luring him into death with her; Eve accuses Adam of not having forbidden her more sternly: "Thus they in mutual accusation spent / The fruitless hours; but neither self-condemning, / And of their vain contest appeared no end." The emotional ups and downs of the invocation to Book 3 is also fugal variation on Book 2, where Satan, on

188

leaving Hell, is blown around the universe as he seeks to find God's newly created world. Finally, the invocation also anticipates Satan's famous soliloquy to the sun in Book 4, where he admits he basks in the sun's warming rays but rejects the source of that comforting power.

## 5. Invocation to Book 7

The next invocation shows the same instabilities as those in the invocation to Book 3 yet in a new key. The fall is less turbulent, more searching. The pilgrim still wishes to fly, not above the Aonian mount but "above the Olympian hill" and "[a]bove the flight of Pegasean wing," but the goal now has something of a Platonic ring to it—"the meaning, not the name." Although the children of God live in a world that is constantly appealing to the senses, they may, Raphael tells Adam, if they understand why they should be obedient, rise to the world of angels. Raphael presents this task as not onerous. After the fall, however, this gentle rise is no longer possible. Indeed, the invocation ends with a differentiation between Urania and the classical muse who could not defend Orpheus. Milton calls this latter muse an "empty dream."

> Descend from Heaven, Urania, by that name
> If rightly thou art called, whose voice divine
> Following, above the Olympian hill I soar,
> Above the flight of Pegasean wing.
> The meaning, not the name I call: for thou
> Nor of the Muses nine, nor on the top
> Of old Olympus dwell'st, but heavenly born.

While the invocation to Book 3 began with praise of the light as if the pilgrim were stunned in admiration, this invocation starts on a lower plane and asks for the Muse to descend to him, bringing a song Urania sang with her sister Wisdom.

> Before the hills appeared or fountain flowed,
> Thou with eternal Wisdom didst converse,
> Wisdom thy sister, and with her didst play

> In presence of the almighty Father, pleased
> With thy celestial song. Up led by thee
> Into the Heaven of Heavens I have presumed,
> An earthly guest, and drawn empyreal air,
> Thy tempering;

The pilgrim is noticeably deferent. Instead of suggesting, as in Book 3, that he had imitated Aeneas in descending to the dark pit, albeit "taught by the muse," here he emphasizes the assistance of Urania ("up led" by her) and—notably—requests her further help. Now he relinquishes his soaring and asks to be returned to his "native element," accepting, it seems, life in a fallen world.

> with like safety guided down
> Return me to my native element,
> Lest from this flying steed unreined, (as once
> Bellerophon, though from a lower clime)
> Dismounted, on the Aleian field I fall
> Erroneous there to *wander* and forlorn. (Italics added)

In Book 3, the falls are like attacks, where bitterness suddenly invades the calm: "Thee I revisit safe .... But thou / Revisit'st not these eyes that roll in vain" (Book 3). Here, however, the poet, aware that he is unsteady, asks for help lest he fall again. Words resonate with danger: *wander, forlorn,* and especially *fall*. He accepts a "mortal voice" that is neither hoarse (presumably like the bold rhetoricians of the devils' "grand consult" of Book 2) nor "mute" (like the bird in "shadiest covert hid.")

> Half yet remains unsung, but narrower bound
> Within the visible diurnal sphere;
> Standing on earth, not rapt above the pole,
> More safe I sing with mortal voice, unchanged
> To hoarse or mute....

He prefers his native element to soaring through the universe, "rapt above the pole." In the sphere designed for human beings, he is "safe," "*standing* on earth," with all the resonance with Adam's lines in Book 8: "up I sprung, / As thitherward endeavoring and upright/ *Stood* on my feet." The pilgrim speaks of a new ease, anticipating the luxurious flora of the descriptions of Paradise in Book 7, and also Raphael's reassurance that an obedient life on earth is the central human concern.

But, again, the hell of despair and alienation from God overwhelm him:

> though fallen on evil days,
> On evil days though fallen, and evil tongues,
> In darkness and with dangers compassed round,
> And solitude.

The mind skids again in helpless repetition: "though fallen on evil days, / On evil days though fallen, and evil tongues." In the earlier part of the invocation, Milton visited as "an earthly guest" in heaven. Subsequently, Milton-the-Pilgrim asks not for the muse who inspires poets to "adventure" ("Taught by the muse to venture down") but for Urania, the muse who governs the universe, and who perhaps will govern his soul. Still, the invocation ends facing a blank wall:

> Yet not alone while thou
> Visit'st my slumbers nightly or when morn
> Purples the east. Still govern thou my song,
> Urania, and fit audience find, though few.
> But drive far off the barbarous dissonance
> Of Bacchus and his revelers, the race
> Of that wild rout that tore the Thracian bard
> In Rhodope, where woods and rocks had ears
> To rapture, till the savage clamor drowned
> Both harp and voice, nor could the muse defend
> Her son. So fail not thou, who thee implores:
> For thou art Heavenly, she an empty dream.

In the invocation to Book 3, he felt safe "in shadiest covert hit." Now the darkness is threatening. As the young author of the *Areopagitica*, Milton thought that the mind's eagerness to wander was a gift from

God, "who gives us minds that can *wander* beyond all limit and satiety." In the invocation to Book 3, wandering was a source of consolation: "Then not the more/ Cease I to wander where the muses haunt" (lines 26–27). Here in the invocation to Book 7, he has renounced wandering and accepted his earthly station, though that acceptance is accompanied by feeling lost. The soliloquy ends with a plea ("who thee implores") and with what seems to be renunciation of poetry. Significantly, the "muse" is differentiated into two kinds, one the classical and the other the Christian. The classic muse could not "defend /Her son"; the "heavenly" muse is more trustworthy. Here the poet is ready to renounce his old allegiance to the ethos of the classical epic poet but has nothing to put in its place.

### 6. Invocation to Book 9

When in Book 1 Satan lay on the lake of fire and told Belial that "to be weak is miserable," he felt the same bewilderment that Milton feels at the end of the invocation to Book 7. Milton-the-Pilgrim does not, however, make commitments that will lead only to self-destruction, as Satan does in Book 4, "evil be thou my good." He does not boldly assert, as Satan does in Book 1, that "The mind is its own place and of itself / Can make a hell of heaven, a heaven of hell." Still, it is hard not to surmise that part of Milton-the-Pilgrim enjoyed writing the bold and defiant words he gave to Satan and his comrades in the earlier books, for they have the same tenor as the anger in the *Areopagitica*. Now he accuses his former self of self-indulgence. The word "indulgent" sounds in the third line of the next invocation. It is used to describe a "rural repast" with an angel, an event that will never occur again.

The invocation to Book 9 starts as the promise to begin a new life.

> No more of talk where God or angel guest
> With man, as with his friend, familiar used
> To sit indulgent and with him partake
> Rural repast, permitting him the while
> Venial discourse unblamed; I now must change
> Those notes to tragic: foul distrust and breach

> Disloyal on the part of man, revolt
> And disobedience; on the part of heaven
> Now alienated, distance and distaste,
> Anger and just rebuke, and judgment given,
> That brought into this world a world of woe,
> Sin and her shadow death, and misery,
> Death's harbinger.

The expression "now I must" announces a duty. The poet sees that the Fall brought misery not just to him but to humanity generally. When he reaches the end of the list of what he must face, the poet seems to choke: "which brought into the world a world of woe."

If in the invocation to Book 7, government of the soul was the aim ("Still govern thou my song"), Milton now seems to have achieved it. He will forgo singing of what is gone, conversations in a beautiful garden with an angel. That activity was a dream.

> Sad task, yet argument
> Not less but more heroic than the wrath
> Of stern Achilles on his foe pursued
> Thrice fugitive about Troy wall, or rage
> Of Turnus for Lavinia disespoused,
> Or Neptune's ire or Juno's, that so long
> Perplexed the Greek and Cytherea's son,
> If answerable style I can obtain
> Of my celestial patroness, who deigns
> Her nightly visitation unimplored
> And dictates to me slumbering or inspires
> Easy my unpremeditated verse.

He will reject the old classical epic and its embrace of pastoral because the one depicts a heroism that is a delusion and the other a release from suffering that is also a delusion. The first three of the rejected examples are of epic anger: the sternness of Achilles, the rage of Turnus. The resolution increases, but it is unsteady. He might be able to continue singing *if … if …* Urania will continue with her help, for, in some sense, he says, her help might be considered his due, since he has pondered the question of a proper subject for a long time and because he now sees more clearly the failures of traditional heroism.

> Since first this subject for heroic song
> Pleased me, long choosing and beginning late,
> Not sedulous by nature to indite
> Wars, hitherto the only argument
> Heroic deemed, chief mastery to dissect
> With long and tedious havoc fabled knights
> In battle feigned; the better fortitude
> Of patience and heroic martyrdom
> Unsung, or to describe races and games,
> Or tilting furniture, emblazoned shields,
> Impresas quaint, caparisons and steeds;
> Bases and tinsel trappings, gorgeous Knights
> At joust and tournament; then marshalled feast
> Served up in hall with sewers and seneschals:
> The skill of artifice or office mean,
> Not that which justly gives heroic name
> To person or to poem. Me of these
> Nor skilled nor studious,
> Remains, sufficient of itself to raise
> That name, unless an age too late, or cold
> Climate or years damp my intended wing
> Depressed, and much they may, if all be mine,
> Not hers who brings it nightly to my Ear.

Having rejected the subjects for epic, which appear to him now as so many toys, a greater difficulty remains. He must find expression for the "higher argument" of patience. Perhaps he will not succeed; England is cold and damp; he himself is old. Furthermore, the pastoral comfort of the nightingale's singing is gone, as are the pastoral memories of the coming of morning and evening, vernal bloom, summer's rose, purple clouds in the east. Here, the demeanor of Milton-the-Pilgrim anticipates Adam's meeting with Eve after she has eaten the apple: "From his slack hand the garland wreath'd for Eve / Down dropp'd, and all the faded roses shed: / Speechless he stood and pale." In Homer, there is nothing so bad that a song cannot be made of it. But here Milton seems to have reached an impasse—his song is silent.

The "higher argument" will not come from Milton as the epic singer.

> Me of these
> Nor skilled nor studious, higher argument
> Remains, sufficient of itself to raise
> That name.

It will come from its truth, "sufficient of itself to raise / That name." Indeed, if the song is his it will fail; it will raise itself only if it belongs to Urania.

> if all be mine,
> Not hers who brings it nightly to my ear.

Unrecognized by Milton-the-Pilgrim, however, is the power of a confession to prepare the soul for the inspiration of a higher muse. Instead, he simply puts down his pen. In sum, in the invocation to Book 9, the exhilaration of imitating classical epic's high style and the exhilaration of meeting artistic challenges has given way to waiting.

## 7. The Ending of the Poem: Pastoral in a New Key

We arrive at the most beautiful of all the beautiful passages in *Paradise Lost*, the ending. The Archangel Michael has assured Adam that although he and Eve can never return to Paradise, they will find a "paradise within … happier far." Eve echoes this assurance when she says that to go with Adam is to carry Paradise within her. She trusts the archangel's promise that through her will be born the greatest consolation for human beings—a savior who will redeem humanity. But the strikingly subdued tone of the last lines is less one of hope than of resignation to the future events that Michael tells of in Books 11 and 12. Human beings will never again feel at home on the earth. Adam and Eve are now silent, and the angels are the ones who act:

195

So spake our mother Eve, and Adam heard
Well pleased, but answered not; for now too nigh
The archangel stood, and from the other hill
To their fixed station, all in bright array,
The Cherubim descended, on the ground
Gliding meteorous, as evening mist
Risen from a river o'er the marish glides,
And gathers ground fast at the laborer's heel
Homeward returning. High in front advanced
The brandished sword of God before them blazed
Fierce as a comet, which with torrid heat,
And vapor as the Libyan air adust,
Began to parch that temperate clime; whereat
In either hand the hastening Angel caught
Our lingering Parents and to the Eastern Gate
Led them direct, and down the cliff as fast
To the subjected plain, then disappeared.

The passage starts with short declarative sentences. The angels perform their job expeditiously; they descend like a mist; they take the human beings by the hand; they lead them down; they disappear. The two human beings are then left alone:

They, looking back, all the Eastern side beheld
Of Paradise, so late their happy seat,
Waved over by that flaming brand, the gate
With dreadful faces thronged and fiery arms.
Some natural tears they dropped, but wiped them soon:
The world was all before them, where to choose
Their place of rest, and providence their guide;
They hand in hand, with wandering steps and slow,
Through Eden took their solitary way.

In comparison to the purposeful activity of the angels, the human beings are small and passive, caught in the gathering and collecting of Milton's long sentence, which here does not move in large waves but with even regularity. Any reassurances are wrapped in ambiguity. The angel's descent is compared to an evening "mist," itself ominous, that "o'er the marish glides" as if it were a snake. Its shapeless form *gathers* round the laborer's heel," perhaps an allusion to Christ's prophecy of the harm that Eve will inflict on the serpent (10.181), but the "gathers" sounds like pursuit and capture. The "Libyan air adust" is also ominous. It marks the end of the fertility of Paradise and echoes God's curse on Adam in Genesis. But it suggests also hope, because, according to Isaiah, dust will be the serpent's meat, which the serpents will compulsively eat, as they do in Book 11. The human pair sets off for a "place of rest," but their steps are "wandering ... and slow." The sentences are short, and the diction is simple. Perhaps "dazed and solemn" is a proper description of the tone of this ending.

I have heard teachers of art history grumble about their students' papers, which are—these teachers say—effusive and lamentably vague. The students gasp, "This painting is magnificent!" But there is little else one can say about the ending of *Paradise Lost*. The poem's energy, which seethes and exults and laments throughout 12 books, now accepts that the idyllic past is gone.

Most significant of all is the poet's retreat from the poem. The five regularly spaced invocations set up the expectation of a valediction, as at the end of *Lycidas*; but here there is none. The poet ceases to dramatize a first-person account of the "refluxes of [his] thought." How easy it would have been for the regenerate Milton to declare his renunciation of his former hope to soar above the Aonian mount! Instead, center stage is given to the two exiles, who depart in silence.

## 8. The End Is in the Beginning: Pastoral in Search of a New Resonance

The principle that the second reading sees deeper into a work is important in appreciating how Milton redefined pastoral. The epic similes that occur at the beginning of the poem have a mysterious poignancy about them. On the one hand, they are, like pastoral generally, a relief from the high-flown rhetoric of the devils. In his Tuscan hills, Galileo is at peace as he peers out toward a planet "to descry new lands" (1.286–91). The "belated peasant" (1.783) returning home in the evening has a moon for "arbitress," and the fairy elves he sees are a charming vision. The little sailor on the Norway foam throwing out his anchor believes he has found safety (1.200–208). But all three of these similes have another side. Galileo exploring the heavens is failing to attend to what "what "lies before [him] in daily life," as Raphael later warns Adam about star-gazing. The peasant enjoying the sight of the fairy elves, "sees, / Or *dreams* he sees," and "at once with joy and *fear* his heart rebounds." The little sailor on the Norway foam prefigures the human ignorance of the monstrous size of evil; he *thinks* he is safe, but he has anchored his boat not to an island but to a large serpent of the deep. The sun "[l]ooking through the horizontal misty air" (1.595) suggests a satanic fog obscuring a clear vision. When Mulciber fell "from morn / To noon ... from noon to dewy eve, / A summer's day" (1.742–45), the subsequent account had errors. In these examples, pastoral ease is mixed with delusion. With the epic similes in Homer's *Iliad*, the poet uses pastoral images to offer a reprieve from the horrors of battle; one can just "turn aside" and focus on something else. Milton had something else in mind.

The similes in the opening book of *Paradise Lost* express the psychological state of fallenness. For Milton, pastoralism promises an ease that is permanent, but which in a fallen world can never be permanent. In his epic, he asks the reader to ponder whether pastoralism is escapism. When the Fall destroyed the mutual courtesy and affection of God's creation (the sun who sups with the ocean, the seas that bring fragrance), then human beings began to swing helplessly between an unknown world they are being exiled to and the memory of a garden perfect for colloquies with wise counselors.

When a second reading sees the ambiguity in these pastoral passages, it leads to speculations about another, larger ambiguity. The imitation of Homer and Virgil in the opening of the poem declares the poet's intention to compete with those great predecessors by writing things "unattempted yet in prose or rhyme." The ending, however, renounces not only the self-assurance of epic high style but also the lyric pastoral, for like those passages when the *Iliad* "turns aside," pastoral can seduce its reader into thinking fallenness can be overcome just by not thinking about it. In the invocation to Book 7, Milton-the-Pilgrim fears coming down to the plain, "erroneous there to wander and forlorn"; similarly, Adam's and Eve's steps at the end are "wandering ... and slow." "Wander" might imply "ease in a garden" or "being at a loss." In the poem's ending, Milton seems to suggest both meanings. "Ease in a garden" may come from the promised guidance of providence, but "being at a loss" is suggested in the slow steps of Adam and Eve as they leave paradise.

There is no escape from fallenness. Perhaps the two most haunting passages in the poem anticipate the Fall long before the Fall has happened. In these passages, Milton is pulling together disparate parts of the poem. In Book 4, long before the moment in Book 9 when Adam and Eve will eat the apple, Milton describes paradise. He says it was even more beautiful than the field of Enna in Sicily:

> Not that fair field
> Of Enna, where Proserpine gathering flowers
> Herself a fairer flower by gloomy Dis
> Was gathered, which cost Ceres all that pain
> To seek her through the world.... (4.268–72)

The passage elicits an intake of breath; we know what is coming. Milton's rolling line, which requires our full attention, is thoughtfully keeping from view the misery to come. But then Milton reminds the reader of that misery, gently but mournfully, in "gloomy Dis" and "all that pain"—phrases that groan with sorrow. There is a similar passage in Book 9:

> O much deceived, much failing, hapless Eve
> Of thy presumed return! Event perverse!
> Thou never from the hour in Paradise
> Found either sweet repast or sound repose. (9.404–407)

"Sweet repast or sound repose": How full of weeping is the elegiac fall of the repetition. Even before the poetic Fall has occurred in the poem, the reader should remember it has already happened. If art offers us beauty, Milton thought the greatest beauty is allied with truth and that the truth is austere. In the chapter on the *Iliad*, I argued the Homer's poem was an elegy. Milton's poem, too, is an elegy, an elegy for a purity that was as natural as breathing—or more properly, *almost* as natural as breathing. Eventually, after much suffering, the Almighty will bring "through the world's wilderness *long wandered man / Safe to eternal paradise of rest*" (12.313–14; italics added). Milton took the poetic of heroism and of pastoral ease and created a new poetics of wandering.

# PURITY IN THE MODERN WORLD

## *1. What* Billy Budd *May Mean*

The image of Billy Budd hanged on the yard arm in the "full rose of the dawn" is so powerful a moment in Melville's story that it is hard not to think that Melville intended it as the story's center, to signal that Billy as Christ is the key to this dense tale:

> Billy stood facing aft. At the penultimate moment, his words, his only ones, the only words unobstructed in the utterance, were these: "God bless Captain Vere!" Syllables so unanticipated in the utterance coming from one with the ignominious hemp around his neck—syllables too delivered in the clear melody of a singing bird on the point of launching from the twig—had a phenomenal effect, not unenhanced by the rare personal beauty of the young sailor, spiritualized now through late experiences so poignantly profound....
>
> The hull, deliberately recovering from the periodic roll to leeward, was just regaining an even keel, when the last signal, a preconcerted dumb one, was given. At the same moment it chanced that the vapory fleece hanging low in the East was shot through with a soft glory as of the fleece of the Lamb of God seen in mystical vision, and simultaneously therewith, watched by the wedged mass of upturned faces, Billy ascended; and. ascending, took the full rose of the dawn.[33]

33  *Herman Melville: Billy Budd, Sailor and Other Stories*, introduction by O. Frederick Busch (New York: Penguin Books, 1986), Chapter 25.

Melville's prose should be appreciated: the images of the beautiful sailor, the vapory fleece of the clouds that seem to have a religious meaning, the mixture of hard reality with the blithe expectation of release ("of a singing bird launching from a twig), the ambiguity of "ascended" and the symbolic richness of "rose of the dawn." The scene could be that of the Crucifixion— the lone body high on the cross and the crowd of stunned onlookers below.

There is also, surely, a Christian hint in the singing bird "on the point of launching from the twig," which echoes a line near the end of Andrew Marvell's "The Garden" and suggests the soul's longing for heaven.

> Here at the fountain's sliding foot,
> Or at some fruit tree's mossy root,
> Casting the body's vest aside,
> My soul into the boughs does glide;
> There like a bird it sits and sings,
> Then whets, and combs its silver wings;
> And, till prepar'd for longer flight,
> Waves in its plumes the various light.

Melville later refers to another of Marvell's poems when he explains how Vere got the nickname "Starry Vere." The bird might be Billy Budd, who, at his death, is serenely going to the next world. For him, the "longer flight" is not to be feared.

Details in the story support the view that the heart of the tale has something to do with religion. Billy's opposite, Claggart, is clearly a figure of evil, human reason degraded to mere cunning and driven by an envy rivaled only by Milton's Satan. In a letter from Melville to Hawthorne in the 1850s, however, Melville says he rejects the notion of a benevolent God. With this information, the reader finds significance in the fact that Melville has Billy's body rise only halfway up the yard arm; the manner of Billy's death, then, becomes a symbol of Melville's *doubts* about religion. Still, if the reader trusts Melville's artistry, then every detail of the story should fit with the whole Melville is driving toward. Neither a religious interpretation nor an interpretation skeptical of religion explains why Melville spends a large amount of time on the advent of steamships, the French Revolution, the mutiny on the Norse, the reading habits of various men, the practice of impressment, and the heroics of Nelson.

By a third interpretation, the concentration should not be on Melville's beliefs but on Vere. Vere, a reader of arcane books, makes an error in judgment. When he might have postponed Billy's trial until the ship could reach a military court on land, he overestimates the threat of the enemy, insists on a "drumhead court," and applies too readily a law whose rigor does not allow for merciful exceptions. By this interpretation, the story is about Vere's failure to uphold justice, that is, in this case, to use his authority as captain to make a judgment of equity by showing mercy.

Melville, however, gives Vere a strong defense of his actions. The *Bellipotent* is fighting a war, and the martial law by which a war vessel operates is an arm of the legal system it is defending. As Vere says to his officers—

> We fight at command. If our judgments approve the war, that is but coincidence. So in other particulars. So now. For suppose condemnation to follow these present proceedings. *Would it be so much we ourselves that would condemn so much as it would be martial law operating through us?* Our vowed responsibility is in this: that however pitilessly that law may operate in many instances, we nevertheless adhere to it and administer it. (Chapter 21; italics added)

Compared to the solutions of his officers, Vere's argument goes straight to fundamental principles. The law operates through official positions. He also warns his officers against the emotional pull of the particular case:

> But let not warm hearts betray heads that should be cool. Ashore in a criminal case, will an upright judge off the bench allow himself to be waylaid by some tender kinswoman of the accused seeking to touch him with her tearful plea?

At this point the sailing master asks the question the reader wants to ask. "Can we not convict and yet mitigate the penalty?" Vere 's answer is political. Any deviation from the established rule will be questioned by the populace, that is, the sailors. His principle is reinforced by the moral differences among human beings:

The people [meaning the ship's crew] have native sense; most of them are familiar with our naval usage and tradition; and how would they take it? Even if you could explain to them—which our official position forbids—they, long molded by arbitrary discipline, have not that kind of intelligent responsiveness that might qualify them to comprehend and discriminate. No, to the people the foretopman's deed, however it be worded in the announcement, will be plain homicide committed in a flagrant act of mutiny. What punishment for that should follow, they know. But it does not follow. *Why?* they will ruminate. You know what sailors are. Will they not revert to the recent outbreak at the *Nore?*... They would think that we flinch, that we are afraid of them—afraid of practicing a lawful rigor singularly demanded at this juncture, lest it should provoke new troubles.

The ship's surgeon also objects:

The thing to do, he [the surgeon] thought was to place Billy Budd in confinement ... and postpone further action in so extraordinary a case to such time as they could rejoin the squadron, and then refer to the admiral. (Ch. 20)

Still another argument holds that we should not give so much credit to Vere. By this argument, Vere is simply not a good leader of men. He contemptuously dismisses the judgment of the sailors; he believes that they do not have "that kind of intelligent responsiveness that might qualify them to comprehend and discriminate." Worse, Vere is also condescending: "You know what sailors are." In still another interpretation, the story is a tragedy because someone reports that on his deathbed, Vere was whispering Billy's name, apparently in remorse for the choice he had made. Good man though Vere may have been, he made a mistake. But if Melville thinks that Vere at his death sees what he should have done, then the tale is a sad story, not a tragedy.

No more than the Billy-as-Christ figure do these interpretations explain the complexity of Melville's novella. They do not explain why it is necessary for Melville to bring up the French Revolution, the mutiny on the *Nore*, sailing ships as opposed to steam ships, the Bible's having fallen out of favor, and Vere's death-bed words.

The story's concern is wider than either the phenomenon of an innocent sailor or the difficult choice of a leader responsible for judging that sailor. The story is instead examining the state of mind of a man who sees the strengths and weaknesses of modernity's "rule of laws, not men." Vere knows that the *Bellipotent*'s officers are the machinery through which the law operates. The principle of "laws, not men" has obvious benefits. Nevertheless, it comes at a price, and the price lies heavily on the man who comprehends that times have changed and that the law has changed, and with the changes in laws have come changes in citizens. Some of those changes have been for good, but some have been less than good. In the extraordinary case at hand, the new law forces the judge to employ too blunt an instrument. Vere sees in Budd a beauty that points to a mysterious goodness having little to do with winning the battle against the French; yet he must put him to death.

For the narrator, "forms, measured forms" are the only means by which man's rebellious nature can be contained (Ch. 27). These forms will always be blunt instruments. The thinkers of the Enlightenment thought that they could, by means of a more finely tuned legal system, make the instrument less blunt; if men can formulate more precisely measured forms, they can ensure that in the future the law will reach a higher level of justice. The story argues that in this view, Enlightenment men were mistaken. The marvel of this tale is coming to realize how patiently Melville plotted his argument and how much he is asking of his reader if his point is to be understood.

## 2. The Strolling Style

The narrator of the story is important to Melville's purpose. At the beginning of Chapter 4, on the history of warships, the narrator establishes a markedly insouciant manner of recounting events. His style has, he admits, "bypaths" whose "enticement cannot be resisted." He asks his reader simply to "keep [him] company," as if nothing but seeing the sights were at stake. The genially slow pace relaxes the reader's attention; he too can enjoy merely seeing the sights. Melville is using this disarming style to move later, with great care, into the change in tone at the tale's end. It is as if the tone were changing in tune with the narrator's perceived changes in the human reactions to his experience. First, the world traveler simply notes this and that in his travels, names and events eliciting no more than a moment's nod at another interesting or bizarre fact; this is how modern man reacts to his world. At the end of the tale, the narrator is no longer ambling around; his tone has acquired a new sonority, as he relates the events leading up to a great mystery.

The narrator in the opening of the story is an amiable, unthreatening type. He has knocked around the world quite a bit; he has remarked the interesting characteristics of different types; he has reflected not only on individuals but on human beings in general; he has a few things to say about historical incidents; and he uses diction so precise that we know he is fully at home with the skill that Plato called "the art of separation," or "the art of discernment." He is astute in his judgment of particular types—what they think about, how they make their decisions, what they enjoy, how seriously they take life. But he is also notably disinterested in those judgments. He is, in short, a sharp but uncommitted observer of human nature. At the end of the tale, we become aware of how much the curious and also dispassionate stance of this teller at the beginning of the tale is important for the feeling of portentous wonder at the end.

The narrator's mention of the category that Bill Budd will fall into is as casual as the rest of his narration. In guiding us around the dock of an unnamed trading city, he notes the various races who work as sailors on commercial ships milling around while their ship is in harbor. One of them happens to be the type of handsome sailor with "offhand unaffectedness" who gathers around him a troop of admirers. The narrator then moves to a description of a particular representation of the type that he happened once to see in Liverpool. Here he drops phrases that turn out to be important later: "[I]n the time before steamships" and "in the less prosaic time." Then he coasts from the bronzed skin of sailors to the star Aldeberan in the constellation The Bull, to Anacharsis Cloots, an orator of the French Revolution famous for his speeches on the universal rights of man (he also points to the origin of Cloots's odd first name), to Prince Murat (Napoleon's brother-in-law), and finally to Assyrian priests. Geographically, he moves from "any considerable seaport" to a Liverpool dock to Scotland as the origin of the hat worn by the African sailor and to the Middle East. The frequent use of double negatives, the historical references, the inclusion of different judgments on events (as in the utilitarian's assessment of Nelson's heroics) establish him as a genial man who, taking care with his many observations, would elicit trust in his observations. As it happens, Billy Budd is also a "handsome sailor" like the one in Liverpool, a person who draws men to him, but in a different way.

### 3. The New Order

Melville does not talk about modernity as the period of "the Enlightenment," as modern history books call it. Instead, the Enlightenment is characterized vaguely as "the new order," or "the time of steamships," or "the prosaic time," all of these phrases implying their opposites—the *old* order, the time of *sailing* ships, and the time of *poetry*. As with his other remarks on the various curiosities to be noted in this world, the narrator more or less wanders into the distinction between the old order and the new. He does not, as would a historian, start from a global view and characterize the time before and the time after and then proceed to analyze the particular social and political changes that followed.

The attentive reader will understand that the heart of the new order is rational procedures. When the narrator praises "forms, measured forms," he is referring to the laws of the new order, which stabilize a polity more successfully than the vaguely defined traditions of the old order. Hence, the new formula of "the rule of law, not men" is measured against the old and vague rules of custom. The rule of law, not men, effectively does away with the old courts of England—Chancery and the Star Chamber. Modern histories, as part of "the new order," have condemned these courts for allowing a King to exercise his royal power against personal enemies. In theory, however, these courts of "the time before" had the advantage of allowing flexibility in a difficult case because they allowed the subjective judgment of a magistrate to overrule the severity of the letter of the law in a particular case. The flexibility of a wise judge could counterbalance a punishment that was inappropriately harsh.

When Captain Vere's officers plead with him to mitigate Billy Budd's punishment by hanging, Captain Vere is aware that they are asking him to use his subjective authority, which is at odds with the modern rationalized law. Since the New Order has brought with it the Rights of Man, the duty of a judge is strictly to uphold the law. The law is the polity's guarantee against the outbreaks of passion after the French revolution and against assaults on the order of command on a navy ship, especially the order of command on a navy ship sponsored by a the "sole free conservative [country] of the Old World," pledged to uphold the law against the breakdown of all institutions (Ch. 3). If Vere, as Captain of the ship, uses his subjective authority to argue for mercy, he will be weakening the objectivity of the law (and, after all, Billy Budd *did* kill a man). To preserve a workable system—the rule of law—Vere must act in a way that does not do full justice in the particular case. But then the story is about how it would be impossible, in any event, to do full justice in the case of Billy Budd.

The changes in courts of law are minor compared to the larger questions Melville has on his mind when, in describing Vere's principles, he refers to "the true welfare of mankind," not as an established fact but as a problem. Modern political philosophy is said to start with Hobbes. For Hobbes, the human being has two fundamental characteristics: the fear of a violent death and the ability to reason. Insofar as human beings fear death, they are beasts; insofar as they fear death, they want protection from violence. They can, however, use their reason to get that protection. Insofar as they use their reason, they are a higher than the beasts.

Using their reason, human beings observe that they were, before the creation of a dispassionate law, accustomed to being on the alert for possible threats. Life was an endless chain of violence and retribution—the state of nature. To break that chain, human beings calculated that they could protect themselves more successfully by putting power in the hands of a disinterested party. That disinterested party is the state, or what Hobbes calls the sovereign. What, then, according to Hobbes, is the characteristic of human beings on which the polity must rely if it is to survive? It is a twisted knot of the passions and the reason, the beast's fear of violent death and the human being's calculation of how that violence can be avoided.

Since the state alone can protect citizens from harm, human beings should give their support to those institutions that are allowed the means of violence to arrest, try, and punish criminals. Interestingly, Hobbes's argument thus rests on the paradox that man-the-passionate-and-fearful-beast is capable of making a *dis*passionate calculation. Whether the combination of bestiality and reason is possible is a question. Still, the highly intelligent Claggart is a case in point, a creature whose actions are dominated by a single, overweening passion to destroy goodness and yet who can control that passion with a debased form of reason. That is, Hobbesian man redefines reason by splitting into two forms: a reason that weighs the worth of a goal and then a reason that calculates the means of achieving that goal. For Hobbesian man, the worth of the goal requires very little pondering because for him it is obvious that the fundamental desire of every man is to stay alive and also to thrive; debating the highest life—whether it is pleasure, or political action, or contemplation—is an idle endeavor. How to set up institutions that punish in a manner that will quash any complaining— this instead is real, this is the work.

According to the ancients, the first work is to create a city capable of protecting itself, but most important, to create a city that foster friendship among citizens and allow some of those citizens to live up to the highest a human being can achieve. As Aristotle puts it, the goal of a city is not to live but to live well. Citizens should be educated to love their city, to be loyal to their fellow citizens, and to honor men of courage and political wisdom. For Hobbes, these goals are too much to expect from most human beings. The human motivation to be counted on is not to live among honor of brave and wise men but fear of a violent death. Because fear of a violent death is the response to be counted on, the law is most likely to gain respect if it promises to protect life and by extension property; therefore, a sound polity will protect citizens and also their right to accumulate stuff.

Thus, the law will do away with honor and virtue-as-nobility as irrelevant to the state's interest and, instead, channel those aristocratic aspirations into commercial activity. In Hobbes's regime, it is of no consequence if a man is a dishonorable person as long as obeys the law. If a citizen fulfills his contracts, he is allowed to be as envious as Claggart. What the ancients called virtue will always be secondary to the guarantees of legality and economic well-being. Plato and Aristotle thought that a good education would persuade citizens to evaluate the various lives that human beings call happy. For Hobbesian man, human reason cannot sift through so difficult a problem. Reason, then, is best put to use not in seeking a truly happy life, about which human beings cannot agree, but rather in allowing human beings to define their goal for themselves and use their reason merely to figure out the means by which that goal can be achieved. The quest for a higher life gives way to calculation— that is, reason splits into evaluation of the goal, which because people cannot agree on the goal becomes a subject not worth spending time on—and calculation of how to achieve whatever goal suits the individual's fancy.

Thus, modern man has accepted a bargain: the law will be strictly fair. In being fair, it will guarantee freedom. Freedom promises the ability to shape one's life according to one's own choice. With that freedom to choose one's own life course comes a sense of personal power. With personal power comes a sense of dignity. But when Hobbesian man turns his quest for happiness into to commercial success, he becomes competitive. He also becomes envious of others' success and self-protective of his own means of winning. Hobbesian man will figure out that if a professor assigns articles in a particular book that the professor has put on reserve in the library, it will dawn on a clever student that he can defeat his student colleagues if he cuts the article out of the book. For the ancients, the state was friendship write large. For Hobbes, it is the contract writ large; and one does not insist on a contract unless one distrusts one's neighbor. Thus, when the new order—the narrator's "prosaic time"—commits to a consistently fair law, it also commits to what the narrator calls "that manufacturable thing called respectability" (Ch. 2)—that is, striving for no higher virtue than simply obeying the law.

Because Hobbesian men are competitive, they are wary. With modern men, says Melville's narrator, "a ruled undemonstrative distrustfulness is so habitual ... they that come at last to employ it all but unconsciously; and some of them would very likely feel real surprise with being charged with it as one of their general characteristics" (Ch.16). The general distrustfulness is exhibited in the "bitter prudence" of the old sea Chiron in his assessment of fellow sailors; he can smell out ill-will and knows how to avoid it; he negotiates the world with "a pithy, guarded cynicism." Respectable men—the Benthamites, among others—get their categories from the latest intellectual chic or from "the journals," i.e., the newspapers (Ch. 11). There, thought is reduced to the watered-down categories of Hobbesian society, in which good is merely prudence and evil merely "rascality" (Ch. 8). By implication, the narrator distinguishes between the respectable yet wary citizen on the one hand, and on the other, the religious citizen whom the wary citizen regards as unsophisticated, that is, lacking the armor of shrewd self-protection. In Melville's story, the unsophisticated types are some sailors, and the type is most clearly represented in the unsophisticated soul of Billy Budd, who is like Adam before the Fall (Ch. 2).

### 4. Leaders

Not all respectables resemble the Claggart type. The relaxed, approachable style of the narrator at the beginning is so disarming that in the introduction of Graveling, captain of *The Rights of Man,* and of Ratcliffe, lieutenant on the *Bellipotent,* we hardly realize that the narrator is giving us a short course in assessing types of leaders. Some leaders are, unlike Vere, not given to musing on life's complexities. Graveling (and what a perfect name for this character—"gravity in a diminished mode"!) has a "musical chime" in his voice that is the heart of "the innermost man" (Ch. 1).

> He had much prudence, much conscientiousness, and there were occasions when these virtues were the cause of overmuch disquietude in him.

"[O]ccasions [of] disquietude" contrast with Vere's steady state of musing.

Similarly, when the narrator moves from Graveling to Ratcliffe, he does not dwell on the moral weight on these two men. In fact, he seems to envelop both in a comedy. In considering an obligation, Ratcliffe is a man who prefers to have some liquor in "irrigating [the] aridity" of obligation and who notes that Graveling is tardy in offering a glass. When Graveling himself starts to talk, however, we realize that the narrator's earlier concession that "he took to heart those serious responsibilities not so heavily borne by some shipmasters" had whispers of irony in it, for after all, he was known to be a "respectable man," who loved "simple peace and quiet." His version of "taking to heart" is simply to remark that he doesn't like quarreling on his ship; it was "black times" for him when the "forecastle was a rat-pit of quarrels." There is little indication in his speech that he sees how singular a figure Billy is. The narrator observes that when Billy must leave Graveling's ship, Graveling has merely "a kind of rueful reproach in the tone of voice" and that he describes Billy with the easy metaphor of "a jewel." The easy metaphors continue. When Billy arrived on the *Rights of Man*, says Graveling, Billy "was like a Catholic priest in an Irish shindy"; his shipmates "took to him like hornets to treacle." The closest Graveling gets to registering Billy's peacemaking qualities is to remark, in a phrase that suggests puzzlement, "a virtue went out of him," but this account of Billy's effect on others is hardly astute. Graveling lacks the seriousness of a strong leader.

The *Bellipotent's* Lieutenant, on the other hand, can go no farther than finding Billy's sunny good spirits somewhat amusing; he smiles when Billy calls out to the merchant ship, "Farewell, *Rights of Man*." On the first reading, the reader finds the comedy of Graveling's modes of speech and of the Lieutenant's eagerness for a bit of drink more arresting than the particular kind of moral laziness in both the not-very-articulate captain, who claims that he is like Billy in preferring to avoid quarrels, and the Lieutenant, who is not interested in analyzing character at all. It turns out that Captain Graveling is right in observing that Billy is a peacemaker, but wrong in his naïve politics; his idea of a community of men on aboard a ship is a "happy family." He is also wrong in failing to note, that, like a Homeric hero, Billy will react with spirit when dishonored, and failing to note also, that, like a guileless child, Billy is, insofar as he is immune to the fear of death, not living in a Hobbesian world. Although both see something in Billy, neither has, as Captain Vere will have, the imagination to ponder what will become of a natural "peacemaker" in a world where people either are evil or are indifferent to the notion of evil. Neither of them sees in this particular handsome sailor what Melville later in the story calls "the moral phenomenon of Billy Budd" (Ch.12).

That Billy Budd is an innocent hardly needs arguing. It takes a little more arguing to hold that he plays a part in the narrator's reflections on leadership, which is an important concern in the story. The most Graveling can muster in the mysterious ways that Billy can bring order on ship is to say "a virtue went out of him." But it is also suggested that like Nelson, Billy might have something of the natural leader in him, an assessment that is corroborated when the narrator says he could be a model for Hercules. The order he brought to Graveling's merchant ship was not the result of establishing democratic rules or negotiating between officers and men, but by the force of his person. But while Nelson's leadership was active in its energetic calls to patriotism, Billy's leadership is passive. He simply draws people to him, as does like the "handsome sailor" at the beginning of the tale. He is unaware of others' reaction to him. On his transfer from *The Rights of Man* to the *Bellipotent,* he is described as a "rustic beauty" transferred to the society of the "high-born dames of court." Other sailors and notice the discrepancy, but Billy does not:

> But this change of circumstances Billy hardly noticed. As little did he observe that something about him provoked an ambiguous smile in one or two harder faces among the bluejackets. Nor less unaware was he of the peculiar favorable effect his person and demeanor had upon the more intelligent gentlemen of the quarterdeck. (Ch 2)

Billy is the true democrat; he is not conscious of social hierarchy. Later, Billy's mentor, the "old sea Chiron" of Chapter 9, is said to have substituted "Baby" for "Billy"—Baby Budd. The narrator puts religious resonance into the connection between a baby and Billy, when, for the second time, he remarks that Billy looked like Adam before the fall (Ch.18).

Another kind of leadership shows the disinterestedness of a good judge. This is the kind of leader Vere is referring to when he says that the civil law acts through the martial law and that he himself is the conduit for that law. The modern leader, then, is almost invisible. It is not he who makes a judgment but the law. In the modern world, if a leader does not have the force of a heroic personality, then rank bestows authority on him. Officers like Ratcliffe and Graveling are examples. Even the authority of "Starry Vere" is legitimized by rank, for as an "undemonstrative man," he lacks the charismatic forcefulness of Nelson. There is the suggestion that he is also unlike Nelson in refusing the appeal to the easily aroused motivation of patriotism. After the mutiny on the *Nore*, Nelson's famous words to his men at the battle of Trafalgar, that "England expects every man to do his duty," is a call for loyalty to the British empire. But Vere fights more for "founded law and freedom" that are threatened by "live cinders blown across the Channel from France" (Chapter 3). Vere fights out of allegiance to principles rather than country, and this is not a motivation that sailors can understand.

## 5. Reading and Pondering

When the narrator gets to Vere, he beings to pay more attention, for Vere is different from most people, and the narrator respects that seriousness. Vere is a man who thinks. He has learned his principles from reading history and biography. Ancient writers in particular have prepared him for accurate assessment of difficult situations:

> In this line of reading he found confirmation of his own more reserved thoughts—confirmation which he had vainly sought in social converse, so that as touching the most fundamental topics, there had got to be established in him some positive convictions which he forefelt would abide in him essentially unmodified so long as his intelligent part remained unimpaired. (Ch. 7)

In this sense, he is a philosopher in the strain of the Plato who wrote the *Republic:*

> ... his bias was toward those books to which every serious mind of superior order occupying any active post of authority in the world naturally inclines: books treating of actual men ... and unconventional writers like Montaigne, who free from cant and convention honestly and in the spirit of common sense, philosophize upon realities. (Ch. 7)

He is "specially adapted for any duty where under unforeseen difficulties a prompt initiative might have to be taken in some matter demanding knowledge and ability in addition those qualities implied in good seamanship" (Ch. 18). As a man of aristocratic habits, Vere contrasts with the other types of modern leaders. He is unlike Graveling, who is "jocosely familiar" (Ch. 7), and he is unlike his officers, who prefer the "companionable quality" and who therefore find their captain "dry and bookish" and "undemonstrative." The men around him, whose judgments come from the newspapers, regard their captain as "pedantic, having a bit of a "queer streak" in him (Ch. 7).

When Vere shows a certain "dreaminess of mood" and "absently gaze[s]

213

off at the blank sea," he is pondering human nature and the law. The fundamental principles that Vere pursues become for him "positive convictions" (Ch. 7). Those fundamental principles derive from his view of politics. As an aristocrat by birth, Vere might be expected as other aristocrats did, to have opposed the reforms of the French Revolution on the grounds that they would curtail their privileges; but in fact he opposed them because they seemed to him "unsusceptible of embodiment of lasting institutions." For Vere human beings need lasting institutions, not a "happy family," which may not always be happy.

As a philosopher, Vere, like Plato in Book 8 of the *Republic*, examines the changes in human behavior that follow upon changes in government. But he is also a philosopher of history. He analyzes historical changes and makes judgments about those changes. He sees that the old order has gone and that a new order has replaced it. In fighting for England against France, Vere believes he is fighting against a disorder he fears will harm humanity. His undemonstrative air and his careful legalism at the drumhead court in defense of securing the new order of freedom and equality show that he has accepted the disappearance of heroes like Nelson, the dismantling of the old poetic political order (where a king was loved by his citizens), and the diminution of the importance of the Bible. His preferred state of mind is reflection. When he is staring out to sea, he is viewing the world from a great height, like that of "a migratory fowl that in its flight never heeds when it crosses a frontier" (Ch. 7). The metaphor implies both comprehension of the many parts of a system combined with a focus on a *telos*—where the bird is migrating to—and the *telos* is the true welfare of mankind. When Vere reflects, he is sifting through the possibilities of human destiny.

Aware of these matters, Vere's reaction to Claggart's death swings in three directions: musing on the world, exasperation with people who do not think (Ch. 6), and swiftness in assessing a situation. At the moment when Claggart is about to inform on Billy Budd, Vere is "absorbed in his reflections" (Ch. 18); when Billy strikes Claggart, Vere sees the significance of the situation; "It is the divine judgment on Ananias! Look!"; but in the next moment, he foresees the consequences of Billy's action and again is "absorbed in thought" (Ch. 19). That Vere reads history in the manner of a philosopher urges on the reader herself the importance of reading history like a philosopher. The greatest deficiency in the modern respectable human being is his inability to see the shortcomings of the new order.

One of those shortcomings is the failure to recognize people or events do not fit into easily recognized categories. Billy Budd and Claggart are great mysteries. Billy Budd seems to come from nowhere; he has no family; he does not know where he was born. Claggart's origins, too, are unknown; he may in fact have been plucked from among from prisoners in jail. Claggart's motivations are also as inexplicable as Billy's. A respectable man might want to find a plausible cause for Claggart's enmity toward Billy Budd, but, Melville says, such enmity is "mysterious"; an "adequate understanding" of the master-at-arms cannot be accomplished by "a normal nature" (Ch. 11). Strangely enough, it is this exceptional and mysterious Claggart who understands that Billy is of another order. "One person excepted, the master-at-arms was perhaps the only person on the ship intellectually capable of adequately appreciating the moral phenomenon presented in Billy Budd" (Ch. 12). That "one person excepted" is Vere.

Vere sees that Claggart and Budd are beings who live on the other side of the great wall of respectable self-preservation where modern man dwells. Moreover, he sees that the difficulty of his position is adjudicating between the abiding truth of good and evil on the one hand, and, on the other, the new orders that modernity has chosen. When Vere is struggling to decide what to do in Billy's case, the narrator asks, in sympathy with Vere's awareness of the problem he confronts: "Was he absorbed in taking in all the bearings of the event and what was best not only now at once to be done, but also in the sequel?" (Ch.19). "In the sequel" is the crux of the matter. The men lacking Vere's wisdom are the officers whom Vere will have to persuade at Billy's trial. The readers who hold that Vere made a mistake in not delaying the trial until the *Bellipotent* reached land are in company with those officers.

If the categories that moderns use to construe the world blind them to mystery, they might, the narrator implies in *sotto voce* asides, reflect on the time of sailing ships, of Nelson, of poetry rather than prose, of moral judgments for the common welfare of mankind rather than immediate calculations, and above all, on the favorite book of the old order—namely, the Bible. The narrator mentions modernity's neglect of the Bible three times. The doctrine of the fall is now "popularly ignored" (Ch. 2); the best resource for examining "obscure spiritual places" might be "Holy Writ," that is, if

Holy Writ "were any longer popular" (Ch. 11); and the narrator wonders if his reader "of today" will balk at the word *depravity* as "savoring too much of Holy Writ" (Ch. 11). The narrator apologizes for referring to holy writ because he assumes that the Bible is not a reference for most of his audience. It is a loss, this reading of the Bible, because, like poetry, it can do something that the prosaic mode cannot—wonder about the mysteries of life.

In this story, any political decision that has as many "sequels" (the narrator's word) as the Rule of Law and the Rights of Man requires understanding the human inclination to evil. For modern man, Exceptional Evil, as in Claggart, is hard to understand; but Exceptional Evil is not as hard to understand as Exceptional Good, for the wary, self-protective creature of the modern world considers every man a danger. Modern man has suffered two falls, one the Biblical Fall, and the other the fall into the Enlightenment. Modern intellectuals may say that any wisdom is out of date that derives from an agricultural society or depends on an affinity for the natural world, or depends on myths, as the Bible does. But the narrator would say that human beings will always have a sense that nature has something he needs to listen to, not because it refreshes his lungs when he goes on hikes but because nature beckons him to the eternal. Only the Bible can argue that the law must be based on something beyond the calculations that guarantee stability in a society; that is, law must somewhere have in it a reference to a higher authority that inspires awe. Only the metaphor of an unfallen pastoral place governed by a transcendent being can give a local habitation and a name to the human need for reassurance that human beings are not a cosmic fluke. The garden of Eden represents a transcendent home, where man is not pre-modern man as opposed to modern man but just "man," who cannot exist without some notion of a transcendent power.

The Bible is good at expressing the ease that modern man longs for, whether he knows it or not, perhaps because in the Hebrew Bible, the Jews suffer so many defeats and so many years of bitter exile. To keep the Israelites going, the prophets are obliged to promise that one day there will be an end to their misery. First and Second Isaiah illustrate the move from grief and desolation among enemies to a place where the garden, or the vineyard, can be renewed. After the conquest of Israel, Jerusalem will be desolate:

It [burning pitch] shall not be quenched night nor day; the smoke thereof shall go up for ever: from generation to generation it shall lie waste; none shall pass through it for ever and ever.

> But the cormorant and the bittern shall possess it; the owl also and the raven shall dwell in it: and he shall stretch out upon it the line of confusion, and the stones of emptiness. (Isaiah 34.10–11)

With the return of the Israelites from Babylon, however, the garden will be restored: "And all of the trees of the field shall clap their hands" (55.1); Israel "will be like a watered garden" (58.11); "And Sharon shall be a fold of flocks, / And the valley of Achor a place for the hers to lie down in" (65.10). Similarly in Ecclesiastes, the weariness of the preacher moves to the next book the happy garden of the Song of Solomon, where the lover worships with his beloved and where the fruits of the garden themselves validate his love.

In the movement from Chapter 8 to Chapter 9 of *Billy Budd*, Melville repeats the movement from First to Second Isaiah and from Psalm 22 to Psalm 23. Chapter 8 deals with Claggart. The prose music is deft and subtle. It starts with the strolling style's characteristic offhandedness, as if Melville were not sure where he is going: "But among the petty officers, there is one who, having much to do with the story, may as well be forthwith introduced." There follows a description which gains in menace as it progresses. Claggart has small hands; "[s]ilken jet curls" frame his brow; his skin is pallid, a color that contrasts sharply with the healthy tan of the sailors. But it is his suspicious background that gets the most emphasis: the sailors do not know where he came from, but rumor holds that he might have been a swindler; in these times when the British navy lacks naval men, he might have been one of those criminals pressed into service out of necessity.

The menace is in the political atmosphere as well; the times were dire: then occurred those wars "which like a flight of harpies rose shrieking from the din and dust of the fallen Bastille," the "genius" of which appeared to thoughtful men like the apparition to the adventurer Camoens, "an eclipsing menace, mysterious and prodigious." Indeed, to Americans, that era, summed up in Napoleon, seemed like revolutionary chaos. New Englanders were anxious that the upheavals of the French Revolution might cross the Atlantic, fulfilling the "judgment prefigured in the apocalypse."

The narrator is, however, conscious of his having drifted into a new register. He retreats from Biblical grandeur and returns to the world of the prosaic, conceding that men appointed to the position of master-at-arms are often resented by the sailors; gossip and rumor tend to be the threads of their judgments. Moreover, in one of Melville's characteristic concessions, it was a "fact" that Claggart worked hard in the "least honorable" section of the crew and rose to the position of master-at-arms. The chapter starts with intimations of disaster and concludes with the account of an individual concentrating on the work in front of him. The final paragraph of Chapter 8 notes how the web of authority can create "mysterious discomfort, if nothing worse," in a ship's crew. The strolling narrator now regains something of the Biblical prophet in his voice.

Chapter 8 then comes to an end. There is a blank space on the page. Then Chapter 9 begins: "Life in the foretop well agreed with Billy Budd." Here we are in a completely different world.

> There, when not actually engaged on the yards yet higher aloft, the topmen, who as such had been picked out for youth, and activity, constituted an aerial club of lounging at ease against the smaller stun'sails rolled up on cushions, spinning yarns like the lazy gods, and frequently amused with what was going on in the busy world of the decks below.

The top men are "aloft." They lean on the sails as if they were "cushions." They form an "aerial club," telling tales "like the lazy gods." They can regard the daily scrambling on a navy ship as so many amusing events in a world below. They resemble the migratory fowl at the end of Chapter 11, "unmindful of circumstance."

### 6. Assessments

We do not stay long in this world of ease. The chapter swings from lazy tranquility to duty as the narrator describes Billy's reaction to a sailor's being punished with a whip and his perplexity in finding that his superiors complain about the towage of his bag and finally the "old Dansker's" suspicion that the master-at-arms must be plotting against Billy. Here the chapter stops, as the narrator uses the old Dansker as his surrogate.

> But after slyly studying him at intervals, the old Merlin's equivocal merriment was modified ; for now when the twain would meet, it would start in his face a quizzing sort of look ... sometimes replaced by an expressions of speculative query as to what might eventually befall a creature like that, dropped into a world not without some mantraps and against whose subtleties, simple courage lacking experience and address, and without any touch of defensive ugliness, is of little avail; *and where such innocence as man is capable of does yet in a moral emergency not always sharpen the faculties or enlighten the will.* (Ch. 9, italics added)

Billy's type cannot be a model for self-protection.

The phrase "speculative query" invites us to consider what will happen to such a man "in a world not without mantraps." Indeed, the reader might ponder whether "in a moral emergency," it might be better not to be so innocent. (The last time I taught this story, a student cited this passage as clear evidence that Melville thinks innocence is going to get you in trouble.) The great busy world of the navy ship, which is the new world of the Rights of Man *in minim*, is a given. Merlin is dubious that innocence can survive in such a world; but of course, an old cynic would have such doubts. Still, the question remains: if we cannot live in the modern world as innocents, how are we to think about our attraction to innocent people? This question will bear upon the difficult decision Captain Vere confronts.

When Vere sees that Billy has struck down Claggart, he understands in an instant what must be taken into account. He knows the limited intelligence of sailors; he knows that they are bound to hold a grudge; if a sailor has killed an officer and that sailor does not hang, the rest of the sailors will regard the officers as weak. Human nature being what it is, grudges and plotting become, in the disaffected, an outright mutiny. Further, Vere knows that after the incident on the *Nore,* commanding officers had to stand with swords behind the men in charge of the cannon. He knows also that the categories by which his junior officers understand the

WHERE THE MUSES STILL HAUNT

world derive from the cant in the newspapers. But if he should delay Billy's trail, as those officers wish him to do, until he can rejoin the fleet or get to land, he risks resistance from the sailors. There may be impressed men on the *Bellipotent* who are "forced to fight for the King against their will." The difficulty for the philosophical man who has been put in a situation where he must act, is his awareness that his soldiers (or sailors) do not have the intelligence to understand the fundamental principles for which they are fighting, nor do they see the threats to those principles.

France must be defeated because Britain is the only country that can defend "founded law and freedom" (Ch. 3) against the tumult of human passions, and human beings are full of ungovernable passions. If Vere should excuse Billy Budd's assault on Claggart, he will be undermining his duty, not duty as the genial Graveling defines it but his duty to the mankind of the modern world that guarantees freedom. At the trial scene, Vere resolves to uphold the law. Earlier in the story, Melville remarked that Nelson's heroism "vitalizes into acts" the nobility that is praised in the poetic lines of epic and drama. Although Vere's death comes after Trafalgar, his leadership stands as an alternative to the romantic heroism of Nelson, not because the narrator disapproves of Nelson's risky heroics, as did other more cynical types (admirers of Bentham), but because his considered judgment approves of the Enlightenment's assault on personal heroics. Only at this point in the story is it clear that the praise of Nelson in the earlier chapter was a concession. Great men are indeed great leaders, but they come along infrequently; better to have solid institutions. Vere then "vitalizes" into an act the full consciousness of an Enlightenment man. Nelson was a soldier; in the case of Billy Budd, Vere is both a soldier *and* a judge. What he judges will affect the stability of the peace he fights for.

The difficulty of his decision is embodied in metaphor of pacing, turning from one side of the ship to another:

> Turning, he to-and-fro paced the cabin athwart; in the returning ascent to windward climbing the slant deck in the sea's lea roll, without knowing it symbolizing thus in his action a mind resolute to surmount difficulties even as against primitive instincts strong as the wind and sea. (Ch. 21)

220

To uphold the rationality that upholds the law, one must fight against "primitive instincts," even when those instincts incline to mercy. If an assessment of modernity's choices is part of the story's meaning, then Vere's pacing is also a metaphor for the complexity of such an assessment. By this point in the telling of the tale, the narrator is moving into prose-epic. At the hanging, we get Billy's cry, "God bless Captain Vere," the cloud looking down like "the fleece of the lamb of God," and Billy's rising "in the full rose of the dawn." Then, as a coda, we get the debate between the purser and the surgeon.

"Steamships," of course, made possible by Enlightenment science, and after Billy's hanging the narrator has science present its case in the conversation between the purser and the surgeon. The purser, for his part, thinks unscientifically: Billy must have used will-power to keep his body from twitching, as bodies, as a rule, do after being hanged. The surgeon, on the other hand, as a man of science, is skeptical: he holds that if Billy's body did not twitch, it was not because of will-power but for some scientific reason that has not yet been found. If scientific man should observe a human action for which he has no medical diagnosis, then he resorts to the categories of the layman; after witnessing Vere's emotions when Billy kills Claggart, the surgeon does not ponder what would make a man like Vere act the way he does; instead, he diagnoses Vere with the crude category of "insane." Scientific thinking, confronted with a puzzle, can turn out to be as much a blunt instrument as the law. The story argues, however, that the complexities of human types and of human actions will always defy the scientist's claim that science is the only tool for understanding the world and human beings.

On the other hand, the purser's belief in will power, may be intended not as a refutation of the surgeon's view but as counterpart; human beings' confidence in their own capabilities may be as much of a delusion as a scientist's confidence in science's explanatory power. As he does in so many places in the story, the narrator is using the purser to introduce another human type—namely, the man who believes in individual will-power who can master anything; it was Billy himself, the purser holds, who roused his courage and controlled his body. Indeed, both views, that of the surgeon and that of the purser, assume that man can master his world on his own.

The narrator offers the example of the "man who though he would always maintain his manhood in battle might not prove altogether reliable in a moral dilemma involving aught of the tragic" (Ch. 21). A Nelson would not have helped in the situation that Vere faces with Billy Budd.

The story moves steadily into tragic mystery, first in Billy's hanging, then in the cry of the seagulls over the place where the body sank, then in Vere's death when his last murmur is, "Billy Budd, Billy Budd" (Ch. 28). If the story were about an unusual character in a realistic story, the ending would occur after the sinking of the body in the ocean. But, in a markedly unpoetic style that is capitalizing on the still-ringing tone of tragedy, the penultimate chapter relates the death of Vere after the *Bellipotent* battled with another ship. The significance of Vere's last words is left to one more uncomprehending listener.

Billy Budd has been "sacrificed," a word Melville used earlier in the story of Nelson's death (Ch. 4). Enlightenment rationality cannot say why we love babies or why it is good to love babies; why we love beauty or why it is good to love beauty; why a beautiful, healthy, happy man attracts people's allegiance; and why in a certain situation, it is tragic that such a man must be put to death. It is the force of moral "compelling" that modern man has lost, "compelling" in the sense of being drawn to something, as the word "draw" is used in the Gospel of John. "No man can come to me, except the Father who hath sent me draw him" (6.44), and "I, if I be lifted up from the earth, will draw all men unto me" (12.32). Making the choice for Enlightenment rationality, modern man has cut himself off from deep loyalties to other human beings and to elemental forces. Billy lying among the cannon is pastoral ease in the midst of modernity's decision that rationally devised institutions and the force that backs them up are more efficacious in creating community than love. Modern man has made his choice for a view of the world that banishes good and evil, love and hate, as useful categories because, after all, these are mysteries:

> Nay, in an average man of the world, his constant rubbing with
> it blunts *that finer spiritual insight* indispensable to the under-
> standing of the essential in certain exceptional characters,
> whether evil ones or good. (Ch. 11; italics added)

Modern man has chosen this world to the exclusion of a higher one, and he has also chosen the lower happiness of guaranteed self-protection over the higher one of true beauty and true freedom, that is, the freedom from the fear of death, just as Socrates maintained.

When Vere chooses the modern version of this life as opposed to the pre-Enlightenment version, he does so with full awareness of what is lost. His lament on his deathbed for Billy Budd is not a recantation of his decision to put Billy to death, as some readers think. It is a lament for a profound difficulty in deciding what the Good is and which world is man's home. The *Bellipotent* can destroy the ship that happens to be named the *Athée* ("atheism"), but the ship stands for a pervasive view that will wreak the cultural destructions accomplished by atheism without having to subscribe explicitly to an atheistic position.

The scene with the chaplain, Chapter 24, is a master stroke in showing the evasions behind the Rights of Man. The new regime will guarantee the safety of individual men, but it will not guarantee the mysterious beauty of Humanity. The chapter starts with a description of Billy Budd lying among the cannon:

> On the starboard side of the *Bellipotent's* upper gun deck, behold Billy Budd under sentry lying prone in irons in one of the bays formed by the regular spacing of the guns comprising the batteries on either side. All of the pieces were of the heavier caliber of that period. Mounted on lumbering wooden carriages, they were hampered with cumbersome harness of breeching and strong side-tackles for running them out. Guns and carriages, together with the long rammers and shorter linstocks lodged in loops overhead all these, as customary, were painted black; and the heavy hempen breachings, tarred to the same tint, wore the like livery of the undertakers.

The scene is dark and forbidding. Billy by contrast is all in white; the bays that house the guns look like side chapels in a cathedral; Billy himself looks like a child in the cradle "when the warm hearth-glow of the still chamber at night plays on the dimples that at whiles mysteriously form in the cheek, silently coming and going there." The Rights of Man claimed to guarantee human beings their freedom, but perfect freedom is being oblivious to the border between life and death, as Vere, who as the migratory fowl, is oblivious to the boundaries that divide the large category Humanity into national allegiances that regard each other with suspicion.

Melville uses the ship's chaplain to emphasize this contrast between one kind of freedom and another. The goodhearted man-of-the-cloth, knowing that ordinary men greatly fear death, sees his job as persuading Billy not to be afraid. He is therefore nonplussed by Billy's ease. He leaves and then returns, greeted cheerfully by Billy. But Melville muses shrewdly on the minister's own implication in the political undergirders of the Rights of Man. Although the chaplain, like Vere, is touched by Billy, he, like Vere, accedes to military law, and like Vere, accedes to military law which guarantees the Rights of Man, "because he too lends the sanction of the religion of the meek to that which practically is the abrogation of everything but brute Force" (Ch. 24). Here the story plummets to the foundation of the Hobbesian doctrine. On the first floor of that doctrine, the polity will allow citizens to be creatures of pleasure—indeed, it will encourage them to be creatures of pleasure—and the doctrine will allow them to imagine that they believe in God. But it also demands a lowering of spiritual aspirations. For modern man, what Milton called the "sweet of life" can come only in isolated and unpredictable intervals—like the appearance of a Billy Budd in one's life. Having made their choice that happiness in this world is man's first duty, moderns imagine a transcendent world in idle moments but then return to "rubbing" against the compromises of the secular world to which they have given their primary allegiances.

Below the first floor of the Hobbesian doctrine is the basement. Ultimately, the enlightened state can guarantee the individual the freedom to live life as he chooses only up to a point. Hobbes's sovereign, in whatever form that may be—king or legislature—will always have to fight enemies, enemies as powerful and as threatening as Napoleonic France. The fight against enemies will erase liberal individualism because a successful army demands a strict order of command and obedience. If this world is man's primary home, then even the representatives of a transcendent world will give their sanction to the swift execution of the law.

The final two short chapters are a descent into the self-satisfaction that accompanies the right not to inquire into the highest happiness. A regime built on institutions that guarantee rights and safety and legitimized by not altogether thoughtful citizens will have to accept the crude terms in which politics are discussed in the newspapers. One source of that crudeness will be government propaganda. Melville makes the point with devastating understatement in Chapter 29's account of the incident on the *Bellipotent* as reported in "the journals." That chapter is the culmination of the various "digressions" in the story that have to do with Vere's preference for reading histories and biographies of men of the past.

One would think that Melville would have felt he had completed his analysis of Hobbesian society. But he moves on. The *thoughtful* Hobbesian man will always gaze over a wall toward a beauty, repose, and transcendent Good from which history has exiled him or from which he has, half willingly, exiled himself. The penultimate chapter shows the inadequacy of the sailor's requiem for Bill Budd. Again, Melville sees both sides: sailors participate in a mob mentality; but some of them have "an artless *poetic* temperament," a phrase that both gives and takes away. The sailors' ballad, *Billy Budd in the Darbies*, is moving in the way country ballads are moving—the simple man's stoic acceptance of his fate in anapestic tetrameter (or at least the first lines suggest tetrameter but the meter stumbles later in the poem), a limited range of diction ("Ay, ay, all is up"), and romantic gestures (the moonlight tipping the guard's sword and "silver[ing] this nook"). The ending shows laconic fatalism: "Just ease the darbies [handcuffs] at the wrist, / And roll me over fair! / I am sleepy, and the oozy weeds about me twist." There is something of a higher poetic register in "oozy weeds"; but the ballad is, generally, metaphorically clichéd, metrically uneven, and morally banal. In the last two chapters then, we have the two most commonly known accounts of the story. One is representative of the degraded thinking of the newspapers. The second is the affecting but jejune art of the common man, who knows a sad story when he hears one but is incapable of understanding tragedy.

And yet perhaps not so. The artistic stroke of the last chapter might be the knife-edge on which the complexities of the ballad rides. One minute it seems coarse and bathetic, for although Melville sees the sailors as connected with the natural force of the sea, he also recognizes their limitations. But then there is the enigma of the "oozy weeds," which "about me twist," a line that is both threatening (death has me in its clutches), and also shruggingly content ("roll me over, boys").

Perhaps the hints of ruefulness in the ballad echo the lament of Vere on his deathbed. Then Vere seems in anguish over the fate of Billy Budd, who could not be protected in a system of rationalized law backed up by force. We know from earlier in the story that Vere prefers thinkers who "in the spirit of common sense philosophize upon realities" (Ch. 7). The reality Vere has faced is his allegiance to the compromises of the modern world. A rational polity of "laws, not men" will lose both a sense of the tragic and also that of perfect ease. Perhaps then Vere's lament is not only for having failed to protect Billy. Perhaps it is a lament—an elegy, even—for the loss for human beings of a "reposeful good nature" like Billy's (Ch. 2). Leaders like Vere, who can see both sides of the border that the migratory bird flies over, will never feel the repose of a Billy Budd and will always have to endure the ease of men like Graveling and Ratcliffe, who have given little thought to what the Enlightenment has abandoned.

In my college course on the novel, when the professor came to the end of *The Heart of Darkness*, she asked the class—all women—why Marlowe felt he had to lie to Kurtz's fiancée when he tells her that the last word on Kurtz's lips was her name. We were young; we had been raised in a sentimental culture; but we also knew we were supposed to grow into some kind of toughness. We said, "Because he knows she wants to hear something romantically reassuring and wishes to protect her fragile world." In short, we said he was a kind man. But like Melville, Conrad saw something deeper. Kurtz's beloved cannot see to the bottom of modern Western culture, as Marlowe has—and, indeed, as Kurtz has. In fact, she wants to remain naive, and she expects that a true gentleman will protect her naiveté. Conrad sees her innocence not as charming vulnerability but an unthinking acquiescence to something false.

In *The Idea of a University*, Newman argued that the goal of a university education is the training of the intellect in calm, in moderation, and in the interrelation of all branches of knowledge. No story that I know of connects all branches of knowledge as much as Melville's *Billy Budd* while, at the same time, lamenting the loss of the calm that could be felt by all. Vere searches for that calm and is prevented from dwelling in it by circumstances. If being innocent of the wisdom of the world (1 Corinthians 3:19) is no longer possible, thoughtful people might try to imagine what it is.

# POSTLUDE

Back in the olden days, the goal of education was said to be thoughtfulness about serious things. Nowadays, colleges say that their goal is "critical thinking," the same thing, perhaps, as "thoughtfulness about serious things" but with a little more snap in it. The Melville of *Billy Budd* would perhaps gloss that phrase as "how to keep someone from putting something over on you."

Hidden in the phrase "critical thinking" is the addendum "critical thinking that is up to date," perhaps even "on the cutting edge." The most admired universities pride themselves on being in the vanguard of scholarship. For some disciplines, this goal makes sense. It is not hard to recognize the scientific vanguard. Science's job is to find better explanations. It can show why a problem that was explained two decades ago was not examined thoroughly enough and how a new experiment comes up with a better explanation. The old explanation, having been found to be wrong, is cast aside and the new explanation is agreed upon as the new, true fact.

In some parts of the humanities, this criterion is also useful. History, which includes the history of philosophy and history of literature, can reveal facts not known before: new documents that show a political leader of the past believed long before he went to war that something was true, and, as it turned out, he was right, or as it turned out he was mistaken; documents that show how this or that philosopher later rejected the ideas he held in his youth; or a diary that helps to explain a writer's puzzling play or novel.

In the arts, however, the goal is first to understand an author and then to ponder his wisdom. That goal has little to do with science's cancellations of past facts. The arts do not reveal facts; they offer a hypothesis about life. As Sir Philip Sidney said ages ago, the artist "doth grow in effect another nature." The artist regards his freedom as an advantage, he can concoct whatever world he sees in his imagination. That other nature is hypothesis, and it is up to the writer, or viewer, or listener to judge if the hypothesis is worth thinking about. The great philosophers argue as if they were presenting a truth; but they do not offer facts; they offer hypotheses about life that may or may not be sound. Judging whether a book of fiction is good or bad is a different endeavor because the endeavor is less precisely defined.

Some of the criteria for judging a literary work are, to be sure, not difficult. Some people do not like mystery stories because, they say, the author's task is rather simple: he deceives the reader until the tale finally reveals who is the murderer. With more complex books, ones that seem to be making an argument about human nature or human life or what is to be celebrated and what is to be grieved over, we cannot prove a judgment right or wrong. We can only measure the arguments against our experience. The judgment depends on how the critic measures artistic difficulties, and how he judges interesting thinking or maybe wise thinking, how well he has taken in life.

How well a person has taken in life is a difficult matter to assess. Perhaps this is the reason the current study of literature has turned to disciplines based on evidence. One of these is cultural history, analyzing how an artwork fits into the culture of its time or place. Here, we judge the work on the verifiable facts, and the facts show that at a certain time, sails for sailing vessels had been newly designed, or that or there had opened up new markets for spices from the east; thus, the optimistic energy of a literary work has to do with a new energy in culture of the times. Or if a literary work gives a lot of space to weavers and history can show that weavers at that time were suffering hardships, then the writer must have been making a point about the financial condition of the working men of those times.

But such conclusions hold limited interest. So one can raise the ante. More interesting is showing how the facts of new designs for sails or the fact of new spice markets or the facts of the social condition of weavers affected the distribution of power in a particular time and place. More interesting still is to show how designs in sails and new spice markets facilitated a country's advance into the future, because new sails or new markets mean more money for somebody, and with money comes power and power affects the course of history. This is the brass ring of semiotics of power—who was winning and who was losing. At this point, an argument built on facts moves to matters not so clearly a matter of facts, for behind that argument is another one, what a human being should be for or against in the great march of history. In these discussions, the loyalty to a particular way of

229

seeing the world overwhelms the detachment that was supposed to accompany "critical thinking," for the conversation has moved into politics.

Persuasion can work in another way. One can use complicated philosophical language. For persuasive power, many English departments have turned to specialized terms. Much study is required to understand how these terms fit into a larger argument. Because there is something very new about these new words, they signal up-to-date thinking. One is not only up-to-date; one is on the "cutting edge," and that is where universities want their faculty to be. Like the persuasion by facts, however, the change in language is also a philosophical change. The new philosophy holds that the study of literature should be a specialty. The person who still discusses literature in the language of the general reader, not that of a specialist, has two difficulties. First, he will have to defend his way of interpreting. At scholarly conferences, some graduate student will ask a speaker, "What is the theoretical background for your analysis?" or "What is your method?" The very question implies that the speaker is using the analytical tools of a particular school or of a particular thinker. Not to have a particular school or particular theorist in mind is a bad sign, for the speaker can be labeled as "out of date" or "unprofessional."

Then the argument moves into a very old debate, carried on by Plato and the professionals, about those who speak to specialists and those who speak to the general public. The specialist's side of the argument claims that its professionalism, arcane though it may be, is the greater wisdom because it is more precise, and Plato, in some dialogues, himself insists on precision. But other dialogues, the more musical ones, show the other side, which has two planks. The first is that good thinking is responsible to the wider community for holding a culture together. If the philosopher is to live in a good city, then he needs to uphold a manner of speech that will bridge the gap between the highly intelligent and the mediocrely intelligent. The second plank is that ultimately the greatest wisdom cannot be articulated. Both great writing and great reading "just see" something, and that something is only weakened by tying it down to historically verified facts or overly refined defining and distinguishing. Good judgment of art also depends on these two planks. Why indeed did Henry James say that *Middlemarch* had a "fatal flaw" in it? Why does it matter? Why did he say that Russian novels were "loose and baggy monsters," and why does it matter?

The old dispensation had its faults, it is true. What was called "new criticism," reading a poem closely, often devolved into hunts for allusions, repetitions, echoes of the ancients, borrowings from contemporary genres and, worst of all, a metaphorical extension of terms that allowed anything to be connected with anything else without an argument about how these allusions, repetitions, echoes, borrowings contributed to the whole. When the old-fashioned scholars spent their careers hunting around in often incidental parts of a text, they were not equipped to imagine a serious debate about the meaning of a work and what a work had to say about a serious life. As a consequence, they were not then equipped to meet the challenges of the 70s and after.

I will conclude with the remarks an author who is usually regarded as one who marks the beginning of modernity. Machiavelli tells a story in a letter written to one Francesco Vettori, in 1513, after he had been exiled from Florence. He starts with an apology for having lost Vettori's letter and then expresses his appreciation for a second letter from Vettori and finally remarks on the unpredictability of Fortune. Then he writes about his daily life in exile in the country, how much he is exasperated by the trivia he must deal with every day. At first, he says, he is more or less struggling simply to find something to do. On an ordinary day, his first occupation is catching thrushes. Then he gets into a quarrel over wood some men bought from him. Then, he endeavors to calm down with reading in an aviary; but then goes to an inn, plays a game of *cricca*, and, disgusted with himself, "become[s] a rascal for the whole day."

Then, with unexpected mildness, the story goes in another direction. He returns where he is living for some dinner:

> When evening has come, I return to my house and go into my study. At the door I take off my clothes of the day, covered with mud and mire, and I put on my regal and courtly garments; and decently reclothed, I enter the ancient courts of ancient men, where, received by them lovingly, *I feed on the food that alone is mine and that I was born for. There I am not ashamed to speak with them and to ask them the reason for their actions; and they in their humanity reply to me. And for the space of four hours I feel no boredom, I forget every pain, I do not fear poverty, death*

*does not frighten me. I deliver myself entirely to them.*[34]  (Italics added)

Machiavelli was talking here about authors who wrote books different from the ones I talk about in this book, but who can nevertheless do what Machiavelli prized. They persuade a reader to "deliver" himself to them, hand himself over in admiration, so much admiration that coming back to them is like returning to an old and still wise friend.

34  Nicolo Machiavelli, *Letter to Francesco Vettori*, trans. by Harvey C. Mansfield, 2nd ed. (Chicago: Univ. of Chicago Press, 1998.)